Tav Chlordane is an all-round sportsman who has taught, lectured, coached, organised and been involved in sport for more than 50 years.

This book is dedicated to all those who are like me but just haven't had the time to write the book.

Tav Chlordane

Interested in Sport

A CIP catalogue record for this title is available from the British Library.

ISBN 9781398448216 (Paperback)
ISBN 9781398448223 (Hardback)
ISBN 9781398448230 (ePub e-book)

www.austinmacauley.com

First Published (2021)
Austin Macauley Publishers Ltd
25 Canada Square
Canary Wharf
London
E14 5LQ

What qualifies me to write a book about sports?

I suppose I should have been the person who took the metro during a marathon and then claimed the victory, or maybe I was the man who ended Jahangir Khan's 555 game win streak in squash or that that I play tennis left-handed like Nadal but that I am actually right-handed, just like Nadal! Well, I'm sorry to say, I can lay no claim to being the subject of any of the content of this book. I am, however, qualified to write about it because I'm obsessed with sport. I've had three nicknames over the years (and probably others behind my back). My names were 'the Cybernaut' when I cycled as a kid. If only I knew then what I know now. I would sit on the front of the peloton and drag them along for as long as possible only to have them ride past me in the last mile. I was also known as 'the legs', and finally 'Competitive Tav!' My first instinct is to make a competition out of anything physical. This stems from often not being able to win fairly, and so an interpretation of a law or the use of a new regulation might be my only way of getting the advantage.
Squash, Enduro MTB and volleyball are sports I currently enjoy. In the past have completed triathlons, mountain biked to Istanbul, ran 90 miles from Birmingham to Reading and cycled from Spain to England for a bet.
This book is meant to be left in the toilet (not literally) and dipped into and used as light reading. Everything inside is deliberately kept short.
I am amazed and totally interested in sport. I apologise to those few friends and family I have left that (somehow) continue to tolerate both me and the content of this book.

Disclaimer

There is no way that I will take responsibility for any of the facts being 100% accurate or authentic. Many originated in pub conversations. They are researched from the interweb, and other forms of media.

Tav Chlordane makes no apologies about the amount of Aston Villa material held within.

This is an English book, written in English that talks about sport facts, trivia and jokes from around the world. A few assumptions are that football is football, not soccer. American football is American football, centre is center, miles are not km, pounds are a currency and weight. I think you get my drift.

The information in this book has been deliberately written without too many records and constantly changing information.

Classifications

- Swimming
- General sport
- Baseball / Softball
- American Football
- Tennis
- Table Tennis
- Golf
- Rugby
- Martial Arts
- Olympics
- Cycling
- Basketball
- Male / Female
- Badminton
- Shooting
- Track and Field
- Archery
- Ice sports
- Cricket
- Aussie Rules
- Handball
- Darts
- Swimming
- Volleyball
- Bowling
- Squash
- Tug of war
- Paralympics
- Boxing
- Water sports
- Equestrian
- Fencing
- Snooker
- Animal
- Joke
- Surfing
- Triathlon
- Human
- Training
- Weights /Gym
- Lacrosse
- Rowing
- Skiing
- Gymnastics
- Skateboarding
- Hurling
- Drugs
- Curling
- Crown Green Bowls
- Running
- Motorsports
- Watersports
- Kayak / Canoe
- Duck
- MTB / BMX
- Football
- Climbing
- Death

A 'try' in rugby was once worth nothing. However, it gave the player, who achieved one, the opportunity to 'try' to score a goal, hence its name. Goals were scored by kicking over the crossbar and between two posts, therefore converting the try into a goal, a goal being worth one point.

In the original set of football rules, there was no 'foul' included. The reason for this was that football was a game played by gentlemen and a foul would have been ungentlemanly behaviour. An apology to the player fouled was all that was needed.

Official baseball rules state that an umpire may not be replaced during a game except if they become ill, injured or they die!

Why if they are square, are they called boxing rings?

The reason that boxing rings are called 'rings' is that in boxing, the original contests were fought in a drawn circle on the floor. The Jack Broughton rules in 1743 had a small circle in the centre of the fight area where the boxers met at the start of each round. The Pugilistic Society in 1838 is who we can thank for the 1st square ring.

I knew my wife was a keeper the first time I ever saw her. She was wearing massive gloves!

The original free kick in football was always indirect (the ball had to be passed before a goal can be scored). This indirect free kick was adopted into the game in 1877. Later, the direct free kick was added to differentiate between the violence and injures caused by the more serious fouls.

The ancient Olympics ran from 776 BC until 393 AD, that's 1169 years! The modern Olympics have been going for just over 120 years!

In the original rules of ping-pong, the ball had to bounce on your side of the table before going over the net after you hit it. In modern day table tennis, the ball must be hit directly over the net onto the opponent's half of the table. It was this extra bounce that gave the game the onomatopoeic name. 'Ping-pong' was also the trade name for the table tennis sets originally sold to promote the game.

The 1976 Montreal Games were marred by the boycott of mostly African countries because of the IOC's refusal to ban New Zealand. The reason the countries wanted the ban was that the New Zealand's rugby union team, the All Blacks continued to play against South Africa, a country banned by the

IOC because of its Apartheid regime. In total, 28 countries felt forced into boycotting the games.

The leader of the 'King of the Mountains' competition in the Tour de France wears a white jersey with red dots ('maillot à pois rouges' in French), which is commonly referred to as the 'polka dot jersey'. The jersey was introduced in 1975. The colours were decided by the then sponsor, Poulain Chocolate, to match a popular sweet which was wrapped in red and white.

Awarding international caps originated from the practice in the United Kingdom of awarding a cap to every player in an international match of association football. Caps are also awarded to cricketers. Other countries mainly from the British Commonwealth follow the same tradition.

Golfer: "I'd move heaven & earth to break 100 on this course." Caddy: "Try heaven; you've already moved most of the earth."

The colour purple (not the film!) has for centuries been associated with royalty, wealth and power. Queen Elizabeth I made it illegal for anyone except for close members of the royal family to wear it. Purple's elite status stems from the rarity and cost of the dye originally used to produce it. Another expensive dye colour is red and that was the reason the red carpet became so prestigious.

The term 'English' can be traced back to the 1870's and was used to describe spin on a pool ball. It was called 'English' because it was the English players who were the first to use the new technique in America. In England, it is referred to as 'side' and 'screw' and in other countries 'backspin' or 'draw'.

In Formula 1 racing and other motorsport, we often hear about the pits for tyre changing and refuelling. These areas are known as the pits because originally there were actual pits where mechanics could service their vehicles from underneath the cars during races.

Are you eligible to play for the Barbarians?

Well, the only criteria a player must fulfil to receive an invitation from the Barbarians to play are that the player's rugby is of a good standard and that they behave themselves on and off the field. Yet a barbarian is a human who is perceived to be uncivilised or primitive! Remember that famous Gareth Edward's 'try', starting in the Ba Baas own 22 and flowing the full length of the pitch with seven passes, three sidesteps and one dummy leading to the first try of the game. Normally, players receiving the ball in their own 22 would kick to touch and play the safe option. I am pleased they didn't.

Golf courses haven't always been 18 holes. Golf courses might have had 5, 7, 12 or even 22 holes. In 1764, the golfers at St Andrews decided to standardise the rules and thus was born the 18-hole round. St Andrews at the time was only 10 holes long, so they had to play eight of the holes twice.

In training and fitness, there is the principle of reversibility or you might know it as 'use it or lose it'. What takes three months to get in fitness, you lose in a month if you stop training. That's the principle of reversibility!

Today a man knocked on my door and asked for a small donation towards the local swimming pool. I gave him a glass of water.

The 1st international rugby match took place between Scotland and England in 1871 at Raeburn Park in Edinburgh. Scotland won 1–0 by converting a try. The scorer, and therefore the first player to score an international rugby goal, was William Cross. If the modern scoring system was used, the score would have been 12–5 to Scotland, who scored two tries and one conversion. England achieved one try but failed to convert.

Husband and wife, Andre Agassi and Steffi Graff, have each won all of tennis's golden slam events at least once. The Australian, Roland Garros (the French Open), Wimbledon, the US Open and the Olympics Singles.

The Lew Alcindor Rule.

'Slam dunking' was banned in the NCAA (US College league) from 1967 to 1976. Many people have attributed this to the dominance of the then-college phenomenon Lew Alcindor (now known as Kareem Abdul-Jabbar). The no-dunking rule is sometimes referred to as the 'Lew Alcindor rule'.

'The Happy Games' was the slogan for the 1972 Munich games which were terrorised by anti-Israeli extremists.

When Roma's kit man, Lombardi, died, Daniele De Rossi laid his 2006 football world cup winners medal in Lombardi's coffin as an amazing gesture of respect for his old friend. Lombardi was given the nickname was 'Spazzolino' (Italian for toothbrush), because of his excellent boot-cleaning skills.

Twenty feet below sea level, a diver notices another guy at the same depth with no scuba gear. The diver goes down another 10 feet, and the guy joins him a minute later. The diver goes below 15 more feet, and a minute later, the same guy joins him. The diver takes out a waterproof pad and pencil and writes, "How are you able to stay this deep without equipment?" The guy takes the pencil and pad and writes, "I'm drowning, you moron!"

During a game for the Chicago White Sox in 1940, Luke Appling managed to foul off 24 pitches during a single at bat. Eventually, Appling drew a walk.

Eddie Shore from the Boston Bruins might have one of the least pleasant NHL records. He has the most scars on his head. Shore allegedly had 19 scars on his head alone. Even worse, these scars only form part of his total of 600 on his entire body!

The same whistle is used to kick off the opening game of every rugby world cup tournament. It is the 'Gil Evans' whistle, first blown by Gil Evans, the referee overseeing a match between England and New Zealand in 1905. Also, it was used in the final rugby match at the 1924 Paris Olympics.

Football was the first team sport added to the Olympics in 1900.

American gymnast George Eyser won six Olympic medals. A feat made more amazing because his left leg was made out of wood.

The BALCO scandal involved the use of performance-enhancing and banned substances by professional athletes. BALCO stands for 'The Bay Area Laboratory Co-operative' and it was based in the San Francisco Bay Area. The business supplied anabolic steroids to professional athletes including Barry Bonds and Marion Jones.

Rafa Nadal is right-handed.

Rafael Nadal is actually right-handed but plays tennis left-handed. Uncle Tony taught him that way in order to get an advantage against other right-handers.

Liverpool FC's famous Kop consists of 132 tiers of steps and can accommodate approximately 20,000 spectators.

Figure skating made its first appearance at the summer Olympics in London 1908 before going on to become a big part of the winter Olympics.

What do they call a boxer who gets upset at getting beaten up in a fight? A sore loser.

Triple-jumper James Brendan Connolly of United States was the first Olympic champion of the modern era. The first final on the opening day was the triple jump which was then known as the hop, skip and jump. Connolly had a unique technique which involved him taking two hops with the right foot. This would not be permitted nowadays, but it was perfectly acceptable back in 1896. His unique style of jumping saw him beat the field by over a metre and win the first ever modern Olympic silver medal (gold medals did not yet exist). He became the first Olympic champion since AD 385, when the Athenian Zopyrus won the pankration.

The only Olympian ever to be awarded the Nobel Peace Prize was Philip Noel-Baker of Great Britain. He was a British politician, diplomat, academic, an outstanding athlete and campaigner for disarmament, who won the silver in the 1500 metres in 1920.

There were more athletes than spectators, at the 1900 Paris Olympic Games.

Michael Jordan appeared on the cover of Sports Illustrated at least 49 times, followed by Muhammad Ali 37 times, Kareem Abdul-Jabbar 29 times, Magic Johnson 22 times and Jack Nicklaus 22 times.

The 1932 Los Angeles Olympic games were the first to use Olympic villages for the athletes. The purpose-built village was just for the male athletes. The female athletes stayed in luxury hotels.

If you buy a racehorse you should name it "Tav takes the lead" Enter it into a horse race and see how the commentator deals with it.

John Daly was the 9th and final alternate for the PGA golf championship in 1991. He shot a first-round score of 69, without the benefit of a practice round. He finished the tournament with scores of 67, 69 and 71, giving him an amazing three shot victory over Bruce Lietzke.

The Maurice Podoloff Trophy is awarded to the National Basketball Association's (NBA) Most Valuable Player (MVP) of the All-Star game. Maurice Podoloff was a US lawyer and an administrator in both basketball and ice hockey. He served as the president of the Basketball Association of America between 1946–1949 and the NBA from 1949 until 1963.

The Masters Tournament held annually at the Augusta National Golf Club begins with an informal par three practice competition. No winner of this event has ever gone on to win the main tournament the same year.

BMX, an abbreviation for bicycle motocross, is an exciting cycle sport raced downhill with a crazy gated start.

The Philips Sport Vereniging (Philips Sports Union), abbreviated to PSV and internationally known as PSV Eindhoven is a sports club from Eindhoven in the Netherlands. It is best known for its professional football department but has various other sports departments. The club was founded in 1913 as a team for Philips (electronics) employees.

- 'Sledging' or 'mental disintegration' as it is also known is the tactic of talking to players on the opposition side with the objective of destroying either their concentration or their confidence/self-esteem. Subjects often used in sledging include opposing player's family, sexuality and body shape.

- Dino Zoff, who in 1982 became the oldest player to lift the football world cup at 40 years and 133 days.

- The 2016 'Race to the Sun' (Paris-Nice), had stage three of the cycle race cancelled because of heavy snow!

The world's most dangerous sport.

- I play the world's most dangerous sport. It's called disagreeing with my wife.

- The three Olympics that were cancelled because of World Wars I and II were Berlin in 1916, Tokyo in 1940 and London in 1944.

- The first game of basketball was played with a football.

- Chris Brasher of Great Britain was initially disqualified during the steeplechase in the 1956 Melbourne Olympics. He was first over the line. His disqualification was for impeding Ernst Larson from Norway. Brasher appealed the decision and his appeal was supported from non-other than the man he was alleged to have impeded, Larson. Judges reversed their decision and Chris Brasher won gold.

- Between 1989 and 1994, ASEC Abidjan of Côte d'Ivoire were unbeaten in 108 games of football.

- Tennis great Althea Gibson was the first Black woman to win the French Open in 1956 and in 1957 she won Wimbledon and what would become the US Open. Repeating the feat again in 1958.

- Arsenal are a team in transition. They're going from bad to worse.

- Pelé is the youngest ever football world cup winner, picking up the Jules Rimet Trophy in 1958. He was just 17 years and 249 days old.

- The first ever University Boat Race was in 1829, after two school friends, decided to set up a challenge. On February 10th, the Cambridge boating club wrote to Oxford, saying: "the University of Cambridge hereby challenge the

University of Oxford to row a match at or near London, each in an eight-oared boat during the ensuing Easter vacation."

The rainbow jersey in cycling only has 5 colours!

Cycling's famous rainbow jersey (awarded to world champions) isn't really a rainbow, it lifted the colours from the Olympic flag!

The Young Boys of Bern, known as 'Young Boys' for short are a Swiss side created at the end of the 19th century. The team name came about thanks to a football game organised by a group of young students at Bern University.

The start and finish of the annual university boat race are marked by large engraved stones on the south bank of the river Thames. These are the official start and finish points of the race and are marked 'UBR' for University Boat Race. The racecourse is 4 miles and 374 yards (6.779 km) from Putney to Mortlake.

You probably know this team from the Greek Super League under the name of PAOK FC. This club was founded in Thessaloniki back in 1926, and its full name is, Panthessaloníkios Athlitikós Ómilos Konstantinoupolitón. Just in case you were wondering, it means 'Pan-Thessalonian Athletic Club of Constantinopolitans' in English.

Up until 2016 there have been 29 modern Olympic games and the USA have topped the medal table 15 times.

Everton football club's roots loosely lie with an English methodist congregation called St Domingo methodist church Sunday school. In 1865, the church bought some land to play football on, in Breckfield road north, between St Domingo Vale and St Domingo Grove. This was located in the district of Everton in Liverpool.

The Champions League began life as Inter City Fairs Cup in 1958. The first final saw Barcelona win 8–2 against London (over two legs).

Golfer: "Do you think my game is improving?" Caddy: "Yes sir, you miss the ball by much less now."

Liverpool was not the first club to be able to boast a Kop, the first was believed to belong to Woolwich Arsenal.

Thousands of 'thoroughbreds' (horses) are bred for racing every year. Unfortunately, only 5% to 10% ever see a racecourse. What happens to the others? Unless they are lucky enough to find another career or owner, they are disposed of, typically at a slaughterhouse.

The yellow jersey in the Tour de France was first awarded in 1919 to make the race leader stand out. The colour yellow was chosen because the pages of the race sponsor's magazine, L'Auto, were yellow.

First sport played on the moon.

Neil Armstrong originally wanted to take a football to the moon. NASA however, deemed it to be un-American. He ended up playing golf instead.

Villarreal in Spain have the nickname 'the Yellow Submarines' after the famous Beatles song.

The United States (that famous rugby-playing nation) are the reigning rugby union Olympic champions. They won the Paris 1924 games, beating the hosts France in front of 50,000 fans. There was a pitch invasion after the game. In the IOC's eyes, the sport already had a poor reputation, and the pitch invasion was the last straw. Baron Pierre De Coubertin stepped down as head of the Olympic movement after 1925 and he was the biggest advocate for keeping rugby in the games. Once De Coubertin was gone, rugby union was immediately removed from the games. Just remember there are three codes or types of rugby. Union, the 15 a side game, League with 13 players and 7's. In the Rio 2016 Olympic games, Fiji smashed GB 43–7 to win gold in the rugby sevens.

Lightning killed an entire football team in 1998. The catastrophe occurred in Congo during a match between the villages of Bena Tshadi and nearby Basangana.

MCC is the abbreviation for the Marylebone Cricket Club.

I thought it was a sure thing, I backed a horse last week at ten to one. It came in at quarter past three!

Footballer's names first appeared on shirts in the 1992 European Championships held in Sweden.

Every member of the University Boat Race crew trains for approximately two hours for every stroke in the race. It takes about 600 strokes to complete the course. That works out at 1,200 hours over six months. That's 200 hours a month.

Thomas Lord (1755–1832) was an English professional cricketer who played first-class cricket from 1787 to 1802. Overall, Lord made 90 appearances in first-class cricket. He was mostly associated with Middlesex and with Marylebone Cricket Club (MCC). Lord is best remembered as the founder of Lord's Cricket Ground.

TMO stands for Television Match Official. It is currently used by the two codes of Rugby Union and Rugby League to confirm certain decisions made or missed by the officials.

Juventus' stripes originated from them borrowing of kit from Notts County whilst touring England.

In scull rowing, the athlete propels the boat by pulling two oars at the same time. These oars are known as sculls, a name since given to the kind of boat the rowers use. Scull is a very old word in the English language dating back to as early as 1345. The word skull in old English is a 'drinking- bowl.' A few etymologists liken the scooped blade of the scull to the hollow basin of the skull, some say that humans once made these drinking-bowls from actual human skulls.

You're a hooker, no problem.

On their honeymoon, the new husband told his bride, "I have a confession to make that I should have made before, but I was concerned that it might affect our relationship." "What is it?" his new bride asked lovingly. "I'm a golf fanatic," he said. "I think about golf constantly. I'll be out on the golf course every weekend, every holiday and every chance I get. If it comes to a choice between your wishes and golf, golf will always win." His new bride pondered this for a moment and said, "I thank you for your honesty. Now in the same spirit of honesty, I should tell you that I've concealed something about my own past that you should know about. The truth is, I'm a hooker!" "No problem," said her husband, "just widen your stance a little, and overlap your grip and that should clear it right up."

Asymmetric bars has always been the wrong name for the gymnastic discipline because the bars are not asymmetric? There is a line of symmetry and they are both the same length and thickness. That's probably the reason they are now known as the uneven bars.

The Englishman, Charles William Miller is considered to be the father of football in Brazil. In 1894, Miller with two footballs and a set of Hampshire FA rules was instrumental in setting up the football team of the São Paulo

Athletic Club and the Liga Paulista which was Brazil's first football league. The league was originally called the Charles Miller League.

- Australian rules football was originally designed to give cricketers something to play during the off season.

- Racehorses have been known to wear out their shoes in just one race. There's no point in having extra weight down there. Experienced mountain walkers say a pound on your feet is like five pounds on your back. I presume the same, or similar can be applied to horses.

- The iconic silhouette on the Major League Baseball logo is Harmon Killebrew.

- During a televised NFL game, you are likely to watch the following: 11 minutes of actual playing time, just three seconds of cheerleaders, 17 minutes of replays and 67 minutes of players just standing around doing not very much at all.

The fastest man before the four-minute mile.

- We all know (and quite rightly so) that Roger Bannister was the first man under four minutes for the mile. He clocked this time on May 6th, 1954. Gundar Hagg is less well known and held the previous record of 4:01.4, which he set in 1945.

- Fencing joke. What's the point?

- A lot of the university boat racecourse goes through the London borough of Richmond upon Thames. In the borough's coat of arms are two griffins holding oars, one light blue, one dark, in reference to the boat race. Cambridge blue is lighter (hex #A3C1AD) than Oxford blue (hex code #002147).

- The Italian national football team is known as gli Azzuri (the blues), from the traditional colour of Italian national teams and athletes representing Italy. However, they haven't always been blue. In its first two matches, the Italian national team wore white shirts with shorts from the club of each player. The azure (blue) shirts were introduced from the third match onwards.

- The modern Olympics normally follow a 4-year cycle. The 1904 in St Louis, the 1908 in London etc. However, there was an official games held in 1906 in Athens. They were called the Intercalated Games. Baron Pierre de Coubertin permitted the games as compensation to Greece for not being able to host every summer games as they did in the ancient Olympics. The Athens

1906 Intercalated games were organised by the IOC and as such are often referred to as Olympic games.

Celtic were the first British winners of the European Cup!

The majority NFL American football stadia are built north to south so that the sun never interferes with a play.

Paris Saint-Germain football club, commonly referred to as PSG are a French professional association football club based in Paris. Their first team play in Ligue 1. The team was formed in 1970 by the merger of Paris FC and Stade Saint-Germain.

How many Liverpool fans does it take to change a lightbulb? None, they just sit in the dark talking about how good the old one was.

Injured American football players in televised NFL games get about six more seconds of camera time than celebrating players that have scored.

Japan beat South Africa in the 2015 Rugby World Cup. South Africa, or the Springboks as they are known, are the proudest, cruel and arguably one of the greatest rugby teams. Many bookies had put them at 500–1 to win the match. Yet Japan, normally group stage cannon fodder, won the match 34–32.

In the 1972 Air Canada Silver Broom curling tournament, Robert LaBonte, the skip of American team, accidentally kicked the stone belonging to the Canadian team at the end of the game. This put the match into an extra end, which Canada won, and they also won the championship. Canada did not win another World Championship until 1980, and it is said that LaBonte put a 'curse' on Canada.

Osamu Watanabe went through the entire freestyle wrestling Olympic championships held in Tokyo 1964 not conceding a single point. His aggregate score was 186–0.

Before Brazil lost the world cup to Uruguay in 1930, the team had been presented with gold watches inscribed 'for the world cup champions' and Jules Rimet, the President of FIFA, had prepared a speech congratulating Brazil. A Brazilian loss was simply not considered to be in the realm of possibility.

Having sleepless nights worrying about which type mountain bike suspension to buy? Well, if you are just starting out, on a really tight budget, or just want to enjoy the simplicity, you should ride a hardtail, a bike with front suspensions forks. If you know you want to complete drops, descend quickly, want to ride rough, technical trails most of the time or if you're an older rider, then you'll likely be happier on a full suspension bike.

NFL cheerleaders typically make $50–$75 a game. However, by the time they spend money on makeup, hair accessories, dance classes, etc., they often end up losing money!

"Jumps for show, corners for a pro!" that's what they say about mountain bike riding.

Jesse Owens wasn't his name.

As one of the most famous and iconic athletes of all time, Jesse Owens is how we knew him. His real name was James Cleveland Owens. James Cleveland was shortened to JC or Jesse.

In the Champions league final of 2005, AC Milan were the absolute favourites when they went in at half time three nil up. But Liverpool scored three goals in 11 minutes and then went onto win the final on penalties.

It wasn't a requirement for American football players to wear a helmet in the NFL until 1943.

In the 1980 winter Olympics at Lake Placid, the United States ice hockey team defeated the Soviet Union team. The teams played in Madison Square Gardens about a week before the start of the Olympics and the USSR spanked the US, 10–3. The USSR were professionals in an amateur era.

In 1908, the Australian rugby league team became known as 'the Kangaroos' to differentiate between them and their rugby union counterparts 'the Wallabies.'

The oldest American football stadium used in the NFL is Soldier Field in Chicago, opened in 1924.

In the 1968 Mexico Olympics Abele Bikila tried to win his third consecutive Marathon gold. This time however Abebe had to abandon the race after 17 km Abebe having broken a bone in his foot whilst running barefoot a few days before the race.

The United States beat England 1–0 in the 1950 football world cup held in Brazil. England were unsure they would even enter the tournament because of the journey. They finally decided to enter and expected to beat the USA easily. England were beaten by a diving header by Joe Gaetjens. Myth has it that England outshot the Americans 125–1 and only lost because they hit the goalposts dozens of times.

In the 1964 Tokyo Olympics, a native American runner named Billy Mills won the 10,000m. He was only the USA's second-best runner in the event, and over a minute slower than the world record holder and favourite Ron Clarke. With just 30m to go, Mills outsprinted Clarke to win the race.

You can swim any stroke in a freestyle race.

In butterfly, backstroke and breaststroke, competitive swimmers can be disqualified for performing the arm techniques or kick incorrectly. In the freestyle event, virtually any technique is permitted. In the medley relay the freestyle leg must be completed in the traditional front crawl technique.

Fans from Liverpool, Manchester United, Boca Juniors and River Plate all meet on the top of a giant cliff to argue about who is the best football fan in the world. The Manchester United fan says, "I am the best football fan of the best football team in the world, and to prove my devotion to football and to Manchester United, I will jump off this cliff. And as I am falling to my death, I will yell "Go Red Devils!" The other three fans don't believe him at first, but he jumps off and yells, "Go Red Devils!" The Liverpool fan, not wanting to be outdone follows suit and jumps off the cliff yelling, "For Liverpool!" The Boca fan, knowing in his heart that he is truly the greatest football fan in the world yells, "Para Boca!" and pushes the River Plate fan off the cliff.

Deion Sanders is the only person in history to both hit an MLB home run and score an NFL touchdown in the same week. He's also the only person to play in the World Series and the Super Bowl.

Why should a bowling alley be quiet? So you can hear a pin drop!

In mountain biking, the larger the wheel size, the faster the ride. Generally, smaller wheel, better manoeuvrability and strength, 29er, weaker wheel, more prone to technical problems but once they are up to speed, they hold it longer and flow over rougher terrain more easily. 27.5 a happy halfway house.

Betty Robinson won the 100m sprint gold medal in the 1928 Amsterdam Olympics. Before the Olympics, she set the world record in only her 2nd ever race and only competed four times before going to games. After the games, she was involved in an aeroplane crash and was so injured that she was thought dead. Doctors realised she was still living, and she eventually regained an element of health, but this was after nearly two months of unconscientiousness. She was left crippled for years. Undeterred, she wanted to compete again and eight years after her first gold, she won gold again as part of the US relay team.

American football's origins.

American football grew out of English sports such as rugby and association football and became popular on American college campuses in the late 1800's.

The rainbow jersey is awarded to a world champion in cycling, road, track or time trial. The cyclist is then allowed to wear the shirt for the year. They do wash them though!

As an incentive to the swimmers, the 1984 Los Angeles games had both A and B finals. The Olympic medals were contested in the A final with the supposed fastest qualifiers. In the 400m freestyle event a B finalist, Thomas Fahrner of West Germany put in an amazing swim and actually finished with an Olympic record time that would have won the A final and the gold medal!

Why did the police officer go to the softball game? Someone stole second base!

Arthur Newton from the USA was one of the 1900 Paris marathon pre-race favourites. The race was won by Théato who was listed as French but really from Luxemburg. Théato was a baker's assistant who lived and worked in Paris. He knew the streets of Paris well from his delivery routes. Newton claimed that both Théato and Émile Champion (the races' silver medallist) must have used their knowledge of the streets to cheat, as he never saw them pass him on the route. Also, that all the other competitors had mud on their legs from running the course but Théato had mud free legs. These allegations have since been disproved, but as a result of them, Théato did not receive the gold medal until 1912. Arthur newton came fifth, over an hour behind Théato.

Golfing is a good walk spoiled, or so the saying goes. Whilst walking the 6 or 7 miles it takes to complete a round of golf, golfers will talk to each other. Competing golfers however can't talk to each other about rules, shot distance, potential hazards or anything that could influence play. They can speak to their caddies for information but asking a fellow golfer would result in a two-stroke penalty.

Brazil were the overwhelming favourites for the 1950 World Cup. They were the hosts and playing in front of 200,000 at the Maracanã in Rio de Janeiro. The game was supposed to be a coronation for Brazil more than an actual football match. To become world champions, all Brazil had to do was draw the final game against Uruguay. This was because of the league format of the tournament. Uruguay won 2–1, the crowd in the Maracanã sat in stunned silence. A few are said to have died from suicides and heart attacks.

The white jersey is awarded to the under-26 rider who has completed the Tour de France in the least amount of time.

55 years to complete a marathon.

Japanese athlete Kanakuri competed in the 1912 Stockholm Olympic games marathon. As you would do when you are tired, he found a nice garden and had a drink and rest and then decided the race wasn't for him and so retired from it. The competition officials were not informed of his retirement and he ceremonially completed the race 55 years later when he ran into the stadium whilst on holiday in Stockholm.

Rocky Marciano is the only undisputed, undefeated heavyweight champion in boxing history. His record was 49–0. Of those, 43 were knock-outs.

FIFA doesn't want the summer Olympics to compete with their world cup, so they only allow players 23 years old and under to participate. As a compromise with the IOC, three senior football players are allowed to compete alongside the under 23's. Also, the use of players under 23 years old got around the tricky Olympic ideology of amateurs only in the games.

Munster played the game of their lives in 1978 and the All Blacks played their worst game on tour, Muster won the match 12–0. It remains the only time an Irish club side has beaten the All Blacks.

What do you call a Cleveland Browns quarterback at the Super Bowl? A spectator.

At the 1988 summer Olympics in Seoul, American Roy Jones Jr dominated South Korea's Park Si-Hun throughout the light middleweight gold medal bout, landing 86 punches to Park's 32. However, somehow, the five judges gave Park a 3–2 decision and the gold medal.

The green jersey is awarded to the rider with the most points. Points are awarded to riders according to the position that they finish each stage, plus points are also awarded for intermediate sprints during some stages. Invariably, it is one of the sprinters who wins this jersey.

The 1972 men's basketball final was one of the most controversial results in the history of the Olympic games. The USSR, down two points, got three chances (thanks to incompetent officiating) to inbound the ball under their own basket with three seconds on the clock. On the third chance, they got the ball down the court and scored for a 51–50 victory.

Does running late count as exercise?

First country out in the Olympic ceremony.

The Greek team always leads the Olympic opening ceremony procession, and the order of the other teams is then alphabetical. The last team out is the hosting country.

Bohola is an Irish village which comprises about 20 houses, a church and two pubs. Martin Sheridan (winner of nine Olympic medals) and Jim Clarke (winner of a silver medal in the tug-of-war in 1908) were both born in this tiny village. Sheridan and Clarke were first cousins and were on opposing tug-of-war teams in the first round at the London 1908 Olympics. Sheridan competed for the USA and Clarke for the United Kingdom No 2 team as a member of the Liverpool police. Sheridan was also a police officer in the USA.

Oval balls are more suited to rugby than spherical balls as they are easier to catch, hold and run with and don't roll as far so don't go out of play as often.

In the 100m final at the 1988 Summer Olympics, Ben Johnson won the race with a world record time of 9.78s. Unfortunately, it was too good to be true, it was discovered that Johnson had tested positive for steroids. His gold medal was taken away and he was banned for life. In what has been described as the dirtiest race ever only 2 sprinters from the 8 racing in the final went on to finish their careers untarnished by drug use or scandal.

Four doubles badminton teams, two from South Korea, one from China (who were the existing world champions) and one from Indonesia were thrown out of the 2012 Olympics for throwing matches. The teams tried to manipulate the draw to avoid the more difficult teams in the semi-finals.

Ralph Rose of the USA won the left and right hand shot put competition to become 1908 Olympic champion.

The first ever internationally recognised male vs female boxing match took place on 9th October 1999. The match was between Margaret MacGregor and Loi Chow in Seattle, Washington. Margaret MacGregor won in four rounds.

Paul is so condescending about my tennis strokes. I can't take any more of his backhanded compliments.

The pommel horse is named 'the pig' by male gymnasts.

What did the bowling pins do because they kept getting hit? They went on strike.

The boxer Hungarian Laszlo Papp won his third successive Olympic gold medal at the 1956 Melbourne games. Coming from a communist country, he was prevented from turning professional. He ignored the rule and travelled to Vienna to train and win the European middleweight title. He was given a world title shot but was prevented from fighting because the Hungarian government were so incensed that he had fought abroad as a professional that they refused him another exit visa!

Doctor's advice.

When I was 40, my doctor advised me that a man in his 40's shouldn't play tennis. I heeded his advice carefully and could hardly wait until I reached 50 to start again.

Football players run an average of 9.65 km during every game.

South Korean épée fencer Shin Lam had a one-point lead over Britta Heidemann with one second remaining in their semi-final of the 2012 London Olympic games. It's virtually impossible to record a strike in only one second, unless the clock sticks and you get extra time. That's exactly what happened, Heidemann got an extra fraction of a second, and scored a touch to win the match.

The Tour de France yellow jersey is the most coveted item of clothing in professional cycling. The wearer is the rider who has completed the race in the least amount of time, and as such tops the overall or general classification (GC) of the race.

The only time a host country of the Olympic games has failed to win a gold medal was the 1976 Montreal games. Canada failed to win a single gold at their games.

In NASCAR, most teams use nitrogen in their tyres instead of air. This is because loss of tyre pressure is slower, because the gas in the tire escapes more slowly than air does giving it a more stable tyre pressure.

- Three men have won the heavyweight championship title three times and they are, Evander Holyfield, Lennox Lewis and Muhammad Ali.

- The first relay event in athletics was included in the 1908 London Olympic games. However, it wasn't in the format we recognise nowadays. It wasn't 4 x 100m or 4 x 400m. The old style was that the first two men sprinted 200m each, the 3rd ran 400m and the final leg was 800m.

Only black underwear permitted.

- All major league baseball umpires must wear black underwear whilst on the job! Officiating, that is!

- People in nudist colonies play volleyball more than any other sport.

- From 1913 onwards, football goalkeepers had to wear different coloured shirts from their teammates.

- I was at a wedding last week. When the bride came down the aisle, the groom was waiting for her with his golf bag and clubs. She asks, "Why the heck did you bring your golf clubs to the wedding?" He turns to her and replies, "Honey, you don't mean to tell me this is gonna take all day!"

- Throughout his entire career in basketball, the great Wilt Chamberlain was never fouled out of a single game.

- A controversial incident happened in the 1984 Los Angeles games. Puerto Rican sprinter and long jumper Madeline de Jesus tweaked a hamstring in the long jump. Not wanting to miss the opportunity of running in the 4x400m final, she got her twin sister Margaret to run in the 4x400m relay heat. The coach withdrew the team upon finding out!

- Australian rugby league player Ryan McGoldrick was a free agent having played both in the UK and Australia. He listed himself on eBay as a '1981 antique rugby league player who is well maintained and comes with a full-service history.' His auction had gained 22 bids at a price of £215 when it was removed for infringing eBay's rules. The selling of body parts and remains is not permitted on eBay.

- Currently no country in the southern hemisphere has ever hosted a winter Olympic games.

- From a complete standstill, a human is capable of outrunning a Formula 1 race car for about 30 feet.

The early Olympic games were celebrated as a religious festival from 776 BC until 393 AD when the games were banned for being a pagan festival. The Olympics were celebrated and were a festival to the Greek god Zeus.

In horse racing, the favourite wins fewer than 30% of the time!

The shot put competition has a long history. Soldiers competed against each other hurling cannonballs. The first recorded shot-put competitions were in Scotland and dated back to the early 19th century. The shot-put competition was also part of the British amateur championships in 1866. The men's shot weighs 7.260 kilograms (16.01 lb), and the women's shot weighs four kilograms (8.8 lb). If you tried to throw an object of this weight, you would most likely injure yourself and that is the reason for putting the shot in this manner. It is also similar in action to loading a cannon ball into the front of a cannon.

No alcohol for rugby players.

Some rugby players, if they are severely bruised from contact, are given prohibition notices by their medical advisors. A bruise is an internal bleed and alcohol thins the blood and can actually make the bruise worse and it will definitely take longer to heal.

The walk from the changing room to the ring is too long, says the boxer. His trainer replies, no worries, on your way back you will come back with the stretcher...

No high jumper has ever been able to stay off the ground for more than one second.

Tennis was removed from the Olympic programme in 1924 because they couldn't determine which players were professional or not!

A 'face-off' in hockey was originally called a 'puck-off'.

Unfortunately, Brunei didn't compete in the 2008 Beijing Olympics because they missed the registration deadline for their athletes.

The Calcutta Cup is the trophy presented to the winner of the England versus Scotland rugby union match. When the Calcutta RFC was disbanded, the memory of the club was kept alive by having the remaining 270 silver rupees in their bank account melted down and made into a trophy.

Top table tennis players can hit balls at speeds well over 100 miles per hour.

The 1956 Melbourne Olympics had the equestrian events hosted in Stockholm. The events had finished five months before the Melbourne games had even started.

A table tennis net is six inches in height. The men's volleyball net height is eight foot. That's 16 times higher.

The first modern Olympics in 1896 only had 300 athletes from 11 countries and just eight British. In Rio 2016, there were 11,303 athletes competing from 207 nations. The 1904 games in St Louis the poorest attended in terms of competitors and sometimes referred to as the worst of all time. Team GB sent no athletes at all!

In China and Sweden, top table tennis players are paid just to practice.

Gianfranco Zola is the only player to be sent off in the football world cup finals on his birthday! The Italian received a red in their second-round victory against Nigeria on his 28th birthday. Some people say, he was desperate to get at least one card on his birthday!

Lucky number 8.

The Beijing Olympics were opened on the 8th August at 8:08 pm because in Chinese culture, the number eight is considered lucky.

Pedro became the first man to score in six different, official club competitions in one season, scoring in La Liga, the Supercopa de España, the Copa del Rey, the Champions League, the UEFA Super Cup and the FIFA Club World Cup

Why did the football coach go to the bank? "To get his quarter back."

American Fred Lorz's marathon victory in the 1904 St Louis games was overturned when it was revealed he had hitched a lift in a car for most of the distance before racing to the finish from just four miles out.

No country has ever won the football world cup during the papacy of a Pope from the same country!

Ryder Cup captain Paul McGinley had a fish tank installed with blue and gold fish to represent the European colours at Gleneagles in 2014. Maybe it was the crucial factor in Europe's 16 ½ points to 11 ½ win over the USA.

The Portuguese, Fernando Peyroteo boasts the world's greatest goals to game ratio of 1.77, having found the net an incredible 331 times in just 187 games for Sporting Lisbon between 1937 and 1949, he reportedly scored four or more goals in a game on more than 30 occasions, and nine in one game!

Australia's Henry Pearce stopped rowing in his 1928 Amsterdam games quarter-final to allow a family of ducks to pass safely in front of his boat. He still won the heat and went on to win gold in the final.

A man waited patiently for his wife to finish playing a round of golf on their 18th wedding anniversary. The two of them went out to dinner at a lovely restaurant. They discussed many happy memories they'd shared during the years. Then he said, "Want to go for another 18?" "No," she replied, "I think it's too dark now."

The 1500m victory of Luxembourg's Josy Barthel at the 1952 Games was so unexpected, that officials had not brought along the music notes to the state's national anthem. With Barthel waiting on the podium, the band was forced to improvise causing him to cry in disappointment.

Bo Jackson played NFL for just three seasons because of injury. He was then able to play baseball playing for the Kansas City Royals, Chicago White Sox and California Angels. Incredibly in 1989, he was picked for both the baseball All-Star game and American Football's Pro Bowl match.

Sometime soon before December 21st 2019 rats ate their way through the wires used for the goal line technology in the Allianz Riviera stadium. The affected match was between Nice and Toulouse. Luckily, there was no controversy as a result and Nice went on to win 3-0.

Modern games founder Baron Pierre de Coubertin introduced an arts competition at the 1912 Stockholm Games. The gold medal winner for literature was… Baron Pierre de Coubertin.

Why did the police officer go to the softball game? Someone stole second base!

The legend that is Sir Ian Botham was not only the greatest cricketing all-rounder of his generation, but also a centre-half (a defender) who had been split between cricket and football as a schoolboy. He made 11 league appearances for Scunthorpe in 1980.

Fifty-six athletes started the 1908 Olympic Marathon. An athlete named Longboat was leading the race until he collapsed after 20 miles. Into the lead went the South African Hefferon, who was coasting until he accepted a glass of champagne. He then vomited and was overtaken by Pietri. Into the stadium ran Dorando Pietri but he was in such a state that he began running the wrong way and had to be turned around, he collapsed five times in the last 200 yards, he was carried over the line. Johnny Hayes, an American, was second. The USA lodged a complaint, saying that the Italian Pietri had received help and should be disqualified. The judges agreed and Johnny Haynes became Olympic champion. As compensation for losing the medal, Queen Alexandra gave Pietri a gilded silver cup as a reward. He became famous after this incident, Sir Arthur Conan Doyle started a fund to raise money to buy him a bakery, he then ran professionally in Europe and the USA. When he finally retired at the age of 26, he invested his quite substantial wealth into an ill-feted hotel business with his brother and lost the lot!

Who can jump higher, a horse or a human?

- The current world record high jump for a mounted horse is 2.47m, the high jump world record is 2.45 m (8 ft 01⁄4 in) belonging to Cuba's Javier Sotomayor. So, a horse can jump higher than a human.

- CSKA stands for Central'nyi Sportivnyi Klub Armii, which means the Central Sport Club of the Army. This club was founded by the Red Army in 1923. Originally, players who played for CSKA were all conscripts in the army.

- There has been talk of bike doping for recent years. Femke Van den Driessche was the first cyclist caught in a cyclocross race in Belgium. The small electric motor which sits in the downtube and drives the bottom bracket round, gives up to 100 watts of power.

- The largest football tournament had 5,098 teams and over 35,000 players participated. The tournament was the second Bangkok seven-a-side league and it was held in 1999.

- Football is the most watched and played sport on earth.

- The state sport of Alabama is figure skating.

Football hasn't changed in more than 120 years.

- The official size of a football is 28 inches in circumference. The ball used in professional football has remained exactly the same size and shape for more than 120 years.

- Where does the majority of an ice hockey player's salary come from? The tooth fairy.

- Pakistan is the centre of the football world. At least when it comes to production of footballs, 75% of the world's footballs are manufactured there.

- After his death, Baron Pierre de Coubertin had his heart sent to the site of ancient Olympia in Greece, where it is still kept in a monument. The rest of him is buried in Lausanne, Switzerland.

- The Houston Rockets did not discover until the 14th game of the 1984–85 NBA season that their home arena rims were set at 9 feet, 7 inches. That's five inches shorter than the official height of 10 feet.

- A practice match Arsenal played at Highbury stadium was the first live coverage of a football match shown on television in 1937.

- If at first you don't succeed, skydiving is not for you!

- A total of 20 red cards were shown in a match played between Sportivo Ameliano and General Caballero in Paraguay.

- In 1978, Sir Alex Ferguson (Manchester United's most successful manager ever) was previously sacked by St Mirren. He then went (with some controversy about taking players with him) to Aberdeen and then finally to Manchester United.

- The grass at Wimbledon was kept two inches long until 1949 when an English player was bitten by a snake.

- The NCAA required college football players to study during the halftime break in matches. This crazy rule continued until 1925.

- The official Major League Baseball rule book states that baseball games 'are to last nine innings or two and one-half hours, whichever comes first'.

- Shakhtyor (Shakhtar in Ukrainian) means 'coal miner'. Coal mining is a very important industry in Donetsk, Ukraine, where the team plays. Originally, the club was called Ugolshchiki ('coal diggers'), then Stakhanovets, after Stakhanov, a hero coal miner of the early Soviet times. In the communist era, the team was made up solely of miners.

- The idea behind handicapping horseraces is to give all entrants an equal chance of winning and therefore making the racing more exciting. The better, faster horses or those with lighter jockeys are penalised by having to carry more weight inserted into pockets on the saddle.

One day, a man came home and was greeted by his wife dressed in stunningly sexy lingerie. "Tie me up," she purred, "And you can do anything you want." So, he tied her up and went to watch a football match.

Gandhi once covered the Olympics as a newspaper reporter. He covered the 1932 Olympics in Los Angeles.

In the 1986 NBA draft, Len Bias was the #2 pick by the Boston Celtics. Unfortunately, he died of cocaine overdose two days after the draft night. He is often referred to as the greatest player not to play NBA.

Who can jump further, a horse or a human?

Well, 8.4m is the longest jump by a horse with a rider on it over water. Andre Ferreira achieved this mark. The current human world record for the long jump is Mike Powell's 8.95m. So, a man can jump further than a horse!

Boxing legend Rocky Marciano was an entrepreneur and after retiring from boxing, his company invented the fax machine.

There are only four players on each polo team.

A Norwegian betting site posted a joke bet and 167 people cashed in big time at odds of 175 to 1. The bet was that Luis Suarez would bite someone during the 2014 World Cup. In the world cup group stage match, Suarez bit Italy's defender Giorgio Chiellini. This was the 3rd time in his career he was caught biting, previously in 2010 whilst playing for Ajax, he was suspended for seven games for biting PSV Eindhoven's Otman Bakkal on the shoulder. Playing for Liverpool in 2013, he was suspended for 10 games for biting Chelsea's Branislov Ivanovic on the arm!

What did the softball glove say to the ball? "Catch ya later!"

Wrestling matches in the ancient Greek Olympics were in the nude and a match would end if one of the competitors became aroused.

Canada were playing the USA in the 2010 Olympic ice hockey final. Nearly 27 million Canadians tuned in to view the gold medal final. That's 80% of the country's population. One flight got delayed because the passengers didn't want to board the plane, they wanted to watch the game instead of travelling.

In 1900 Paris Olympics, winners got paintings instead of gold medals. Gold, silver and bronze medals weren't given out until the third modern Olympics, in 1904. The French gave the winners paintings because they believed they were more valuable. The average weight of an Olympic medal is about 175g. In London, the gold medal weighed about 400g. 175g of 18k Gold is worth about $7000. Current gold medals awarded, I'm afraid to say are merely gold plated!

Luckiest ever Olympic winner?

Steven Bradbury won a gold medal in 2002 Salt Lake City Olympics in speed skating, because everyone in front of him crashed. Three races in a row!

Wilt Chamberlain, one of the greatest players in NBA history, was a noted scorer on the court. He was also quite good scoring off the court as well. As a lifelong bachelor, he claimed to have had sex with over 20,000 different women.

In English football you (for those of you with eagle eyes) will see teams with either square corner flags or triangular ones. The use of triangular corner flags in English football is a regular occurrence based upon a traditional achievement. Tradition holds that only clubs that have won the FA Cup have the right to use triangular corner flags rather than the regular square ones. However, some clubs that have never won the FA Cup use triangular corner flags, such as AFC Wimbledon, because they see themselves as the true successors to Wimbledon who did win the 1988 cup with the crazy gang.

The Kennett Curse is the name given to AFL club Hawthorn's 11 match losing streak against fierce rivals Geelong. In 2008 after the Hawks won the 2008 Premiership, the then-Hawthorn President Jeff Kennett proclaimed that Geelong 'lacked the mentality to defeat Hawthorn in big games'. Quite the contrary happened though. Geelong defeated Hawthorn eleven times in a row!

Times were tough for Paris in 1900 and they didn't want to spend much on their Olympics. They held the track and field events in the bois (woods) de Boulogne on an area of grass because they didn't want to build a cinder track! They refused to cut trees down and both javelins and discuss were hitting and getting stuck in them. They used the river Seine for the swimming events and when the current was running fast, world records tumbled!

If self-depreciation was a sport. I'd probably be pretty rubbish at that too.

Károly Takács, a right-handed Hungarian shooter, severely injured his right (shooting) hand in a grenade explosion. He retrained himself with his left hand and went on to win two Olympic golds 10 years later.

- In the 1970 Mr Olympia final, even after some delay the judges could not decide between Arnold Schwarzenegger and Sergio Oliva. So the two of them, exhausted, agreed to walk off. Sergio left, but Arnold, after taking one step, turned back to the judges, made fun of Sergio for leaving and started posing again and won.

- Pistol duelling with wax bullets was a popular pastime in the early 20th century. It even featured as a sport in the 1908 Summer Olympics.

- When a 7ft NBA player named Reggie Harding attempted to rob a Detroit gas station with a mask, the attendant said, "I know it's you, Reggie." To which he replied, "No, man, it ain't me." Reggie had a career littered with controversy with rape, drugs, violence and more. He was murdered in 1972 and unfortunately the grave dug for him was too short for his 7-foot coffin and so he had to be buried at an angle!

- A football world cup qualifying match between Chile and Brazil was cancelled after an opposing fan supposedly hit the Chilean goalkeeper with a flare. Photos later proved that the flare never touched him. The goalkeeper faked the injury by cutting himself with a hidden razor blade.

- Eric Liddell was born in China as the son of a missionary. He won the men's 400m gold for Great Britain in the 1924 Paris Olympic games. The story is immortalised in the film 'Chariots of Fire'. He died in 1945 in a prisoner of war camp in China. On Eric Liddell's memorial in the Tientsin province of China, there are the simple words taken from the Book of Isaiah and they read 'They shall mount up with wings as eagles; they shall run and not be weary'.

Civil war ceasefire to watch Pelé

- The two factions involved in the Nigerian civil war agreed to a 48-hour ceasefire. The agreement in 1967 was so they could watch Pelé play an exhibition game in Lagos.

- In the 1977 NBA draft, Bruce Jenner was selected 139th overall by the Kansas City Kings, despite not having actually played basketball since high school. Jenner had just won the gold medal for decathlon at the 1976 Olympic games. He never played a game of professional basketball.

- China didn't win its first medal until 1984. It's hard to believe now, since China seems to be a medal-winning machine. Xu Haifeng won their first gold in the 50-metre pistol event.

Lob is a funny word. Literally, as its early meaning derives from the old English word 'lobbes' which meant 'clown.' And there's no funnier sight to see, than drawing your opponent into the net and lobbing the ball over their head seeing them scramble back after it.

Having a population of less than one million, Qatar hires migrant workers to fill their empty stadiums in the Qatar Stars football league, paying them one dollar an hour to watch the matches.

On the 9th June 1984, Marion Woronin ran 9.992s for the 100m and it would be the first time ever a white man broke the 10s barrier. But in track and field back then, the time were rounded up to the nearest 1/100th and not 1/1000th. Therefore, his actual time of 9.992s was rounded up to 10.00s dead.

The 1912 Olympics was the last time that gold medals were solid gold. Ever since, they've been silver with gold plating.

The first Olympic drug suspension wasn't until the 1968 Mexico games, Hans-Gunnar Liljenwall, was the culprit. He was a Swedish pentathlete and was suspended because he tested positive for the banned substance alcohol. He drank several beers before the pentathlon and was disqualified for it.

Hitler grew to hate soccer because he couldn't fix matches to ensure German victories.

The Moors of northern Africa ruled the area of the Iberian Peninsula now known as Spain for nearly 700 years. Their language was Arabic, its influence on the Spanish language is significant. One of those words is olé. Ancient traditions among many Moors were to have great celebrations that included dancing. When a dancer performed at the highest levels of grace and intensity, for that moment, they were believed to be vessels through which Allah was acting, and the moment allowed the witnesses to see a glimpse of Allah's power through the artist. So, it was customary for the Moors of northern Africa centuries ago to exclaim Allah! Over the time and many centuries this became olé and is used not only in the barbaric activity (I won't call it sport) of bullfighting but it is also by spectators celebrating beautiful sport. The Brazilians crowds were first to use it whilst watching Garrincha.

John Boland from Great Britain travelled to the Athens games in 1896 to spectate. His friend, who was also the secretary of the 1896 organising committee, entered him into both the men's singles and doubles tennis competition. Boland went on to become Olympic champion in both competitions. His doubles winning partner was Friedrich Traun from Germany.

Sex is like sport.

☺ Sex is like sports. I don't do it myself, but I love watching other people do it.

✺ In May 2011, Oklahoma City Thunder small forward Kevin Durant tweeted an insult directed at cult rapper Lil B. In response, Lil B cursed Durant, claiming that he would never win the NBA championship.

✺ In 1908, the London Olympics went on for 187 days, they started in April and didn't end until October. The Tokyo games of 2020/21 are just scheduled for just 18 days.

✺ In 1985, English soccer hooligans killed 39 people and caused 600 injuries, resulting in all English club teams being banned from international competition for five years.

✺ Drogheda United FC, an Irish football team, has a logo based on the Ottoman Empire. The Ottomans secretly smuggled food into Drogheda during the great famine of Ireland.

☺ In the 1984 sheep dog trials, none were convicted!

✺ Colombian football player, Andres Escobar, who scored an 'own goal' in a 1994 World Cup match against USA, was murdered as the scapegoat for the team's upset. One of the gunmen shouted 'goal!' every time he fired a shot whilst killing him!

The oldest and youngest Olympians.

✺ There's a 62-year age difference between the oldest and youngest Olympians. The youngest ever was Greek gymnast Dimitrios Loundras, he was 10. The oldest was Oscar Swahn, a Swedish shooter in the 1920 Antwerp Olympics. He was 72 years old when he won gold, making him not only the oldest Olympian but also the oldest Olympic gold medal winner.

☺ A Rangers and Celtic fan get into a nasty car accident in Glasgow. Both vehicles are really badly damaged, but amazingly neither of them is hurt. After they crawl out of their cars, the Celtic fan says, "So you're a Rangers fan, that's interesting. I'm a Celtic fan. Wow! Just look at our cars. There's nothing left, but fortunately we are unhurt. This must be a sign from God that we should meet and be friends and live together in peace the rest of our days." The

Rangers fan just about managed to nod and replied, "I totally agree, this must be a sign from God!" The Rangers fan went on, "And look at this, here's another miracle. My car is completely demolished but this bottle of whisky didn't break. Surely God wants us to drink it, to celebrate the fact we both got out of this terrible crash alive." He hands the bottle to the Celtic fan who nods his head in agreement, opens it and takes few big swigs from the bottle, then hands it back to the Rangers fan. The Rangers fan takes the bottle, immediately puts the cap back on and hands back to the Celtic fan. The Celtic fan asks, "Aren't you having any?" The Rangers fan smiles and replies, "No thanks, I think I'll just wait for the police."

Nine months after hosting the 2006 football world cup, the birth-rate in Germany was up to 30% higher compared to the same period in the year before that.

Greek footballer, Giorgos Katidis, was given a life ban from playing for the Greek national team after giving the Nazi salute after his winning goal in AEK Athens 2-1 victory over Veria.

The Olympic flame was first used in the 1928 games in Amsterdam.

Football evolved out of mob football, a game played between whole villages, any means could be used to move the ball, as long as it did not lead to manslaughter or murder, the goal being to get the ball into the centre of the other village.

Norway is the only national football team in the world that has never lost to Brazil. They have currently played each other four times and have won twice and drawn twice.

Muscle means mouse.

The word 'muscle' has its roots from the Latin word 'musculus', which itself is a diminutive of 'mus' meaning 'mouse'. Some people used to describe muscles as little mice moving about under the skin.

FC Barcelona paid UNICEF 1.5 million euros each year to have their logo on their shirts. A few years ago, Aston Villa gave their shirt rights away for free to the Acorns Charity in Birmingham.

The UK had National Service after the WWII. Rugby League great Alex Murphy was on service and his commanding officer wanted him to play rugby union for the Royal Air Force. Murphy wanted to continue playing rugby league for St Helens. His commanding officer threatened to post him to Guam if he did not play for the RAF. At first Murphy didn't even know where Guam was, he quickly learned the union rules once he realised its location in the Pacific!

Why was the tiny ghost asked to join the football team? They needed a little team spirit.

Greenland can't join FIFA because they don't have good enough grass pitches there for a football game. FIFA stipulate minimum standards of international football pitches.

In the tug of war event at the Paris 1900 games, only two teams entered, and the joint Danish and Swedish team beat France to win.

Not surprisingly, North Korean world cup soccer fans are actually hand-picked by the government. The fans are made up of Chinese volunteers since North Koreans are not allowed to travel.

What did Mike Tyson say to his girlfriend? You're EARresistable.

The fastest red card in football history was just two seconds. Lee Todd was sent off for foul language after he exclaimed '#uc! me that was loud' after the starting whistle.

The 'Pat Venditte rule' and named after the switch pitcher in Major League Baseball. Venditte can throw with either arm. The rule states that he has to declare which arm he will use before each at-bat. He is however allowed to switch arms from batter to batter, or even the same batter in different plate appearances. This prevents switch-hitters from also switching from side-to-side to get a favourable matchup while Venditte also would be switching from arm to arm. Obviously, baseball gloves are handed and so for Venditte to wear a glove suitable for either hand throughout a game, Venditte has a special six-fingered glove allowing it to be worn on either hand.

The famous wartime game of football played between England and Germany in no man's land in WWI saw England beat Germany 1-0. The East Surrey Regiment represented England with their staff sergeant acting as the referee.

Originally, in early Olympics, football, rugby and hockey were classed as winter Olympic sports.

At just 4, football star Abby Wambach from the USA was transferred from the girls team to the boys. This was because she scored 27 goals in just three games!

It's like football coming home again, West Ham have taken over the use of the 2012 Olympic Stadium. Football was first played in the 1900 Olympic Games in Paris. Great Britain beat France in the final 4–0. The team representing GB was Upton Park FC, who had players that also played for West Ham United or as they were known back then as Thames Ironworks.

Cycling gears are still measured in inches, and whilst it may seem old fashioned to refer to them in that way, it's a very simple calculation that gives us an easy way to compare all sorts of pedal cycles. To calculate gear size, you enter the diameter (in inches) of the actual wheel, and the numbers of teeth on the crankset and rear sprocket, into the following formula: Gear = Wheel × Chainwheel ÷ Sprocket

Biggest winning margin.

AS Adema 149–0 SO l'Emyrne was a football score in a match played on 31st October 2002 between the two teams in Antananarivo, Madagascar. SO l'Emyrne intentionally lost the game against their arch-rivals AS Adema in protest over refereeing decisions that had gone against them during a four-team playoff tournament. They scored 149 own goals! Their opponents didn't touch the ball once they started scoring the own goals! The previous biggest loss in a senior game was when Arbroath smashed Bon Accord 36–0 in 1885.

Brazilian football star Ronaldinho first gained media attention when he was just 13. His team won a game 23–0. The score was quite amazing but even more amazing was that Ronaldinho scored every single goal in the game.

A man and his wife are playing the fifth hole at their club when he slices his drive so far to the right it rolls into an equipment barn. He finds the ball and plans to take a drop when she says, "Let me go down to the other end of the barn and hold the door open. Then you can hit your ball through the door and back to the fairway." He thinks this is a good idea, so she holds the door. He takes a big swing, but rather than flying through the door, the ball hits his wife in the head and kills her. A year later, the same man and his new bride are playing the same hole when he again slices the ball into the shed. He finds it and plans to take an unplayable lie when she says, "Let me go down to the other end of the barn and hold the door open. Then you can hit your ball through the door and back to the fairway." He looks at her, shakes his head and explains, "No way. The last time I tried that, I took a triple bogey on this hole!"

The eternal flame at the Arc de Triomphe in Paris has only been extinguished once. Unfortunately, it was done by drunken Mexican football fans. They urinated on it after the final of 1998 world cup, when France defeated Brazil.

Ø   Rugby league and union split in 1895, at first rugby league stuck with the 15 a side game but in 1903 the sport experimented by reducing the numbers to 12. In 1906 it was finally decided on 13 a side to allow more space and therefore more open play.

⊕   German football player Mesut Özil donated his €300,000 World Cup victory bonus to pay for medical treatment for 23 poor children in Brazil.

⊘   If there was ever a special award for the heaviest baseball player then the clear winner would be Walter Ernest Young Jr. He was listed at 372 lbs. He played 10 games for the Orioles in 2005, with stats of 0.303 (10 for 33) batting average, 1 home run, and 3 RBIs and quite predictably no bases stolen.

🏃   In an Olympic ice hockey qualifier in 2008, Slovakia women beat the Bulgarian women 82-0. That's a goal every 44 seconds. As good as the Slovak ladies were in that game, they didn't go on to qualify for the 2010 Vancouver games. Canada beat the USA 2-0 ultimately to become the Olympic champions.

🏈   The NFL has 32 teams, 28 have made it to a Super Bowl final. Leaving the Houston Texans, the Jacksonville Jaguars, the Detroit Lions and Cleveland Browns. Of those four, however, Houston, Jacksonville and Detroit at least have hosted a Super Bowl in their city. Unfortunately, the city of Cleveland has neither hosted nor played in a Super Bowl final.

🐾   Reebok, the sports shoe company named itself after an antelope native to South Africa. The reebok is part of a family that also include springboks. You might be familiar with this animal because the South African rugby union team has it as their emblem.

❀   The first winter Olympic games were held in 1924 in Chamonix, France. 16 nations sent 258 participants to compete in six different sports. Sochi had 88 nations and more than 2,800 participants to compete in 98 events across seven sports.

⊕   A simple way of thinking about weight loss is all about a calorie deficit. If you consume more calories than you use you will get fatter. If you are in a deficit, you use more calories than you consume you will lose weight. It all gets a bit more complicated with Atkins, Keto, Zones, South Beach etc.

❀   Per capita, Norway has won one winter Olympic medal for every 16,556 residents. The United States, on the other hand, has one medal for every 1,237,154 residents!

Are you allergic to sport?

I think I'm allergic to sport, I keep breaking out in sweat!

Two counties on the all-time top 10 list of medal winners don't even exist now. The top 10 medal winners at the winter Olympics include both the Soviet Union and East Germany. The USSR collected 194 medals, between 1952 and 1991, making it third of all time. Meanwhile, East Germany's participation only lasted from 1968 to 1988, but in those 20 years, they managed to win 110 total winter medals during that time, placing them 10th on the all-time list.

Aston Villa won the 1982 European Cup 1–0. Peter Withe scored in the 67th minute against Bayern Munich. I don't think we can tire of Brian Moore's commentary, "Shaw, Williams prepared to venture down the left. There's a good ball in for Tony Morley. Oh, it must be and it is! It's Peter Withe!"

In 2002, the baseball all-star game went 11 innings with the score at seven each before it was finally called off due to a lack of pitchers.

Swimmer Henry Taylor was one of Great Britain's greatest ever Olympians. In the 1906 Interim Olympic games in Athens, Taylor won gold, silver and bronze medals, three Golds at the 1908 London games, a bronze at the 1912 Stockholm Olympics, and a bronze at Antwerp in 1920. In growing up, he was so poor he could only afford to swim in Chadderton baths on 'dirty water days', this was because the entrance fee was cheaper. As an amateur, he had little time to train and would swim in the reservoir near the mill where he worked in his lunch hour and after work in his local boating lake. His haul of three golds in one games was a feat that remained unmatched by any Briton for a century. That was until Sir Chris Hoy matched him by winning three cycling golds in Beijing.

Handball is the second largest sport in Europe.

A couple of old boys are talking and one asks the other, "Are you going to watch the school football match this afternoon?" "No, it's a waste of time," came the reply. "I can tell you the score before the game starts." "Can you? What is it then?" "Nil nil!"

Is it worth it?

An hour of vigorous swimming will burn up to 650 calories. That's 2½ Mars Bars approximately!

Only three teams have won the FA cup without conceding a single goal during the entire competition. They were the Wanderers, in 1873, Preston North End in 1889 and Bury in 1903.

Over 50% of world-class swimmers suffer from shoulder pain.

The keirin is a massed start cycle track race where riders are paced by a derny (small motorbike) up to 50 km/h and then the derny peels off to leave the riders to race the final three laps.

The female athlete Stamata Revithi ran the marathon route the day after Spyridon Louis won the Athens 1986 event. Stamata was born into poverty, had children and walked 9km to Athens to get a job. On route there, Stamata met a male runner who advised her to run the marathon to become famous and then she would be able to get a good job. As a child, she had enjoyed running and thought she would beat the male competitors! She was prevented from running and so she completed her own run on the same course in 5 hours 30 minutes as a protest. She wasn't however, allowed to enter the Panathinaiko stadium at the end of the race.

An old joke here, the East German pole vault champion who is now the West German champion.

Ozeki is the title given to a sumo wrestler who has won 33 fights in three consecutive tournaments.

'Mr Irrelevant' is the nickname given to the player picked dead last in each year's NFL draft. Most of these players never go on to big NFL careers or are dropped in the preseason training camps.

What are Arsenal fans going to do after they win the Champions League? Shut down the play-station.

The only summer and winter Olympic champion.

Only one person in the Olympics has won gold medals at both the winter and summer Olympic Games. At the 1920 Antwerp summer games, American Eddie Eagan won the light-heavyweight boxing gold. Years later, Eagan was a member of America's gold medal-winning four-man bobsled team at the 1932 Lake Placid games.

Julio Iglesias played for the Real Madrid youth team before a car crash ended his career.

With 303 total medals and 107 golds, Norway starts certain events in the winter Olympics as favourites, especially in cross-country skiing and speed skating, the country's two best sports.

Blackburn Rovers get their name from their lowly beginnings. The team lacked an official ground for quite some time after its formation, causing them to be dubbed the 'Rovers'. Likewise, a team with Wanderers in the name, such as Bolton or Wolverhampton would also have had to originally share grounds.

An average pro cyclist can ride anywhere around 25,000 miles in a year. That's more than cycling around the world! The circumference of the earth around the equator is 24,901 miles (40,075 km).

I've always wanted to be somebody, but I should have been more specific.

Fidel Castro, the Cuban revolutionary, was once University of Havana's star baseball player.

The following distances in golf became officially recognised in 1911

- Par 3 is up to 225 yards
- Par 4 between 225 and 425 yards
- Par 5 between 426 and 600 yards
- Par 6 are over 601 yards

Before Babe Ruth joined the Yankees, professional cyclists were the highest paid athletes.

Back in 1927, the Great Britain Ryder cup teams took six days to cross the Atlantic on RMS Aquitania. The competition was held at the Worcester Country Club in Massachusetts and the journey must have taken it out of the players because the British team were walloped 9½–2½ by the USA.

First ever cycle race.

The first ever cycle race was first recorded in 1868 and took place just outside Paris, France.

My wife said, "I can think of 14 reasons to leave you, plus your obsession with tennis!" I replied, "That's 15 love!"

An eerie coincidence happened on May 26th, 1955. Two-time world F1 champion Alberto Ascari died at the age of 36. His father Antonio Ascari was killed while leading the 1925 French Grand Prix in an Alfa Romeo was also 36 when he died. Both father and son had won 13 championship Grands Prix. Both of them were killed four days after surviving serious accidents. Both drivers had crashed fatally at the exit of fast but easy left-hand corners and sadly both left behind a wife and two children.

A snooker break is a bit vague in its definition and history. To break or a break off in snooker is the first shot at the tightly packed reds. It is obvious why this is named so, breaking up the reds. A maximum break is scoring the maximum number of points available on the table. You would need to go from the break off, red, black all the way through the reds and then clear the colours in order. I get the maximum break name and logic. Also, a break (of how ever many points) from the first red potted in the frame I get. A break (nowadays) however has no logic in its title because it is used for any points accumulated from pots in successive strokes made in any one turn by a player during a frame. You could have a break of 50 half the way through a frame!

The five continents of the world are commonly accepted as Australasia, Europe, Asia, Africa and America. That is why there are 5 rings on the Olympic flag. Have a look at the names of 5 continents again and compare the first letter and last letter in each one.

In 1992, the Camp Nou hosted the Olympic games final and La Roja, the Spain (under 23's) national football team, defeated Poland 3-2. La Roja team included players such as Pep Guardiola, Toni, Luis Enrique and Kiko.

The nine original modern Olympic events were: athletics, cycling, fencing, gymnastics, shooting, swimming, tennis, weightlifting and wrestling.

The football championship playoff game in England is often referred to as the most lucrative sports teams match. The winners gain promotion to the payday of the Premier League and a minimum payment of £170 million!

Do you remember the green water in the Rio?

The water in the diving pool of the 2016 Rio Olympic Games wasn't the only water to turn green in the Olympics. Unfortunately, the pool in the 1908 London Games which had no filtration or cleaning system also turned green.

Baseball has only seen 23 official perfect games by the current definition. No pitcher has ever thrown more than one.

'Birdie', meaning a score of one stroke under par in golf, comes from the early 20th century American slang term 'bird', meaning anything excellent.

- The national sport of Japan is sumo wrestling.

- Rebecca Romero won a silver medal in the quadruple sculls at the 2004 Olympics in Athens but was forced to retire from the sport in 2006 due to back problems. Romero took up cycling, she won a silver medal in her first international cycling event, the track world cup in Moscow in December 2006. She then went one step better and became Olympic champion in the individual pursuit in Beijing in 2008.

- Lokomotiv means 'locomotive'. Lokomotiv Moscow was founded in 1935 (and is still owned) by the Ministry of Transportation. Before that, it was a railroad workers' team in Moscow.

- What do you get if you cross a ball and Romelu Lukaku? A goal kick.

- Baseball's first perfect nine innings game was achieved by John Lee Richmond on 12th June 1880.

- Sébastien Loeb won the world rally championship a record nine times, taking the title every year between 2004 and 2012.

- Approximately, one out of four injuries in athletes involves the wrist and hand.

Football matches start a war!

- There were a super highly charged series of matches in the 1970 football world cup qualifiers between El Salvador and Honduras. It started with a 1–0 Honduran victory. This was followed on 15th June by a game in San Salvador which El Salvador won 3–0. Both games were marred by violence and the bigger consequence was that the two countries embarked on a 3-day war!

- A wicket is a set of three stumps with two wooden bails on top of them. They can be stumped, hit, kept, taken or given away. A wicket or wycket as it used to be spelled is also a small gate embedded into either a huge decorative door often found in cathedrals or it is a fence. Wickets, in the early days of cricket, were made of only two stumps and one long bail, so they looked very similar to a small gate. The third stump was introduced in 1775 after a bowler called Lumpy Stevens (it's true!) bowled three balls in a row that went straight through the two stumps rather than hitting them.

- The first ever African country to play in the football world cup was Egypt in 1934.

- Between the 1947 and 1965 seasons in baseball, the minimum salary rose by just £1,000 from $6,000 to $7,000!

- Salt Lake City made a $101 million profit from hosting the 2002 Winter Olympic Games.

- In an effort to sell more licensed apparel, the minor league baseball teams were often changing their names. To stop the fleecing of the fans, the sport's governing body implemented limits that name changes may only happen every three years.

- An eagle in golf is a score of two under par for a given hole. This was an extension of the theme of birds for good scores from a 'birdie'. It would be natural for American golfers to think of the eagle, which is their national symbol and the term seems to have developed shortly after the 'birdie'.

- What is a banana's favorite gymnastic move? The splits!

- Endomorphs physically have a soft body, undeveloped muscles. They are round shaped and have an over-developed digestive system. Their personality traits include a love of food, they are tolerant, they have an evenness of emotions. They love comfort. They are sociable, good humoured and relaxed.

- The total audience for the first televised American football game in 1939 was 500. More than 100 million watch the Super Bowl nowadays.

- Gordon Ramsay was scouted by Glasgow Rangers but turned to cooking after his football career was cut short due to a knee injury.

- Swimmer Duncan Goodhew had alopecia universalis, to those of you unsure, that means a complete lack of body hair. As the winner of the 100m breaststroke in the Moscow games of 1980, this lack of body hair would have given him an advantage in the hydrodynamic department.

What weighs more a human or a Formula 1 car?

- A Formula 1 racing car weighs around 550 kg. There have been a lot of humans more than this weight.

- White City stadium was the major venue for the 1908 London games. It had a 100m swimming pool in the centre of a third of a mile (536m) running track. Alongside the pool was an area for football, lacrosse, hockey and archery, around everything there was a cycle track. Often three or four different sports were taking place at the same time. There was also changing facilities for 3000 athletes.

Pitcher Nolan Ryan played 27 seasons in major league baseball. During this time, he struck out more batters in his career than any other pitcher.

Al Oerter is the only athlete to win the discus in four consecutive Olympic games. Not only did he win gold medals but he also set new records in the 1956, 1960, 1964 and 1968 games.

Before Carl Weathers was trying to beat up Sylvester Stallone in the Rocky films, he played professional American football for two seasons with the Oakland Raiders in the early 1970's.

FC Barcelona has not always been playing its home games at the Camp Nou stadium. Earlier, Camp de Les Corts was its home stadium and even before that, Camp de la Industria was used. Camp de Les Corts or simply Les Cortes was inaugurated in 1922 and Camp Nou (which means new field) was inaugurated in 1957.

If laziness was an Olympic sport, I would've placed 4th so I wouldn't have to climb onto the podium.

Why do cyclists shave their legs?

The shaving does serve a purpose. As much as cyclists like to show off their muscular calves, it is much easier to scrub gravel off your injuries and apply ointments and bandages. I spent some time cycling for an amateur French team and the result of a big crash, the affected area was likened to pizza on my right butt cheek. Also, cyclists get frequent massages, the therapist is happier to work your legs when they are clean-shaven. The hair on cyclists' legs makes little or no difference in terms of aerodynamics.

Albertville lost $67 million whilst hosting the 1992 Winter Olympics.

In darts, there are 3944 different ways of achieving 501 with nine darts, of which 2,296 finish with the bull's eye, 672 end on double 20, 792 on double 18, 56 on double 17, 120 on double 15 and just eight finishing on double 12.

The madison is a team event in track cycling, named after the original Madison Square Gardens in New York, and known as the 'American race' in French (course à l'américaine) and in Italian and Spanish as Americana.

The 1904 games in St Louis the poorest attended in terms of competitors and sometimes referred to as the worst of all time. Team GB sent no athletes at all!

The word 'tournament' comes either from the old French 12th century word tornement which was a contest between groups of knights on horseback or from the word tornoier which is to joust or tilt. The 'tournament' is now a word used across all sports.

Dale Earnhardt Sr. earned 76 Cup Series wins and is the all-time race winner at Daytona International Speedway, with 34 wins. Tragically, Earnhardt died in an accident on the last lap of the Daytona 500 on 18th February 2001.

Futsal directly translates into foot room, and that's what the sport is. It is football played in a room.

Designed to knock riders off their horses.

Taekwondo is a Korean martial art. Taekwondo was developed during the 1870's and has big kicks designed to knock people from their horses.

In snooker, the maximum break is 147, or so we are led to believe. It is possible to score 155 though. Starting the break with a free ball after a foul.

Why are baseball umpires fat? They always clean their plate!

'Recuperate' is from the Latin word of recuperare 'to get again,'

A heptathlon is a track and field combined events contest made up of seven events. The name derives from the Greek hepta (seven) and áthlon, meaning 'contest' or 'prize'. A competitor in a heptathlon is referred to as a heptathlete.

The southpaw is more commonly associated with boxing, denoting the left hand or a punch with the left hand. Its origin is in baseball, from the orientation of the diamond to the same points of the compass, causing the pitcher to have his left hand on the south side of his body.

The bleacher seats are the seats facing the batter in baseball. With the orientation of the diamond, those sat in these seats would be in the sun and the seats became bleached by the sunlight.

A man rushes into his house and yells to his wife, "Pack up your things. I've just won the lottery!" His wife replies, "Shall I pack for warm weather and the beach or cold and skiing?' The man responds, "I don't care. Just so long as you're out of the house by noon!"

Sedatives such as diazepam, propranolol or even alcohol have been used by athletes in certain sports which require accuracy and steady hands. Stress and nervousness can be overcome with sedatives.

The wooden spoon was originally associated with the Cambridge University mathematical tripos exams and was a kind of booby prize awarded by students to their fellow student ranked lowest in the final exams. It is now used in sport, especially the Six Nations rugby tournament.

The verb 'nutmegged' is listed by the Oxford English dictionary as "arising in the 1870's which in Victorian slang came to mean 'to be tricked or deceived, especially in a manner which makes the victim look foolish'.

Why do we shout 'fore!' in golf?

We shout 'fore' to warn others of wayward shots in golf. The term comes from 'forecaddie', this was a person employed to go ahead of players to mark the lie of balls once played. The player would shout 'fore!' to alert the forecaddie a shot was on its way and so they could keep an eye out for it.

What do you call and Englishman in the knockout stages of the world cup? A referee.

In basketball we love the 'alley-oop'. Its origins are from the French term alley-oop, which circus acrobats would scream as they performed. The 'alley-oop' was 1st used by the San Francisco 49ers to describe a high-arching pass to wide receivers. The term then became used in basketball when player would grab a pass out of the air and slam the ball through the rim.

An American football coach walked into the locker room before a game, looked over to his star player and said, "I'm not supposed to let you play since you failed math, but we need you in there. So, what I have to do is ask you a math question, and if you get it right, you can play." The player agreed, and the coach looked into his eyes intently and asks, "Okay, now concentrate... what is two plus two?" The player thought for a moment and then he answered, "4?" "Did you say 4?" the coach exclaimed, excited that he got it right. At that, all the other players on the team began screaming, "Come on coach, give him another chance!"

Par is derived from the stock exchange term that a stock may be above or below its normal or 'par' figure. In 1870, Mr AH Doleman asked the golf professionals David Strath and James Anderson, what score would win 'the Belt', then the winning trophy for 'the Open.' Mr Doleman called this 'par' for the course.

Ayrton Senna's funeral was one of the largest ever in history. He was loved and idolized in Brazil. There were 3 days of national mourning declared across Brazil. Millions filed past his closed coffin, and millions more lined the streets for his funeral procession.

Bill and Earl are out playing golf. They get to the 17th tee, which overlooks a small lake, and see two guys out on the lake fishing. Bill says, "Hey Earl check out these two idiots fishing in the rain!"

The ancient Egyptians used wrestling as a training method for their soldiers. As well, the ancient Greeks organised wrestling and started competitions. They created wrestling schools, known as palaestras. Every Greek city would have at least one palaestra.

The 'bicep' muscle literally means 'two-headed', from bi 'two' + ceps which itself comes from the latin caput meaning 'head'. There are a couple of 'monoceps' but no one talk about these. The sphincter muscle is one and it only has one head.

A 'volley' in 1570 meant the firing of a number of guns at the same time. It was from the French word 'volée,' based on Latin volare 'to fly'. A volley in sport eventually became hitting the object before it had finished flying.

To throw your hat into the ring.

To throw your hat into the ring is often used to signify one's candidacy for (political) office or election or to enter a contest. In early days of boxing, a boxer would signify a challenge by throwing their hat into the boxing ring.

The game of darts itself is generally thought to have stemmed from the Middle Ages. Legend has it that the sport was originally invented by bored soldiers who had too much time on their hands in between waring campaigns. They would turn to alcohol to alleviate the boredom. Once the barrel of wine was finished, they would then aim and throw their arrows at the end of the barrel which would now be on its side. They referred to it as the game of 'butts'. As the game became more popular, dart boards were made out of cross sections of logs and the reason for the doubles, triples and bull stem from the cracking in these logs caused by the drying out process. Throwing long arrows inside isn't particularly practical and so their arrows were shortened. There is a rumour that Anne Boleyn had a set of darts made for Henry VIII. Maybe Henry didn't like the darts and that was the real reason for him having her head cut off, and that it was nothing to do with the adultery and witchcraft she was convicted of.

Jules Rimet was one of the founders of the Fédération Internationale de Football Association (FIFA) in 1904. He went on to become its 3rd president, serving from 1921 to 1954. He was also president of the French Football Federation between 1919 and 1942. Jules was involved in running of the football tournament in the 1908 Summer Olympics. It was Jules Rimet's initiative that brought about the first FIFA World Cup which was held in 1930. The Jules Rimet Trophy awarded to world cup winners was named in his honour

With 24 seconds remaining in a 1975 wild card playoff game against the Vikings, Cowboys quarterback Roger Staubach threw a 50-yard, game-winning pass to Drew Pearson. After the game, Staubach told reporters: "I closed my eyes and said a Hail Mary prayer." The name stuck.

How many snowboarders does it take to screw in a lightbulb? 50: three to die trying, one to actually pull it off and the other 46 to say, "Man, I could do that!"

The expression 'down to the wire' came from horse racing and is used in a close finish. Horse races would have a length of wire stretched across a racetrack at the finish line to help determine the winner.

A G (gravitational) Force is either the force of gravity on a particular extra-terrestrial body or the force of acceleration anywhere. It is measured in G's. One G is equal to the force of gravity at the earth's surface, which is 9.8 meters per second per second. During an F1 race, a driver will experience up to 5G's under braking and cornering and 3G's under hard acceleration, meaning that their neck has to support up to 24kgs during a long corner. Go and pick up a 24kg dumbbell in the gym and imagine it on your head whilst driving!

An 'albatross' is the term for three under par and is a continuation of the birdie and eagle theme. 'Double eagle' for three under which is still used by some golfers though.

Charles Goodyear (who Goodyear tyres were named after) created the first vulcanized rubber football in 1855. Over the next 20 years he developed the design with an inflatable rubber bladder and it was adopted as the official size and weight of all footballs. The same size and weight we play with today.

Prize money in sport is still unequal. 30% of sports reward men more highly than women.

Blindfold archery!

Have you guys tried the new sport of blindfold archery? You don't know what you're missing.

Practice makes perfect. What a load of rubbish, practice makes permanent! That's all. Learning the wrong way will reinforce the wrong thing. Only 'perfect practice makes perfect!'

In early boxing, having a 'whip round' would take place after the fight. The losing boxer would be given some money. This money was extracted from the crowd by the person controlling them with a whip!

Painkillers mask athletes' pain in order to continue competing beyond their usual pain thresholds. They range from common over-the-counter medicines such as non-steroidal anti-inflammatory drugs like ibuprofen to prescription narcotics such as morphine.

Why did the soccer ball quit the team? It was tired of being kicked around.

It has been an ongoing debate as to whether stretching before exercise can minimise your risk of injury. Of course, stretching holds many key benefits such as improving flexibility and joint mobility but injury prevention, I'm afraid there isn't much evidence that supports the prevention of injury though.

The word 'hooligan' derives from a notorious Irish family in the London borough of Southwark in the 1880's. The O'Hooligan's were quick to fight and steal. The characters became famous in theatres and in cartoons and slowly the word hooligan became a byword for violence amongst men. The family name O'Hooligan is likely a variant of the Irish surname Houlihan.

Turning fat into muscle.

This is a great one we've probably all heard in our time! There is no way we can convert fat into muscle, it just doesn't work like that! Exercising and participating in sport, can burn fat and build muscle but the two are completely different tissues.

Throughout the 3-week race, the peloton uses over 790 tyres in total. That's about four tyres per rider.

The hattrick is now used in numerous sports for three of something. It originated in cricket and was for three wickets in consecutive balls by a bowler. If a bowler managed this, they did a trick with their hats (which they used to wear).

The word 'coxswain' comes from the early 14th century. He was the 'officer in charge of a ship's boat and its crew,' from cock 'ship's boat' + swain 'boy'. Swain coming from Old Norse sveinn 'boy, servant'.

Eddy Merckx averaged 485 watts of power for his world hour record set at altitude in Mexico in 1972. He cycled 49,432m on a traditional bike.

No pain, no gain. Depending what you want, this is rubbish. Pain in sport is often an injury or overtraining. Both need recovery. Most sport is meant to be hard and possibly uncomfortable but not painful!

How do baseball players keep in touch with each other? They touch base every once in a while.

'The Tiger Woods/10,000 hour myth'. This myth says that any sport can be mastered in just 10,000 hours. Whilst 10,000 hours is a lot of training and competition, the evidence just isn't there to support it that guarantees final excellence.

South Africa's 15–12 victory against the All Blacks in the 1995 World Cup final was affected as some of the All Blacks had been struck down with food poisoning. They even cited a waitress named Suzie as the person who had tampered with their food! The manager at the Johannesburg hotel where the All Blacks were staying, said, 'There was no Suzie, she didn't exist'.

Only in the US and Canada can you have a World Series.

The 'World Series' title implies that nations all over the world take part, but only teams from the United States and Canada compete. Some say that the USA's major baseball tournament was called the 'World Series' because it was sponsored by the now defunct New York World newspaper. Some also say that the North Americans just love the idea of ruling the world!

In cycling, 20% of the rider's power output is used just for pushing the bike through the air.

Masking drugs prevent the detection of other drugs and unfortunately, they evolve as quickly as the testing methods. An example of this is Probenecid, which is primarily used to treat gout. This now banned drug would ensure the athlete's urine sample had exceptionally high levels of Probenecid thus masking any performance enhancing agents.

In American pool, you might see six red dots on the white cue ball. This is to show spectators the amount of 'English' (spin) has been put on the ball. It is a purely visual thing.

The first athlete to die in Olympic competition due to doping was Danish cyclist Knut Jensen, who died on 26th August 1960 at the summer Olympics in Rome. It was an incredibly hot day with temperatures reaching 40 degrees. He collapsed during the 100km team time trial race, banged his head and died in a hospital tent soon afterwards. His autopsy revealed traces of an amphetamine called Ronicol.

I used to dream of playing golf like Tiger Woods. Now I can.

Velodromes vary in size from venue to venue, some are indoor and are 250m in length, others that circle athletics tracks can measure 500m. The steepness of the curves on indoor tracks is generally about 42 degrees.

The Olympic sport of water polo gets its name from the original form of the sport, which was played on horseback and involved mallets. Polo, itself was last an Olympic sport in 1936. Polo is a rendering of a Balti Tibetan word, 'pulu', meaning 'ball,' that is the target of the sport's swinging mallets.

The fuel pump on a Formula 1 car delivers fuel at a greater rate than your domestic tap does water.

Did Denis Law really get Manchester United relegated?

Denis Law played for both Manchester United and then Manchester City in his career. With Manchester United fearing relegation from the league, the Manchester derby came around. When Law scored for City against his old club in 1974, he hardly celebrated, but it was not the Scot's goal that doomed United to relegation, as many think. When Law scored five minutes from time, he did no more than change the goal difference and United were doomed anyway!

Golfers encourage one another to take 'the tiger line', the tightest and bravest shot to the green. You might assume it's what Tiger Woods would do, but you'd be wrong! James Bond plays against Goldfinger and Fleming describes the 2nd at Royal St George's, as 'a 370-yard dogleg to the left with deep cross-bunkers daring you to take the tiger's line'. The meaning is more to do with taking the line closest to edge of the fairway. Which is as far as the wild animals might venture onto a golf course before losing their camouflage.

In 1929, the Tom Thumb golf course was the first miniature (crazy) golf course to be opened in the United States. It was built in Chattanooga, Tennessee by John Garnet Carter.

Ref: I'm sending you off. Player: What for? Ref: The rest of the match!

The years in which tennis grand slam tournaments were first contested: Wimbledon was established in 1877, the US Open in 1881, the French Open in 1891 and the youngest is the Australian Open which recently started in 1905.

The first instance of global electronic communications took place in 1871 when news of the Derby winner was telegraphed from London to Calcutta in under five minutes.

Chris Boardman has still ridden the furthest in an hour on a bicycle. He rode a heavily modified time trial bike in Manchester and set the distance of 56,375m on September 9th, 1996. This record isn't currently recognised because of the outlawed riding position.

In 1986, yellow balls were used at Wimbledon for the first time to make them visible for the TV cameras. Tennis balls used to be white, it was only really after the introduction of televised tennis that they were changed to the yellow and much more visible ball we know and love today.

Why we ban performance enhancing drugs.

A substance can be included on the 'world anti-doping code prohibited list', if it meets two of the following three criteria:

- it is performance-enhancing
- it is harmful to the athlete's health
- it violates the spirit of sport

A women's university football match in China had to be called off, the women's teams of Fuzhou and Jimei universities were due to play each other when the match was threatened with cancellation because of breaches of the strict code on physical appearance. Before the match, there were multiple players rejected from the match for violating a rule which requires that all players do not dye or curl their hair. The offending players tried to prevent the abandonment by quickly dyeing their hair black. Officials decided that one of the players hair wasn't black enough and so the match was forfeited. The concerned leagues rule states the 'athletes are not allowed to dye their hair, grow long hair [for boys], wear weird hairstyles, or wear any accessories.'

The largest ever sports trophy measures more than 22 feet tall. The trophy was presented to both the Marquette Informal Longboarding Foundation and the NMU Skate and Snow Club on 10th April 2011.

Kurt Angle of WWE fame was men's heavyweight freestyle wrestling champion in Atlanta, 1996.

Swimmer Zoltan Halmay from Hungary clearly beat the American J Scott Leary in the 50m freestyle event in St Louis Games of 1904. A cheating USA official awarded the race to the American. Incensed by the decision Halmay started fighting Leary, a rematch was ordered and justice prevailed when Halmay won the re-race. Halmay also won the men's 100m freestyle at the same games.

Blood boosters such as Erythropoietin (EPO), increase the oxygen-carrying capacity of blood and are often used in endurance sports.

Races in the 1908 Olympics were held on a track of 536.45 metres (1/3 mile) in circumference. Instead of the standard 400m we have today.

Where do old bowling balls end up? In the gutter!

Carl Schumann from Germany not only won three golds in the gymnastics at the Athens 1896 games, but he also won the men's Greco Roman wrestling and also entered the weightlifting, long jump, triple jump and the shot put.

In 1900, Dwight Davis gave his name to a tennis competition between the United States and Great Britain. Annually more than 60 countries now contest the Davis Cup.

World's highest golf course.

The highest golf course in the world is the Tuctu Golf Club in Morococha, Peru, which sits 14,335 feet at its lowest point above sea level.

A bit of cycling science for you, amazingly, a bicycle can stay upright without a rider as long as it's moving at 8mph or faster. My thought is that it takes hardly any effort up to 15mph. Then it's up to you.

An F1 car can accelerate from 0 to 160 kph (100 mph) and decelerate back to 0 in just four seconds.

A 'derby' match is linked with a 'football' match that takes place on Shrove Tuesday every year in Ashbourne (England), which is close to but not Derby. However, it is in the county of Derbyshire. The term is used as to describe two local teams playing each other.

A bowling pin only needs to tilt 7.5 degrees in order for it to fall over.

The longest golf hole in the world is the 7th hole (par 7) of the Sano Course at the Satsuki Golf Club in Japan. It measures an incredible 909 yards. Even with Bryson DeChambeau's massive hitting it would take him at least three to the green.

Yokozuna is the highest level a sumo wrestler can achieve. In the history of the sport, there have been less than 100 achieve it, there is never normally more than one or two competing at this level at the same time in history.

Only 1 runner in the final

The 400m final was the most controversial event of the 1908 London Games. Due to disqualification of a runner and subsequent protest withdrawals from other athletes, Halswelle, a British athlete was the only runner in the 400 metres final. He ceremonially ran to Olympic gold.

Zenit (St Petersburg) means 'zenith'. For some reason, this is what they called teams that represented military-industry plants and factories in those days. One of the definitions of the word zenith means 'the highest point or the point above your head. Zenit St Petersburg was owned by the Leningrad Metalworks Plant, which amongst other things made military equipment.

Golfer: "How do you like my game?" Caddy: "Very good sir, but personally, I prefer golf."

Jeu de paume is a ball-and-court game that originated in France. It was an indoor precursor of tennis and played without racquets, though these were eventually introduced. It was an Olympic sport and has the honour of the oldest annual world championship in sport, first established over 250 years ago. It was originally spelled jeu de paulme, it is sometimes called courte paume or real tennis.

Racket derives from the Arabic rakhat meaning the palm of the hand.

✗ Goldie is the second boat of the Cambridge University Boat Club, which competes against Isis (the second boat of the Oxford University Boat Club) on boat race day. The boat is named in tribute to CUBC's legendary President, John Goldie

🚲 A one-piece skinsuit in cycling and triathlon can give a 2% reduction in drag over more traditional jersey and shorts.

⛳ Before 1850, golf balls were made of leather and were stuffed with feathers.

🚲 Up until the 1960's cyclists in races such as the Tour de France, Giro Italia and the Vuelta España would drink alcohol during racing. They thought the numbing of the pain would help them ride quicker. Quite the opposite is true, and the blood would in actual fact have less red blood cell carrying capacity.

🎾 In 1931, tennis star Lilí Álvarez became the first-ever woman to wear a pair of shorts at Wimbledon.

🏃 Vanderlei de Lima carried the Olympic torch up the stairs at the Maracanã Stadium in Rio and went on to signal the official start of the 2016 Olympic Games. De Lima replaced soccer legend Pelé, who could not make an appearance due to poor health.

⚽ One of the trains used to transport the materials for building the old Wembley Stadium was buried beneath the stadium.

⛳ Phil Mickelson, who plays left-handed, is actually right-handed. He learned to play golf by mirroring his father's golf swing, and he has used left-handed golf clubs ever since.

🪁 'Charlie Browner', is a term used for a kiteboarder.

⚽ Unfortunately, CSKA Moscow goalkeeper Igor Akinfeev went 40 Champions League matches without keeping a clean sheet. That's 10 years! The Russian nearly broke his hoodoo in the 40th game but conceded in the 87th minute against Monaco. The last clean sheet he kept in Europe's top club competition was a goalless draw against Arsenal on 1st November 2006.

You can't trust teachers!

🏃 I was always told by my physical education teachers that four laps of the 400m track was a mile. Four laps of four hundred metres is 1600m but a mile is 1609m! They lied to me.

For some time, my wife has had this crazy idea that I'm playing too much golf. Things finally came to a head at about midnight last night. She suddenly shouted at me. "Golf, golf, golf. All you ever think about is bloody golf!" I'll be honest, it frightened the life out of me. I mean, you don't expect to meet anybody on the 16th tee at that time of night.

'Win' comes from old English 'winnan', meaning to fight, endure or struggle.

'Lactic acid' is the main acid produced in the souring of milk by bacteria, the lactic acid produced by bacteria and that produced by animals are molecular mirror-images. Lactic gets its name from the Latin word 'lac', and its genitive lactis meaning milk. Lactic acid, or lactate, is a chemical by product of anaerobic respiration, the process by which cells produce energy without oxygen around. Bacteria produce it in yogurt and our guts. Lactic acid is also in our blood, where it's deposited by muscle and red blood cells.

The word 'yoga' is derived from the Sanskrit 'Yuj', meaning 'to join' or 'to unite'.

The oldest sport.

Wrestling can be traced back to at least 4000 years ago. There was evidence of it in the ancient civilisation of Mesopotamia. 'The Epic of Gilgamesh', the first great work of literature was written in 2100 BC. In the poems, the two main characters Gilgamesh, King of Uruk and Enkidu, who was sent by the gods to challenge Gilgamesh over his appalling abuse of power. The two of them wrestled and afterwards became friends.

Stéphane Peterhansel holds the record for most Dakar Rally wins. In total, he has won the race 11 times. He won the motorcycle category (on a Yamaha) six times and has won the car category five times.

Both Valencia and Stade De Reims are teams that have made the Champions League finals twice each They also have the unviable record of both having lost twice in these finals.

Milkha Singh, nicknamed 'the Flying Sikh was the first Indian track and field athlete to reach an Olympic final.

Did you know that 49% of all tweets are about sport.

A low-fat meal will empty from the stomach faster than a high-fat meal, so be sure to eat a low-fat meal before exercise.

Golf balls can reach speeds of 170 miles per hour.

Thirst is not a good indicator of when to drink. Ideally you should drink little and often, and dehydration is a prevention thing not something to treat in sport.

You would think the world's highest paid model Gisele Bündchen would be used to walking along catwalks. However, in the opening ceremony of the 2016 Olympics, her 400ft walk across the Maracanã stadium was so slow that it meant a homage to Tom Jobin, composer of 'The Girl from Ipanema', had to be dropped right at the last second. Her appearance at the ceremony led to a 1,850% rise in Google searches for her name 'Gisele'. She is also married to American football quarterback Tom Brady.

Dynamo Kiev was founded in 1927, as an electricians' team, but was soon afterwards transferred to the police. Later on, the USSR Sporting Society 'Dinamo' was created, unifying all police teams in the country. This is why there are so many 'Dinamoes' out there now.

Track athletes are most likely to break records later in the day when their body temperatures are highest.

In 2010, almost twice the number of Americans played basketball (26.3 million) over baseball (14.5 million).

Addicted to swimming.

I used to be addicted to swimming but I'm very proud to say I've been dry for six years.

Sir Steve Redgrave of Great Britain is widely hailed as the greatest rower ever. He won gold medals at five consecutive Olympic games.

Football teams that have United in their title, will have been the result of a merger of clubs at some time in their history or represent a large area that might include more than one town or city. Teams that have Albion in their title are just British teams as Albion, is the earliest-known name for the island of Britain. The name Albion has been translated as 'white land' and the Romans explained it as referring to the chalk cliffs at Dover. So maybe Brighton and Hove Albion are the only correct users of the name? Teams that have Athletic in their title would have been formed from track and field athletic clubs. Teams with a day of the week in their title, such as Sheffield Wednesday will have only played on that day because they had workers in their teams that had to work over the weekend or that ground shared with another team who played on the traditional Saturday. Spanish football clubs might have Real in their names such as in Real Madrid, Real Sociedad, Real Zaragoza and Real Club Deportivo Mallorca. This means they will all have received a royal charter from the King of Spain.

Full 15 a side rugby union was played for the first time as an Olympic sport in the Paris 1900 games. However, the depth of competition wasn't the greatest as only three teams entered. My old team of Moseley Wanderers represented GB. They lost to France. The whole story thickens around the event as Moseley had played a match the day before in England. Then travelled to Paris to play France. They travelled back to Great Britain the next day. The team was so worn out, their next scheduled match against Germany was cancelled and France was awarded gold and Germany and GB joint silver!

Spectator comes from the Latin spectātor, which derives from spectō meaning 'watch', which in turn came from speciō meaning to 'look at'.

The 'funny bone' didn't get its nickname because of that funny feeling you get after you hit it. The bone itself is called the humerus hence the name, funny bone. Running down the inside part of your elbow is a nerve called the ulnar nerve and this is the part of the reason things hurt so much when you bang your funny bone!

A 'prize' comes the from the old French word 'pris' meaning price, value, worth or reward.

Rugby shouldn't exist.

When William Webb Ellis picked up the ball as a 16-year-old at Rugby School, what was the referee doing and why was he allowed to get away with it. Imagine if they had VAR or TMO? He would have yellow carded and Rugby wouldn't exist!

The 'pike' in gymnastics, diving and trampolining is quite simply the position when the body is bent forward at the hips with the legs straight.

According to manufacturer Spalding, the average lifespan of an NBA basketball is 10,000 bounces.

The Comrades, widely regarded as the one of world's greatest ultra-marathon races is 89km long. Bruce Fordyce won the event on nine occasions: in 1981, 1982, 1983, 1984, 1985, 1986, 1987, 1988 and 1990. I know what you are thinking, why didn't he win in 1989? Well, he didn't run that year, good of him to give someone else a chance.

A forfeited game in baseball is recorded as 9–0.

In 1894, the United States Golf Association (USGA) was founded. They are the governing body of golf in the United States.

Tommy Simpson died whilst climbing Mont Ventoux in the 1967 Tour de France. His last words were 'put me back on my bike', his autopsy revealed amphetamines in his system and he is also thought to have drunk brandy at the foot of the climb to help ease the pain!

Up until 1859, baseball umpires sat in a padded rocking chair behind the catcher

The Dallas Cowboys hired the NFL's first professional cheerleading squad in 1972.

A VAM is a measure of climbing speed of cyclists. It is measured in metres-per-hour. The largest values ever seen in professional cycling, over a series of sustained climbs, were in excess of 1800 Vm/h. The two cyclists with the highest measurements were Marco Pantani and Lance Armstrong. Tour de France winner Chris Frome has been measured at about 1600 Vm/h.

Rubin (as in the football team Rubin Kazan) is the Russian word for 'ruby'. No idea why this name was chosen, other than the fact that ruby is a nice-looking stone. True to the name, the team plays in red kits. I drove to Kazan for charity on route to Mongolia. Beautiful Kremlin there!

The legend Billy Casper continued as a golf professional during the Korean War. He was serving in the Navy and was assigned to operate and build golf-driving ranges for the US Navy.

Tarzan prevents a clean sweep.

In the Los Angeles games of 1932, the Japanese swimmers almost completed a clean sweep (winning all the races). The person to foil their attempt was none other than Tarzan. Buster Crabbe won the 400m freestyle event. There has also been another Tarzan in the Olympics with Johnny Weissmuller winning five swimming golds in Paris, 1924. In Montreal during the 1976 Olympic Games, Team USA nearly won a clean sweep of all the men's gold medals. They won 12 of the 13 available. The man to stop them winning the lot was Great Britain's David Wilkie in the 200m breaststroke.

What are the rules for zebra baseball? Three stripes and you're out.

When the itinerary for the first modern Olympics was being drawn up, it included both cricket and yachting. The yachting event was cancelled because they couldn't get enough good boats and the cricket wasn't played either.

In 2018, France became world champions and received $35 million, Croatia, as runners up won $25 million. Even teams eliminated in the group stages received at least $8 million per team. Just in case you wonder whether this is too much or an unsustainable amount of money, the 2018 men's world cup generated nearly $5.4 billion in total revenue, with about $3 billion coming from the sale of broadcast rights.

The Tzukahara is named after the Japanese gymnast, Mitsuo Tzukahara. He was credited with this move. It is used on the vault by both men and women. The gymnast performs a quarter or half onto the vault and a back salto off.

Prize money in the football world cup has skyrocketed. Listed below is the prize money awarded in recent competitions.

Year	Country	$ in millions
1982	Spain	20
1986	Mexico	26
1990	Italy	54
1994	USA	71
1998	France	103
2002	Korea and Japan	156.6
2006	Germany	266
2010	South Africa	420
2014	Brazil	576
2018	Russia	791

We all know that the home team provide the match balls. In American football, the home team must provide the referee with 24 footballs for each national football league game. 12 are used as primary and the other 12 as back-up ones. The referee will conduct an inspection and record the PSI measurement of each football.

The term 'freestyle' means that you can swim in any style you like. In a technical sense, you are free to swim backstroke, sidestroke or any other stroke you choose in a freestyle race.

The largest football stadium in the world is the Maracanã in Rio de Janeiro, which hosted the 1950 world cup final in front of a crowd of 199,854. Today the crowd capacity is limited to under 80,000. I was there for its reopening in 2013.

✂ The only time a dead heat occurred in the university boat race was in 1877. The result, however, was shrouded in controversy, as the judge on the winning line was asleep under a bush when the race finished.

🏊 Japan gets the credit for holding the first swimming races in 36 BC.

⚽ It is theoretically possible to have a square football pitch. The dimensions of a pitch are given as 50–100 yards wide and 100–130 yards long. Maximum width and minimum length equals a square!

🏏 A little like 'love' in tennis, a duck (scoring 0 in cricket) gets its name from its resemblance to an egg which is oval in shape. Out for a chicken didn't work, out for a love bird neither and so it was decided 'out for a duck.'

There are different types of ducks, too:

> 🏏 A regular duck is when a batter is dismissed without any runs scored but having faced more than more delivery.

> 🏏 A golden duck is when a batter is dismissed on their first ball bowled to them.

> 🏏 A diamond duck could be considered unlucky for it given when a batter is dismissed without facing any legal balls. This would usually happen from the non-striking side, maybe a Monkad, but a batter could get out for a diamond duck after a wide ball on the striking end, too.

> 🏏 A platinum duck or royal duck is when a batter is dismissed on the first ball of the first innings of the entire match.

> 🏏 If you are unlucky or bad enough to get a 'pair', then you will have been out for a duck in both innings of a match.

> 🏏 Just to finish off the different ducks, a 'king pair' is when you are out to two golden ducks.

⚽ Only 13 countries contested the first football world cup in 1930, which saw Uruguay winning the trophy. Of those 13 countries, 8 were from South America, 4 from Europe and the remaining team was the USA.

Mark Spitz was in the Olympic village at the time of the anti-Israeli terrorist acts. The 7-time gold medallist is Jewish and had to be evacuated for his safety.

Marco Pantani aka 'il Pirata' (because of his shaved head, the bandana he wore and his large earrings). Pantani won both the Tour de France and the Giro D'Italia, although Pantani never tested positive during his career, his career was beset by doping allegations. Following continued accusations of doping, Pantani went into a depression. He tragically died of cocaine poisoning in 2004.

Tennis scored on clocks.

There is an opinion that the tennis scoring system came about because of the use of a pair of clocks to keep the score on. They rotated the hands to signify 0, 15, 30, 40 and game (60).

Why is football sometimes referred to as soccer? In the 18th century, the rules of the game were codified, and a number of football associations were formed. In fact, it is an abbreviation of the word 'association' that gave rise to the term 'soccer'.

The word 'sport' itself has been around in the English language since the mid-15th century, when it was derived from the old French word desporter, meaning 'to amuse, please or play'.

Cuban Alberto Juantorena won both the 400m and 800m in the 1976 Montreal Olympics. 100m/200m, 200m/400m, 800m/1500m, 5000m/10000m are all recognised as normal combinations. The 400m/800m is not something you hear about. Juantorena was nicknamed the 'White Lightning'.

The 2011 collegiate ice hockey game between Michigan and Michigan State, played at the Big House in Ann Arbor had an attendance of 113,411. Making it the largest ever ice hockey live viewed game.

The first ever Tour de France in 1903 had six stages and 70 entrants. Riders would start at night and race through to the following afternoon.

The 'hack-a-Shaq defence maybe worked! Shaquille O'Neal was not the best from the free throw foul line. When Shaq retired in 2010, he missed a total of 5,317 free throws over his career. You will read later about how many he did make though.

From 1900 until 1920, the tug of war was a sporting event at the summer Olympic games. Great Britain was awarded the most medals in the event with five, including two golds.

Psychological science looked at 60,000 MLB games played between 1952 and 2009. They found that temperature was the most effective indicator of whether a pitcher would retaliate if a teammate was hit by the opposing pitcher. Also, the chances of a pitcher purposefully retaliating against a batter went up 5% in temperatures above 90 degrees.

During a marathon, there was one runner dressed as a chicken and another runner dressed as an egg. Not that old debate again!

Former welterweight boxer Aurele 'Al' Couture passed away in 2000, but his record of delivering the fastest knockout in pro boxing history is likely to remain. In his bout against Ralph Walton in 1946, Couture knocked the fighter out in just 10.5 seconds, this time included the mandatory 10-second count by the referee. Apparently, Walton had been distracted by his corner man, when he was caught by the punch.

There was live pigeon shooting at the 1900 summer games in Paris. The event actually entailed hundreds of pigeons being released, who were then shot in front of the spectators.

The Inazawa Bowling Centre in Japan opened in 1972, with 116 lanes! Making it the world biggest.

Pro golfer Kevin Na broke a PGA record at the 2011 Valero Texas Open. Na set a new record for most strokes on a par-4 hole, when he shot at 16 on the ninth. The hole took him 20 minutes to complete.

During Olympic qualifying between the Peru and rival Argentina football teams in 1964, a controversial refereeing decision sent the crowd into a rage. When police fired tear gas into the stands, the fans panicked and tried to flee. The gates of Lima football stadium were locked, resulting in a deadly stampede that took the lives of 328 spectators.

Cycling inspiration.

Whilst racing, 'le Tour' Italian cyclist Mario Cipollini taped a picture of Pamela Anderson to his handlebars for inspiration.

Average lifespan of a major league baseball is just five pitches.

On the velodrome, there are a series of lines – red, black and blue. The red line is known as the sprinter's line, riders are not allowed to overtake under this line. Then there is the black line, this is the shortest route around the track. A little further up the track is the blue stayer's line. This line is used in 'madison' races for riders to rest between attacks or riding down of opponents.

Manager to player: "I'll give you 100 pounds a week to start with and 200 pounds a week in a year's time!" Player to Manager: "Well, I'll come back in a year's time!"

Slalom is the form of skiing that requires competitors to ski around gates on a downhill course. It gets its name from the Norwegian for 'gentle slope or track'. Anyone skiing on a world cup slalom course will testify these are not gentle slopes.

The Boston Celtics have won the most NBA championships. Their 17 victories included seven straight between 1960 and 1966. I saw them in London against the Timberwolves with Eugene.

Hugh Laurie only found out his father was an Olympic gold medallist when he went fishing as a teenager with his mother and father. His father said he would row. Hugh asked his mum if his dad knew what he was doing. His mother said that his father knew what he was doing. The father being such a modest man stored the Olympic gold medal he won in London 1948 in the sock draw and hadn't told his son of his success.

A soigneur is an assistant to professional cyclists. They give post-race massages as well as numerous other activities such as taxi driver to the riders, they do the food prep, wash the kit, fill the bidons (water bottles) and musettes (bags filled with food worn whilst racing), handing out of the musettes during the race and finally anything else that needs to be done!

150 years salary for winning Olympic gold!

Hoang Xuan Vinh, a 41-year-old army colonel, made history in the 2016 Rio games taking gold in the shooting. Vinh received $100,000 from his country, Vietnam. The average income in Vietnam is only $150 a month!

During a cold winter in the 1880's, a group of tennis players in England were unable to play their preferred sport so they placed a rack of books at centre of large dining to act as a net, they used books as rackets and a golf ball to hit. This game is evolved as table tennis.

A 'flic-flak' is a common gymnastic move where a gymnast takes off from one or two feet, jumps backwards onto their hands and then continues the move to land back on their feet. This is also referred to as a 'flip-flop.'

A young man, who was also an avid golfer, found himself with a few hours to spare one afternoon. He figured if he hurried and played very fast, he could get in nine holes before he had to head home. Just as he was about to tee off, an old gentleman shuffled onto the tee and asked if he could accompany the young man as he was golfing alone. Not being able to say no, he allowed the old gent to join him. To his surprise, the old man played fairly quickly. He didn't hit the ball far but plodded along consistently and didn't waste much time. Finally, they reached the 9th fairway and the young man found himself with a tough shot. There was a large pine tree right in front of his ball and directly between his ball and the green. After several minutes of debating how to hit the shot, the old man finally said, "You know, when I was your age, I'd hit the ball right over that tree." With that challenge placed before him, the youngster swung hard, hit the ball up, right smack into the top of the tree trunk and it thudded back on the ground not a foot from where it had originally lay. The old man offered one more comment, "Of course, when I was your age that pine tree was only three feet tall."

More than 1,800 medals are awarded at Olympics games.

Baltimore Orioles shortstop Cal Ripken, Jr didn't miss a game in 16 years. He played in 2,632 consecutive games from 30th April 1982 to 19th September 1998.

Shaquille O'Neal wears size 22 shoes. He wore a brand-new pair before every game. Nate Robinson loved them as well. Have a look at the YouTube clip of it if you don't believe me.

It takes 3,000 cows to supply the NFL with enough leather for a year's supply of American footballs.

Unfit to serve.

In 2003, Roger Federer was classified 'unfit' to serve in Swiss military due to back problems.

The Irish Greyhound Board said they drug test between 5,000 and 6,000 greyhounds per year and that their sport has the 'most intensive testing regime of any sport in Ireland'.

It's not chalk weightlifters or rock climbers cover their hands with, but it looks like it. It is in fact magnesium carbonate and it keeps your hands free of sweat and improves your grip. It comes in a block form and then gets broken off and ground into powder.

Wouldn't competitive swimming be more exciting if there was a loud bang or even a gunshot to start the races? It might sound more exciting but the bleep you hear was designed with pool acoustics in mind. It echoes less and helps prevent false starts.

The Kazakh fighter Gennady Gennadyevich Golovkin generates the power of boxers two weight divisions or around 15lbs heavier. He also often lands 10 blows a round more on average than others in his middleweight division.

What did the baseball glove say to the ball? Catch ya later!

Football Club Barcelona got their famous maroon and blue colours from a rugby team based at a school in north west England. Arthur and Ernest Witty were both students at Merchant Taylor's School in Crosby, Liverpool. Their rugby team played in maroon and blue. Both went on to be heavily involved in the early years at Barcelona FC. Arthur captained the side alongside founder Joan Gamper before going on to serve as the club's president.

American football got its name from the sport of rugby football because of the similarities between the two.

Cat gut has been used as the name for strings in tennis rackets since the 1800's. One of the first manufacturers was Pierre Babolat who was making cat gut strings way back in 1875. However, contrary to its name, the source of natural gut tennis string is the cow. More specifically, part of the cow's intestine called the serosa. Whilst looking for other tennis string sources, sheep's guts were tried and fortunately for them, their intestines were too weak and prone to snapping whilst hitting the heavy tennis ball.

Ever wondered why the weightlifting area doesn't break. I guess, probably not. I will tell you anyway, there are several reasons why hundreds of kilos of weight being dropped from 2m does not destroy the frame. Firstly, the competition platform is extremely strong and is a metal-framed platform with a concrete base and a hardwood surface. The multi-layered wooden surface also acts a little like a shock absorber. Also, the weights themselves are covered in rubber.

The term 'seed' originated in tennis tournaments. The better players are 'planted' into the draw (to avoid them meeting each other in early rounds of knock out tournaments) and from these seeds, the tournament would then grow. The seeding method has now been adopted into many other sports and their tournaments.

Not even god can hit a one iron.

After being struck by lightning during a golf tournament in 1975, Lee Trevino offered some advice to anyone who might find themselves caught on a golf course during an electrical storm. "Hold up a 1-iron. Not even God can hit a 1-iron!"

In the 1941 Yorkshire Cup, Huddersfield beat Castleford in the strangest circumstances. At full time the rugby league match was tied at 3 each. Extra time loomed. Being war time some of the Castleford players had to report for duty. Huddersfield ceremonially kicked off against no opposition and scored a converted try. History shows the final score as 8-3.

At the beginning of the 2017 Premier League football season there was a match between Burnley and West Bromwich Albion at Turf Moor. What was unique about this game was the ball was in play for only 160 seconds more than it was out of play. Also, in the first 19 games of the season, none featured more than 61 minutes of actual play!

In 1921, the World Boxing Association (WBA) was formed. A lot of fans like the WBA since it's the oldest, however some people prefer the WBC because it's a more popular organisation. The WBC then came in 1963 and was the first organisation to reduce fights to a 12 round maximum limit. Then came the IBF in 1983, it formed because a man who didn't get elected to become president of the WBA got fed up. The IBF used to be the USBA, a regional boxing organisation but transformed into the IBF in 1983. Then came the WBO in 1988 after some people got fed up with the WBA at their 1988 convention and started their own organisation. Oh dear!

Michael Phelps took 730ms to leave the starting block in the 2012 Olympics. Usain Bolt took 146ms to react to the starting gun in 2009's 100-metre race. However, an arm wrestler's reaction to the referee's starting whistle is actually as fast as an incredible 123ms!

In the 1984 sheep dog trials, none were convicted!

In the 2018 Australian Open, Denmark's Wozniacki and the Romanian Halep met in the final. What made this a bit more unique was that for the first time ever in the open era, both players faced and saved match points against them en-route to the final.

Spanish clubs protect their investments by putting 'buyout clauses' in their contracts. Should a player or other club want to activate this clause, the player must pay the buyout clause. Remember Neymar Jr leaving Barcelona to join PSG with its reported 'buyout clause' of £200 million!

Fast tracks.

Supermondo is a type of running track that is quicker by 0.15s for a 100m than a non Supermondo track. The track used at the London 2012 Olympic games is made of it and also the tracks used in the Diamond League.

Abebe Bikila, the Ethiopian was the first man to successfully defend the Olympic marathon title. He won it both in 1960 and 1964. In 1964 Bikila won the race in trainers in a time of just 2 hours, 12 minutes and 11 seconds. His previous Olympic winning time in the 1960 games was 2:21:23, however he won this race barefoot!

Football in the UK was first screened live on television in 1937. The BBC broadcast just a quarter of an hour of a specially arranged friendly between Arsenal versus Arsenal reserves from Highbury.

Only about 1500 athletes have run a four-minute mile and this number only increases by about a hundred a year and no woman has yet to break the barrier.

PEDs are banned in sport for the following reasons, they are detrimental to your health, it is against the spirit and fair play of the sport and finally they create an unfair advantage. First of all, most of the drugs are pharmaceutical grade and produced for their medical benefits. EPO to increase red blood cell count before operations etc. Secondly, I have not known an industry as unfair and corrupt as sport, think Sepp Blatter, financing of teams in leagues and competitions, selection of athletes for events etc., and finally sport is so unfair anyway. Think of tall basketball players against shorter ones, fast twitch against slow twitch in the sprint. Rich teams and warm weather training, latest expensive equipment, support, massage etc., etc. There are sportsman and teams who have a massive legal unfair advantage. Drugs (PEDS) could be argued make sport fairer!

Bowling has 10 pins in triangle formation, Skittles has 9 pins in a diamond.

What kind of stories are told by basketball players? Tall tales.

Lis Hartel represented Denmark in the Helsinki games in equestrian. She was one of the first women to compete against the men and won a silver medal.

Something that made her achievement even the more remarkable was that she was paralyzed below the knees due to polio. She even had to be helped on to and from her horse.

The sport of rowing began in London back in 1715, when the Thames watermen held organised races between themselves.

Father John Coates from Australia was ordained into the priesthood by the Pope. He is the only member of the clergy to have played rugby league at the highest-level representing Australia in the 1960's and 70's.

Duathlons can take various forms but the most common involves cycling and running. Often following the run, cycle, run format.

The average male has a grip strength of 108lbf whilst the average male arm wrestler's is a whopping 203lbf. Professional muscle man Magnus Samuelsson has a grip strength of 365lbf. That's even stronger than the bite of a rottweiler!

Biathlon is a winter sport that involves cross country skiing and shooting. It became a men's Olympic sport in 1960 and the women were kept waiting another 32 years. A couple of technical issues in the sport, a competitor's skies must be at least 4cm shorter that their height and their poles must not exceed their height. The shooting must also be taken from standing or prone and alternates between the two depending on the number of laps the race is. The distance is 20km and the target distance from the athlete is 50m. In the original races between 1958 and 1965, the 20km distance was the same but there were four separate shooting ranges and firing distances of 100 metres, 150 metres, 200 metres and 250 metres. Real bullets were also used!

Apartheid.

South Africa was banned from the Olympics between 1964 and 1992 because of their apartheid regime. Apartheid comes from the Afrikaans word meaning 'separateness', or 'the state of being apart', literally 'apart-hood'.

Aladár Gerevich might have won more than his seven gold medals in six different Olympics! He was a fencer and he was an expert at the sabre. He won his first in the LA games of 1932 and his last in Rome (1960), we can only imagine what might have happened if the 1940 and 1944 Games of Tokyo and London weren't cancelled due to World War II.

In Australian rules, football teams are made up of 22 players. There are 18 players on the field of play and four interchangeable players.

All thoroughbreds descend from three stallions.

- The Beverley Turk, 1689
- The Darley Arabian, 1704
- The Godolphin Arabian, 1730

The original decathlon took just a day for all 10 events. Also, the events haven't always been what we see today. Thomas Kiely won in the 1904 games held in St Louis. Two of the events were the 800m walk and the 56lb weight throw. The weight throw was measured in height, similar to events in the Scottish highland games.

Ice hockey players are like goldfish. Just tap on the glass to get their attention.

Flyweight to welterweight boxers wear 8oz gloves, super welterweight up to heavyweight wear the heavier 10oz gloves.

The name given to the object ball in crown green bowling is called the jack. There are a couple of competing theories as to etymological origin of the word 'jack'. Some say that the name 'jack' is derived from the latin word jactus, meaning a cast or a throw. However, the most straightforward theory is that it appears that the word jack in some contexts meant a slightly smaller version of something. EG a jackrabbit is a little rabbit. As the object ball is smaller than a bowl, it was known as a 'jack-bowl', or little bowl, and then later shortened to 'jack'.

To bowl comes from the 15th century and means 'to roll a ball on the ground'. In cricket, we normally bowl overarm, but the bowler is allowed to roll the cricket ball along the ground. This, however, would be classed as unsporting because it would prevent the batsman hitting the ball any significant distance. Remember the match in 1981 between Australia and New Zealand? New Zealand needed a six of the last ball to tie and Australia then bowled underarm preventing the opportunity of a 6 and won the match.

Antifreeze.

The 'antifreeze' is an extremely difficult shot in curling. The stone is delivered so that it will come to rest behind another stone already in play. The phrase is used because they appear to be frozen together.

The name 'colosseum' is believed to be derived from a colossal statue of Nero that once stood nearby. It comes from the Greek word 'kolossos', meaning 'gigantic statue.'

- Snooker balls were originally made of ivory. Unfortunately for the African animals, they were more sought after because of their denser ivory.

- The maximum weight of a dart is 50g.

- Taekwondo translated from Korean is 'the way of kicking and striking'.

- Teams in korfball are mixed with four males and four females. When playing against other teams, players of the same sex are only allowed to defend against each other. Korfball gets its name from the Dutch for basket.

- They say the best way to beat the rush at Villa Park is to stay and watch to the end of the game!

- Ayrton Senna is the only F1 world champion to die during an F1 race. Other F1 champions have died driving but not in F1 races are:

  - Jochen Rindt who tragically died in practice at Monza in 1970, eventually became a world champion posthumously. He had amassed enough points from his 5 wins out of 10 Grand Prix's to win the championship. Jackie Stewart presented the championship trophy to his widow Nina.

  - The 1952 and 1953 world champion, Alberto Ascari, who died in 1955, whilst having a go in a Ferrari at Monza, this was after crashing his Lancia into the sea 4 days earlier in the Monaco Grand Prix.

  - Scotland's, Jim Clark, a 2-time world F1 champion in '63 and '65 and Indy 500 winner in '65 died on the 7th April 1968. He was competing in the Deutschland Trophäe, a F2 race. In those days F1 driver would drive in other championships because of the long 4-month break between racing seasons.

  - The 1967 F1 world champion, New Zealander Denny Hulme. Hulme's death was caused by heart attack, whilst driving a BMW M3 during the 1992 edition of the Bathurst 1000 race in Australia.

- In the UK, rock climbing routes are classified 4a, 4b, 4c, 5a, 5b, 5c, 6a, 6b, 6c, 7a, 7b. The smaller the number, the easier the route, within the grade the letter A is easier than B and C even more challenging.

- In Japanese, ju means 'gentleness' and jitsu means 'art'. Thus, ju jitsu means the gentle art.

Level 6 on a Concept 2 rower is what the resistance of water on the river feels like.

White water kayaking courses have six classifications of waters. From one to six, one is the easiest and six, the hardest.

Ryu are Ju Jitsu schools.

Both breaststroke and butterfly require the swimmer to finish two handed when touching the end of the pool. A single-handed finish results in a disqualification. Some swimmers don't cut their fingernails short in order to be able to complete the race in a faster time!

'Golf', usually taken as an alteration of middle Dutch 'colf or colve' meaning stick, club or bat.

Competition bullets.

For the obvious safety reasons, in shooting competitions only soft nosed bullets such as those tipped with lead are allowed.

Joe Davis was the first world champion in snooker and was also the organiser of the tournament. Joe would go onto win the first 15 world championships between 1927 to 1946.

In curling the players sweep in front of the stone to speed it up should it be going too slow and also then the opposition have the opportunity to move it further on once it is past the seven circle (centre) thus making it less of a counting stone.

Average distances run in sports

- Rugby – 12km in 80 min
- Football – 7 miles in 90 min
- American football – 1.25 miles for receivers and cornerbacks
- Ice hockey – 2856m (I know its skating)
- Baseball – 0.0375 miles
- Basketball – 2.55 miles in 48 min
- Tennis – 3 miles
- 10k track – 6.2 miles

One in 50 Canadians are registered as ice hockey players.

The moguls we have come to hate in skiing get their name from the Bavarian word 'mugel', which means mound or small hill. I once told a pupil I took on a school ski trip they were called moguls and shaped as they are, because it was the snow covering mole hills!

The perfect hat-trick.

In football, the perfect hat-trick is a right foot goal, a left foot goal and a header.

The biggest difference in points in an international rugby union game is 152. It has happened on two occasions. In 2002, Japan beat Chinese Taipei 155–3, and in the same year Argentina beat Paraguay 152–0.

"How was your golf game, dear?" asked Jack's wife Tracy. "Well, I was hitting pretty well, but my eyesight's gotten so bad, I couldn't see where the ball went." "You're seventy-five years old, Jack!" admonished his wife. "Why don't you take my brother Scott along?" "But he's eighty-five and doesn't even play golf anymore," protested Jack. "Yes, but he's got perfect eyesight and can watch your ball for you," Tracy pointed out. The next day, Jack teed off with Scott looking on. Jack swung and the ball disappeared down the middle of the fairway. "Did you see where it went?" asked Jack. "Yup," Scott answered. "Well, where is it?" yelled Jack, peering off into the distance. "I forgot."

Rugby sevens has its origins in the Scottish town of Melrose. It was originally invented as a charity game in the 1880's. Its inventor was the butcher, Ned Haig.

You know you are one of the greatest when you have numerous nicknames.

- Babe
- The Great Bambino
- The Sultan of Swat
- The Colossus of Clout

All were names for George Herman Ruth.

Bandy is a sport that resembles football on ice. Not Bambi on ice!

Are you sleepless at night wondering why there is both the 1500m and mile distance in track and fields? We go from 100m, 200, 400m, 800m and then 1500m? What is that all about? Well, the reason is that the French used to have 500m tracks in the 1800's. The French played a large role in establishing the first modern Olympics, remember Pierre de Coubertin was a major instigator of the first Games.

The US Open (tennis) is different.

The US Open is the only grand slam that has a final set tie break as a way of deciding the outcome. Their reasoning is that it suits the TV networks. They like to know when the match is going to finish and also the ability to schedule advertisements.

To 'lose', now this is quite an interesting one for me, because I have heard about this word. It's the word that describes others when I play them but having no first-hand knowledge of it, I thought I would investigate it a little. To 'lose' comes either from the old English 'losian' meaning 'to be lost or perish,' and/or 'los' which means 'destruction, loss.' These in turn may well have come from the old Norse word 'los', meaning 'the breaking up of an army;'

'Fore' is from old English meaning before, in front of. Used in other words like forecourt. In golf, fore is shouted to warn others in front of you of wayward shots. Along time ago in golf a fore caddy was used to go in front of the player to watch where the ball finished up.

Penny farthings were bicycles raced in Victorian times. The name penny farthing comes from the British coins, the penny and the farthing. With one much larger than the other, like the wheels on this bike. The penny-farthing didn't use gears, so the only way to go faster was to have a bigger wheel. Pedals were directly attached to the front wheel, so the bigger the wheel, the further a single pedal push can propel you. Another reason why the penny-farthing uses a large wheel is that to keep the rider comfortable. Back in the olden days, the roads were in poor condition, and the large wheel of the penny-farthing could roll over potholes and small rocks. It led to a smoother ride than smaller-wheel bikes, which were often called boneshakers.

Dale Ellis played 69 minutes in a single basketball game! On November 9th, 1989, the Seattle Supersonics (for whom Dale played) met up with the Milwaukee Bucks in a game that went to five overtime periods, the Sonics lost 155-154.

A win streak of 81 is an all-time record of any professional tennis player on a particular surface. The record is held by Rafael Nadal on clay. He went undefeated for more than two years.

Harrow School in the 1800's is the birthplace of squash rackets, which then became known as squash.

Table tennis grips.

Penholder and handshake grip are the two styles of holding a table tennis bat.

Badminton gets its modern name from where it was first played in England by the Earl of Badminton, at Badminton House in 1873. Originally the sport was called 'Poona' after the Indian city (Pune) where it was invented before the British soldiers brought it to England.

Jimmy Connors has won more matches in the modern era than any other player. His career lasted 21 years and he won 1337 matches.

Four nuns were attending a baseball game. Four men were sitting directly behind them. Because their habits were partially blocking the view, the men decided to badger the nuns hoping that they'd get annoyed enough to move to another area. In a very loud voice, the first guy said, "I think I'm going to move to Utah. There are only 100 nuns living there." Then the second guy spoke up and said, "I want to go to Missouri, there are only 75 nuns living there." The third guy said, "I want to go to Texas, there are only 50 nuns living there." The fourth guy said, "I want to go to Maine. There are only 25 nuns living there." The mother superior turned around, looked at the men, and in a very sweet and calm voice said, "Why don't you go to hell, there aren't any nuns there!"

Players of Chinese hacky sack, featherball, kinja and chapteh will all see the similarity of them to jianzi.

Skeet shooting sees the shooter having to aim at targets that are fired both low and high. The shooter shoots from eight different positions around a semicircle. The targets are released both singularly and also as doubles. Only one shot is allowed at each target. Targets are released in a set pattern and happen within three seconds of the shooter calling for their release. This variation in time increases the difficulty.

Within gymnastic circles, the rings are referred to as roman rings. However, they are nothing to do with romans or Rome but in fact they were first used in Germany.

In the Salt Lake City winter Olympics, something quite unique happened after some controversial scoring. There was a tie for first place in the pairs figure skating. The original winners were Elena Berezhnaya and Anton Sikharulidze of Russia but they were joined afterwards by the original silver-medallists Jamie Salé and David Pelletier of Canada once it had been decided the scoring had been unfair.

A yard sale.

A 'yard sale' is a term used by skiers and mountain bikers to describe a horrendous crash that leaves all your various 'things' – water bottles, ski poles, pump, tool bag, sunglasses etc., scattered as if on display in a yard sale.

The cold rubber squash ball has little or no energy in it and must be warmed up. Once it is warm, the ball flies much quicker. Players are given five minutes on court to warm both themselves and the ball up. The warmup involves hitting the ball to each other, sometimes the player will do a combination of shots back to themselves. Sometimes they play too many shots to themselves in the warmup and in which case will be given a warning by the marker.

Why is the sport of cricket called cricket? Because it's boring.

Al Oertar won three consecutive golds in the discus. His third and final gold was won despite him wearing a neck brace!

A man went to doctor, "Doctor every night in my dream I am playing soccer." The doctor says, "Take these pills, they will help you sleep better." The man, "I can't take them, tonight is the semifinal."

In the 1968 Grenoble winter games, the East German luge team placed 1st, 2nd and 4th. However, they were found to have heated their runners and were disqualified as a consequence.

There are 67 different types of throw in kodokan judo.

It is thought the reason the men do not use the balance beam as an apparatus in gymnastics is quite simply because of them wanting to protect the old crown jewels.

The Cuban, Ángel Valodia Matos was so incensed because of his disqualification in the 2008 Beijing Olympics taekwondo bronze medal match that he took his own retribution by kicking the referee in the face. He received a lifetime ban.

Michael Johnson was the first man ever to be ranked number one in both the 200m and 400m distances. He also held both world records for nearly 10 years.

- The Atlanta 1996 games were unique in that all 197-member nations of the IOC competed in the games for the first time.

- Kersten Palm, a Swedish fencer, competed in 7 consecutive Olympics. She didn't actually win an Olympic medal but did place 5th in Mexico.

If you drink, don't drive.

- If you drink, don't drive... Don't even putt."

- There were 18 nations (Soviet Union, Bulgaria, East Germany, Mongolia, Vietnam, Laos, Czechoslovakia, Afghanistan, Hungary, Poland, Cuba, South Yemen, North Korea, Ethiopia, Angola, Albania, Iran and Libya) who boycotted the 1984 Los Angeles games. These nations just eight years before had won more than half of all the gold medals available.

- Innsbruck lit two flames because it was the second time they had hosted the winter Olympic games.

- Dressage wasn't always a sport but was a form of military training for both horses and rider.

- The Vatican City national football team surprised everyone and caused an upset by beating Portugal 2–1 in the opening match of the 2012 London Olympics. The Portuguese coach said that his players' fear of scoring against the 'God's football team' which could be seen as desecration was the reason for the defeat. Unfortunately, San Marino and Sao Tome and Principe were more professional and beat the Vatican City. The Vatican national football team finished last in that group with three points.

- The first racing sleds were made of wood but were soon replaced by steel sleds that came to be known as bobsleds, so named because of the way crews bobbed back and forth to increase their speed on the straightaways.

- My wife returned home from a round of golf and said she'd been injured. She told me she'd be hit between the first and second holes. To which I replied: That doesn't leave much room for a band aid!

- The Munich 1972 Olympic games were the first to use a mascot.

- A sure-fire way of losing your money at the dogs is to back the first three lanes assuming that they are the shortest route to the first bend. I tried this and lost every race.

The etymology of the sport of parkour is from the French, parcours du combattant. This is the obstacle course used in French military training.

There are principally four different tennis surfaces played on.

- Grass – Wimbledon
- Clay – Roland Garros
- Hard – Australian and US
- Carpet – Indoor competitions

Sir Roger Bannister completed his morning house rounds at Paddington Hospital (he was a doctor there), he caught the train to Oxford, was paced to 3 mins 59.4 seconds, the first ever four-minute mile. The members of Parliament once receiving the news adjourned for 3 mins 59.4 seconds as a tribute. Just a little challenge. Run (safely) next to car at moving at 15 miles an hour (that would give you a four-minute mile pace), and I think you will be shocked at how fast you have to go.

First use of electronic timing.

Electronic timing was first used in the 1968 Mexico Games before that handheld stopwatches were used.

In the 1908 summer Olympics, Oscar Swahn won two gold medals in the running deer, single shot events (individual and team) and a bronze medal in the running deer double shot individual event. Before you go speaking to your MP, the deer in this case were targets in the shape of deer. Unlike the live pigeon shooting event in the 1900 games, where the object was to shoot as many live pigeons as possible.

London 2012 Olympic torch bearers ran an average 300m each and the 8000 bearers carried the torch a total distance of 24000km.

One of the 2016 Rio Olympic Venues of Barra Tijuca was the old site of the Brazil Grand Prix. The Grand Prix is now held at Interlagos, Sao Paulo.

The long jump run up must measure at least 40 metres and there must also be a minimum of nine metres of landing pit.

The current world records for the javelin are not the furthest distances ever thrown. For safety reasons, in 1986 they changed the rules and the 104.80m mark of Uwe Hohn (GDR) set in 1984 was no longer the record. It was next held by Klaus Tafelmeier (FRG) with a new best of 85.74m. The reason for the rule change is the athletes were throwing their javelins nearly onto the track at the other end of the stadium. The javelins centre of balance was changed thus bringing them down earlier.

The Greek word 'athlos' means a contest or competition gives us the modern-day word athlete.

She was a he!

Stella Walsh was really born Stanisława Walasiewicz. She won gold in the 100m at the 1932 Los Angeles Olympic games breaking the 12 second barrier. Unfortunately, she was killed in robbery quite a few years later. In the autopsy on her, it was revealed that she was indeed a man and then the truth came out about his real name. The most bizarre part of the whole story that even though Stella Walsh was a man, she is still the female 1932 Olympic 100m champion!

I met a couple of Aston Villa supporters at the pub the other night. "Do you often go to Villa Park?" I asked. "Yeah, of course!" they said. "We've found the perfect way. Ten minutes after kick-off we climb over a fence!" "That sounds great," I replied. "Yeah, but last week we were caught and had to sit down and watch the rest of the game."

One of the original sports in the first modern Olympics, the shot put would see the athletes standing still whilst competing. The sport developed with 'the glide' coming into the sport in the 1950's. It was USA shot putter O'Brien who is credited with the first glide technique. The rotation that is often seen today originated in the 1970's and is credited to the Soviet athlete Aleksandr Baryshnikov. He adapted the discuss technique to suit the shot.

On Thanksgiving Day in Chicago in 1887, the sport of softball was first played.

There are only about 50 real tennis courts in the whole world.

Lifting in the sport of race walking is where both feet are off the ground simultaneously. Australian walker Jane Saville was leading with just 150m to go in the 2000 Sydney Games 20km event was disqualified for the offence. You do get warnings though before you are finally disqualified.

Judo is Japanese for the 'gentle way' and the aim of the sport and art of fighting is to turn your opponent's aggression to your advantage.

The 'ollie' is a trick used by skate boarders to jump over obstacles.

The indy car motor racing sport gets its name from the Indianapolis 500 race.

To ensure competitive and fair games of polo, all players are given a handicap rating. The best players have a 10-goal handicap, the worst will have a two-goal handicap. The total for the team is calculated and the difference between the two teams is given to the lower rated team in goals. For example, a team with a total handicap of 40 would give away 10 goals, if they are playing against a team with a total of 30 handicap.

In trap shooting the shooter requests the release of the clay usually by shouting 'pull'. The target is released immediately, and two shots are permitted at each target. Targets are released from in front of the shooter.

'Why do scuba divers fall off their boats backwards?" "If they fell forwards, they'd still be on the boat!"

Refrain from violent behaviour

The dojo kun is a set of guidelines that karetekas (karate fighters) adhere to both in the dojo and their everyday lives. They are:

- Perfection of character
- Be faithful
- Endeavour
- Respect others
- Refrain from violent behaviour (I presume this doesn't mean whilst you are kicking and punching your opponent!)

The world's first ever luge race was between the town of Klosters and Davos in Switzerland. The actual race ended in a dead heat.

In track cycling bikes, there are no brakes as you might expect on a normal road bike, rather the fixed gear is used to slow the bikes down. A fixed gear is where the chain drives the sprocket on the rear wheel with no freewheel mechanism. Fixed gear bikes can (but I see no reason to do so) be ridden backwards.

Water polo might have got its name from its association with polo. Competitors would sit on barrels (simulating horses) in the water.

Control of the cue (white) ball in snooker, pool, billiards and the like can be gained by hitting it in certain areas. Hitting towards the top of the ball causes it to continue on after impact with its top spin, towards the bottom sees the ball spinning back towards to you. Side can also be put on the cue ball which gives the cue ball an element of sideways movement.

What are the most athletic rodents? Track and field mice.

The cross-country art of skiing known as 'telemarking', got its name after the Norwegian (Telemark) mountainous region in which is what was founded. The foot is attached on the top and the ski grips the snow with the skis unique underside and shape allowing for uphill skiing.

The Japanese founder of judo was a man named Jigaro Kano, a Russian Vasili Oshchepkov developed the sport of Sombo having been inspired by judo. All sounds fine so far. Enter Stalin and his views of things. Stalin wanted everything in the Soviet Union to be good and great, outside ideas were frowned upon. Oshchepkov paid the ultimate price for telling Stalin where his inspiration had come from. He was imprisoned and died whilst serving time.

Weight categories for tug of war teams.

There are five men's categories of weights for tug of war teams:

- Up to 560kg
- 600kg
- 640kg
- 680kg

For women, the weight categories are:

- 480kg
- 520kg
- 560kg

You can have as many in your team, as long as the sum total doesn't exceed the maximum weight capacity. All competitors must tug with their weight written on them to prevent cheating.

The Iron Dog Classic is the longest snowmobile race in the world. The competitors have to race 2000 miles in Alaska between Wasilla with Fairbanks.

The number of clubs a golfer can carry, and use is 14. This can be a personal choice but is usually the three driving woods, a full set of irons and a putter.

Nico Rosberg won the inaugural 2005 GP2 series. Lewis Hamilton won the second series a year later.

A bagel in tennis.

A 'bagel' in tennis is losing the set to zero. 6-0.

Makushita is the title given to apprentice sumo wrestlers.

Trinquet are a type of pelota court where spectators can actually sit inside the court on the steps at the side of the courts. Players aim for the steps because of the uncertainty of the bounce. Spectators are often known to be hit by the ball.

Trampoline is from the Italian 'trampoli', meaning 'stilts.' Further explanation is unclear, but some think it's related to the English word tramp, meaning 'to stamp around,' and the word that is slang for 'vagrant.' The trampoline was invented in the USA in the 1930's by George Nissen.

Why didn't the dog want to play football? It was a boxer.

The 3 swords of fencing.

There are three different types of fencing. Each has its own type of sword.

Foil

A very light and flexible blade with the pressure sensor (a push button) on the tip of the blade. The torso of the opponent is the target area that scores in the foil discipline of fencing.

Sabre

The sabre blade has sensors on the edge as well as the tip of the blade. It doesn't have a push button sensor and indeed the tip of the sabre is folded over for safety. The head, body and arms are all targets.

Epee

The epee has a push button sensor on the tip of its blade and scoring can be made anywhere on the opponent's body.

Pelota is a similar game to squash but played with a hard ball. It was first invented in prisons as a game played in the yards. Eventually, it became a respected game once it was played by public school boys in the 1800's. In Spain and France where the sport was invented, Pelota is known as 'jai alai' which translates from Basque to 'happy festival'.

✕ Most competition dragon boats have 18 oarsmen, there are bigger ceremonial swan boats that have up to 50 crew but these are much less raced.

🏸 What's the difference between a 'let' and 'stroke' in squash? To stop all the arguments on the squash court, here is the difference very simply. A let is when your opponent stops you getting to play the ball, and a stroke is when your opponent is in the way of the ball travelling towards the front wall when you are going to hit it.

▢ There are two juries in gymnastics awarding scores. The A jury is made of two judges and sits in front of the apparatus and the B jury has six judges and they are positioned around the apparatus.

✕ In hurling, the sliotar can be hit nearly the length of the 130m pitch. It can also travel as fast as 90 miles an hour.

🚲 The omnium is a 6-event cycle race on the track. There are three sprints and three endurance events that decide the winner.

 - 🚲 250m flying sprint
 - 🚲 30km/20km points race
 - 🚲 Elimination race
 - 🚲 4km/3km pursuit
 - 🚲 Scratch race 15km/10km
 - 🚲 1km/500m time trial

🏌 America's Babe Zaharias won two golds and a silver at the 1932 Olympics in the 80m hurdles, javelin and high jump. In 1935, she took up golf and went on to win 82 tournaments around the world, including 10 Major championships. She even competed 3 times on the men's tour and made the cut twice.

🥊 At 20 years old, Mike Tyson was the youngest man to win the heavyweight boxing title.

🏆 The British motor racing legend that is John Surtees is the only man ever to be crowned world champion in both Formula One and motorcycle racing. He kickstarted his career, becoming world champion four times in 500cc racing in the five years from 1956 to 1960. In his final season racing motorbikes he was simultaneously racing cars. Making his debut at the 1960 Monaco Grand

Prix before finishing second in his Grand Prix at Silverstone a few weeks later. He went on to win the championship with Ferrari in 1964.

Excess consumed energy usually calories from fats or carbs, is stored in fat cells in the form of triglycerides. This is how your body preserves energy for future activity. Over time, this excess energy (energy not used by your body) results in a fat surplus that can affect your body shape and health.

The three elements of the triple jump are not equal in their distances. The 'hop' is the longest at about 37%, the 'step' makes up 33% and the final 'jump' makes the final 30%.

How long to run around the world?

It would take you 958 days to run around the 24901 miles of the earth's equator if you ran 26 miles (a marathon) a day.

In archery, men shoot 90m in some competitions, the Olympic distances is 80m for both sexes and there is also the indoor distance of 50m.

Drag cars can accelerate to more than 600 kilometres an hour whilst racing the 400m straight-line race distance. Parachutes are used to slow them down and the drivers experience 5G in the deceleration. Just in case you fancy giving it a go, there are only approximately 300 drag strips in the whole of the world.

Three fans were bemoaning the sorry state of their American football team. "I blame the general manager," said the first fan. "If he signed better players, we'd be a great team." "I blame the players," said the second fan. "If they made more of an effort, we'd score some points." "I blame my parents," said the third. "If I'd been born in New England, I'd be supporting a decent team."

Since 2009, the Paris – Dakar was moved to South America because of the threat by terrorists on its original route which passed through North Africa.

It takes two crewmembers to race at the top forms of powerboats. The formula 1 and class 1 boats have a driver to steer and a crewmember to throttle the boat. These boats can reach more than 135 miles an hour and the sport is extremely dangerous. The boats are so wide they have to be transported on their side on the back of low loader lorries.

Adolf Hitler enjoyed handball and the sport made its Olympic debut in Berlin because of this. Hitler wasn't a particularly popular man after the war and as a consequence handball was dropped from the programme until 1972.

In the 1920 Olympic Games, Suzanne Lenglen won the gold medal for tennis, on route she played 10 sets, won all 10 and indeed she only lost a total of four games throughout the tournament.

A 'let' used in tennis and squash gets origins stem from the old Saxon word 'lettian' which meant to hinder or prevent something from happening.

Mars the Roman god of war.

Martial as in martial arts dates back the medieval Latin word 'martialis' meaning 'of Mars or war.' Mars, of course is the Roman god of war.

A man loved to play golf. It was the one activity he looked forward to every week. One Saturday, he returned home from a scheduled foursome much earlier than his wife had expected. She asked him why he was home so early? "Do you want to play golf with someone who whines about every shot, complains about everything on the course, and makes noises when you're trying to make an important shot?" he replied. "No, I don't," answered his wife. "Well, neither did they!"

Figure skater, Gillis Emanuel Grafström from Sweden won three consecutive gold's in the 1920, 1924 and 1928 Olympic games. He was also an innovator and invented the spiral and the flying seat spin moves in the sport.

'Steady Eddie', Charlton was one of the slowest snooker players. After one match, fellow player Cliff Thorburn observed. 'Before the match I had a suntan, now it's gone.' Away from the table, however Eddie was part of a winning team in the Australian surfing championship and he also played in the Aussie rules first division for 10 years. In 1956, he was selected to carry the Olympic torch on its journey to Melbourne.

In the Los Angeles games of 1932, Babe Didrikson competed in and won both the javelin and the 80m hurdles. She also won a silver medal in the high jump. She wanted to compete in more events but women were prevented from entering more than three events back then.

What's a baseball player do when his eyesight starts to fail him? He takes a job as an umpire.

In the 1900 Olympics, Alvin Kraenzlein won four individual gold medals in the 60m dash, the 60m and 200m hurdles and also the long jump. This individual feat in track and field has not yet been equalled. Alvin loved athletics so much he preferred to become a coach rather than a dentist for which he was qualified.

Aerobic sports quite simply are those that require oxygen for the muscles like the running a marathon or playing football. Anaerobic means without oxygen and these sports have actions in which the muscles work without oxygen for example power lifting and 60m dash.

Largest regulation basketball score.

On February 27th, 1959, the Boston Celtics beat the Minneapolis Lakers 173-139. This is the highest ever basketball winning score in regulation (no overtime). Boston managed 52 fourth quarter points.

Dennis Compton was as a test cricketer and footballer, he scored 17 centuries for England, averaging 50 in 78 matches either side of World War ll. He also played for Arsenal, winning an FA Cup winner's medal in 1950. When he was asked to explain his success, he said 'Lucky... went to a decent school, you see.'

The only man to play in both the rugby and cricket world cup finals tournaments, was the Namibian Rudi Van Vuuren. He completed this amazing feat in 2003. He was a rugby union fly-half and a medium-pace bowler. Unfortunately, both he and Namibia did not have too much success in either tournament.

The martial art 'karate' began in Okinawa in the 17th century. It is the most practised of all the arts and there are more than 70 styles of karate.

The sport of fencing gets its name from the word 'defence'. Which in turn comes from the Latin 'defendere', meaning to 'drive away.'

West Auckland were the first winners of the football world cup. We all know that Uruguay won the first FIFA world cup in 1930. In 1909, a team made up of miners raised the money to travel to Italy to represent England. They beat FC Winterthur of Switzerland 2–0 in the final of the first football world cup.

Professional cyclists don't have time to stop and urinate once the racing starts in earnest. To stop the rider losing ground, they are pushed by a teammate and the lycra shorts are pulled up and you can imagine what happens next.

In athletic relay races, the handover zone is just 20m. Both runners must be completely in this zone whilst exchanging the baton to prevent any disqualification. When you consider the male runners are sprinting at more than 10 metres a second, which means less than two seconds is spent in this handover zone.

Mintonette becomes badminton.

Mintonette (referencing its similarity to badminton) was the original name for volleyball. It was invented in 1895.

Maria Mutola was the first athlete to win the IAAF Golden League jackpot outright on her own. If there are multiple winners of the award, the prize money was shared. She was an 800m runner and won the league in 2003.

A clean round in mountain bike trials is rewarded with a score of zero. Points are added for dabbing feet on the ground, leaving the course or running out of time.

Judo is partly derived from ju jitsu which was the hand-to-hand fighting method used by the Samurai.

How do hockey players kiss? They pucker up.

Sumo wrestlers are known as 'rikishi' informally and in a formal way, they are referred to as 'sumotoris'.

A 220lb (100kg) person burns approximately 150 calories running an 8-minute mile. However, that figure reduces to just 82 calories if the person weighs 120lbs.

Mexico City was the first games to use a synthetic track. Before that, cinder tracks were used. The first few modern Olympics saw their track and field events run on the grass.

A batter in cricket hitting 160 not out is a good score but that nothing completely unheard of or something to be in this book. This 160 not out, however, was Shania-Lee Swart who was the only player in her team to score a run. She hit 160 from 86 balls against Easterns in Pretoria, South Africa. Her amazing innings included 18 fours and 12 sixes. Her eight teammates scored a grand total of 0. The final score for the innings was 169–8 in 20 overs. The other nine runs were gained from the bowlers as extras.

In 1933, Garrincha was born in the state of Rio de Janeiro. His father was an alcoholic, drinking cachaça (a rum) heavily, a problem which unfortunately Garrincha would inherit. He was a boy with a carefree attitude, he was a lot smaller than other kids his age.' Because of his size his sister Rosa started calling him Garrincha, Brazil's north-eastern name for the wren, a little brown bird. The name stuck and by the age of four years, he was known as Garrincha to his family and friends. Garrincha was born with a deformed spine and one leg slightly shorter than the other but is often described as the best ever dribbler of the ball in football.

Some football firsts.

◦ Some football 1ˢᵗ's

- ⚽ 1857 – Sheffield FC – 1ˢᵗ football club in the world founded in 1857.
- ⚽ 1860 – 1ˢᵗ non-British team in the world. Lausanne, Switzerland.
- ⚽ 1885 – 1ˢᵗ Non-European International. Canada beat USA 1–0.
- ⚽ 1887 – Gimnasia y Esgrina de la Plata, Argentina, 1ˢᵗ South American team formed.
- ⚽ 1888 – 1ˢᵗ football league is founded in England by Aston Villa director William McGregor.
- ⚽ 1898 – Athletic Bilbao 1ˢᵗ club in Spain.
- ⚽ 1899 – Barcelona FC is founded.
- ⚽ 1900 – Bayern Munich started just a year later.
- ⚽ 1902 – Real Madrid Football Club founded.
- ⚽ 1910 – Corinthians were founded.

◦ The new ball in cricket is introduced after 80 overs. The bowlers don't want it, the batsman do!

◦ In 1891 when penalties were first introduced, Corinthian's CB Fry called the new law: 'a standing insult to sports men to have to play under a rule which assumes that players intend toe tip, hack and push opponents and to behave like cads of the most unscrupulous kidney'. Corinthians were touring South Africa in 1903, a referee adjudged one of their players to have committed a foul in their own penalty area, such was the ignominy and insult that the Corinthian goalkeeper stood to one side to give the opposing team a free shot.

◦ "I was playing chess with my friend, and he said, 'Let's make this more interesting.' So, we stopped playing chess."

◦ Falkirk (Scotland) and River Plate (Argentina) are the only two football clubs outside of Italy, England and Spain to have broken the world record transfer fee. Sydney Puddlefoot joined the Scottish side for a then record £5,000 in 1922, whilst the Argentinians splashed out a record £23,000 on Bernabe Ferreyra ten years later.

◦ Shigeki Tanaka survived Hiroshima's bombing and went on to become the winner of the 1951 Boston Marathon. It was the first post WWII athletic competition to invite Japanese athletes, who had also been barred from the 1948 London Olympics. The Boston Globe nicknamed him 'atomic boy.'

Triathlon distances

	Swim	Bike	Run
Sprint	0.5mi (750m)	12.4mi (20km)	3.1mi (5km)
Olympic	0.93mi (1.5km)	24.8mi (40km)	6.2mi (10km)
ITU Long	1.86mi (3km)	49.6mi (80km)	12.4mi (20km)
Half/70.3	1.2mi (1.9km)	56mi (90km)	13.1mi (21.09km)
Ironman	2.4mi (3.8km)	112mi (180km)	26.2mi (42.19km)

Sergio Batista (1986) and Gennaro Gattuso in 1986 and 2006 respectively are the only two players to have won the football world cup whilst sporting a full beard.

Ex Manchester United defender Nemanja Vidic has a surname that is completely made up of roman numerals: V (5), I (1), D (500), I (1), C (100)!

England rugby union prop Joe Marler's 10-week ban for grabbing Alun Wyn Jones' genitals ended without him missing a match because of the coronavirus lockdown.

Getting your knee down.

Whilst cornering on motorbikes, riders often actually rub their knees on the floor. The friction obviously wears things out. To stop the expensive protective once piece suits getting damaged, stick on replaceable knee sliders are used.

Abebe Bikila defended his Rome Olympic marathon title in Tokyo. He won in Tokyo in a new Olympic record time of 2:12:11.2. Most people including elite runners are normally exhausted after a marathon but Abebe not appearing the least bit tired started a routine of stretching exercises. He later stated that he could have run another 10 kilometres.

The powerhouse nations of Algeria, Ghana, South Korea and Saudi Arabia are part of an elite group, they being the only countries in the world to boast an undefeated record against England in football.

Why don't grasshoppers watch soccer? They watch cricket, instead.

Baseball team owner, Joe Engel, in 1931 decided to trade his shortstop for a turkey. Johnny Jones was a Chattanooga Lookouts player that, if we are being honest, wasn't any good. He was such a weak-hitting shortstop that even the press complained about him. Joe Engel decided to trade him to the Charlotte Hornets of the Piedmont League. In return, Engel and the Lookouts received a 25-pound turkey. Joe Engel even went as far as to say, "the turkey was having a better year."

Only baseball team to go bankrupt.

The Seattle Pilots are the only Major League baseball team to go bankrupt. The club started well with a win over the Chicago White Sox on the 11th April 1969. Less than a year later on 1st April 1970, the Seattle baseball franchise was moved to Milwaukee because of lack of funds!

The sport of bowling has quite a vague history. There is, however, evidence that the Egyptians were playing a form of the game as many as 5000 years ago.

US President Gerald Ford played American football as a University of Michigan undergraduate. George HW Bush played in the first two college world series.

We all know how good health wise cycling is for you but there is evidence that it causes impotency! The pudendal nerve is involved in sensation of the penis and perineum and is intimately involved in the process of ejaculation. Sitting on a bicycle seat can put a lot of pressure on the pudendal nerve and the blood vessels in the area. The theory is that this pressure causes nerve entrapment and dysfunction of the nerve. 'Pudendal nerve entrapment' has been associated with pelvic pain, loss of sensation in the penis, erectile dysfunction and difficulty ejaculating.

The basketball legend that is Michael Jordan packed in his first love in order to play professional baseball. Some said he could have continued onto the Major League but he delighted the world by returning to basketball, and was arguably a better player after his return.

The American figure skater Tonya Harding became a hate figure in 1994 when her Olympic rival Nancy Kerrigan was assaulted with a metal bar. Harding's husband later admitted being involved in a plot to attack Kerrigan. After refusing to co-operate with the investigation, Harding received a fine and community service. She entered a 'reality TV' fight and subsequently turned professional in 2003. She has had six boxing bouts as 'America's Bad Girl', finishing her career with 3 wins and 3 loses.

The CONMEBOL football Federation is made up of Argentina, Bolivia, Brazil, Chile, Colombia, Ecuador, Paraguay, Peru, Uruguay and Venezuela.

In 1951, the first year of night games of American football, the balls were white with two black stripes so that players and spectators could easily see the ball in the dark. Advancements in stadium lighting were made, making the white ball unnecessary, and by 1956, they were officially replaced with the standard brown balls we see today. The white stripes on some footballs are used to differentiate between collegiate and NFL games.

The bail, two of which are found on top of the wickets in cricket was originally a French word that described the top part of the gate of a sheep pen.

Whilst many people in the USA call American footballs 'pigskins', the official nickname of the football used by the NFL is the 'Duke' after Wellington Mara. Mara, who was named after the Duke of Wellington, was the co-owner of the New York Giants and the son of the founder of the Giants. The nickname was used between 1941 and 1969. It fell out of use in 1970 when the AFL and NFL merged, but bounced back into play in 2006, a year after Mara's death.

Scrambled eggs and Tottenham.

How are scrambled eggs and Tottenham Hotspur the same? They've both been beaten a lot!

Championship American football games are called 'bowls' thanks to a stadium designed by Myron Hunt. The Rose Bowl was modelled after the design of Yale's stadium, Yale Bowl, which got its name from the fact that it resembled a bowl. Gradually, other cities and universities with American football teams saw the money-making opportunities and promotional value of these tournament games, like the Rose Bowl, and began creating their own 'bowl' games. Even though many of these games were not played in bowl shaped stadiums! The NFL eventually borrowed this terminology when they created the Pro Bowl in 1951, and later, of course, the Super Bowl.

Jules Rimet was one of the founders of the Fédération Internationale de Football Association, (FIFA) in 1904 and he went on to become its 3rd president. He was also president of the French Football Federation between 1919 and 1942. He was involved in running of the football tournament in the 1908 Summer Olympics. It was Jules Rimet's initiative that brought about the first FIFA World Cup which was held in 1930. The Jules Rimet Trophy awarded to world cup winners was named in his honour.

Romanian tennis superstar Ilie Năstase was the first professional athlete to sign a contract to play in Nike shoes. In 1972, legendary American runner Steve Prefontaine became the first track athlete to wear Nike.

The word 'mascot' probably derives from the French word 'mascoto', meaning 'witch, fairy or sorcerer'. This, in turn, gave rise to the slang word 'mascotte', meaning 'talisman' or 'sorcerer's charm' in the 1860's. The word 'mascotte' was first used in the context of a good luck charm in sporting events around the 1880's in American baseball.

It is interesting to notice that the oldest British sports still use the term 'handicap' in a way that resembles the old uses. A handicap in horse racing still refers to a race, not to the extra weight. In golf (a game almost as old as horse racing), the handicap is a benefit given to inferior players, not an extra burden on superior players.

Pankration

Whilst today we have MMA, the ancient Greeks had something known as pankration, which was something like a free-for-all hand to hand fight that mixed boxing, kicking and wrestling. The only two rules of pankration are don't bite and don't gouge out your opponent's eyes. Everything else was fair game. There were no time limits and, except in rare cases where a judge might intervene, the fights lasted until one person was coerced into giving up or died.

Pato, Argentina's official sport was originally played with a live duck, although after many government interventions, the game now uses a ball instead. With players on horseback, it's something of a cross between polo and basketball, the objective being to get the ball to your own side. If you are wondering 'why a live duck instead of a ball?' In the original version, the goal was to get the duck back to your 'ranch house'. In some cases, this was a literal thing as a match might be played such that your farm might be your team's base and your neighbour's the other team's base. In the early days, it was common for the duck to be killed during the match and knife fights would often break out between competitors. In the late 18th century, trying to discourage the game and the extreme violence in it, there were some catholic priests who refused to give a Christian burial to any person who died during a pato match.

Standing on the sidelines, during a game being played by my school's American football team, I saw one of the players take a hard hit. He tumbled to the ground and didn't move. We grabbed our first-aid gear and rushed out onto the field. The coach picked up the young man's hand and urged, "Son, can you hear me? Squeeze once for yes and twice for no."

Alan Shearer has missed the most Premier League penalties, missing 11. In fairness, he's also scored the most, netting 56.

In 1992, Lance Armstrong competed and came 14ᵗʰ in the summer Olympics in Barcelona, Spain. He turned professional after the Olympic games and finished last in his first race.

A chukka is a time period in polo. A match is made up of six chukkas. Each chukka lasts seven minutes. Chukka comes from the Indian word for a circle or round.

In the 1928 Olympics, the women competed in the 800m but because one of the runners collapsed, the event was withdrawn and wasn't run again by females until 1960!

Tensions were so high between fencer's Aldolfo Contronei and Giorgio Santelli that they actually had a real duel! It was only after Santelli had drawn blood that honour was restored, and things went back to normal.

Rope a dope.

'Rope a dope' is the boxing style made famous by Muhammed Ali, he deliberately leant back on the ropes letting George Foreman punch himself into exhaustion. Once Foreman tired, Ali came off the ropes and knocked him out in the 8ᵗʰ round.

John Dillinger was a notorious bank robber from the USA. He was also a star second baseman and pitcher, he even earned a $25 bonus from a local furniture store for being the best hitter on the Martinsville, Indiana team. The 1924 baseball season ended, and Dillinger didn't have a job. He turned to banking robbing and was caught and sent to prison. In 1929, he became eligible for parole. He played a prison baseball game the day before the hearing and the governor told a reporter, "That kid ought to be playing major league ball." Next day, his parole was denied! Dillinger was sent to Indiana State Prison, because they wanted him to play shortstop for their baseball team. Even when he was on America's most wanted, he still kept up with his beloved Chicago Cubs and even had the audacity to watch them play live whilst on the run from the law!

The first puck ever used in an ice hockey game was reportedly a frozen piece of cow crap.

Where do catchers sit at lunch? Behind the plate.

Zlatan Ibrahimović almost secured a move to Arsenal when he was at Swedish club Malmo, and the club even had a shirt made up with his name on the back.

The one spanner in the works? The then manager, Arsène Wenger wanted him to do a trial. Maybe he wasn't sure if he was any good!

Give me a gun.

When the race walker Jane Saville was asked if she needed anything after being disqualified in the 2000 Sydney Games, she replied. "A gun to shoot myself."

Crown green bowls are designed to travel a curved path because of a weight bias. Originally the bias was produced by inserting weights in one side of the bowl. This, however, is no longer permitted and the bias is now produced entirely by the shape of the bowl.

The Dutchman Clarence Seedorf has won the champions league four times and he did so playing for three different clubs. They were Ajax, Real Madrid and AC Milan.

A retiree was given a set of golf clubs by his co-workers. Thinking he'd try the game, he asked the local pro for lessons, explaining that he knew nothing whatever of the game. The pro showed him the stance and swing, then said, "Just hit the ball toward the flag on the first green." The novice teed up and smacked the ball straight down the fairway and onto the green, where it stopped inches from the hole. "Now what?" the fellow asked the speechless pro. "Uh... you're supposed to hit the ball into the cup," the pro finally said, after he was able to speak again. "Oh great! NOW you tell me." said the beginner.

The javelin comes from a French word for a 'light spear'. Where the French javeline comes from, is a bit vague some says it has a Celtic root that means 'forked,' and is related to a branch of a tree that spears were first made from.

Jim Hunter became baseball's first free agent. After contractual issues, he was allowed to leave the Oakland A's.

Nearly 6000 calories a day.

The average amount of calories used by a Tour de France rider per day is 5,900. An average man uses about 2500 calories a day.

At the time of writing, the two Spanish giants of Barcelona and Madrid are yet to meet in a Champions League final.

Polo players must wear white jodhpurs. Polo is a very traditional game originating in India. It was played by nobility and later introduced to British army officers stationed there in the nineteenth century. Players competing in the Indian heat, preferred clothing that was light in weight and colour. Jodhpurs, the tailored riding britches still worn by some players, took their name from the Indian state of Jodhpur.

The overall winner of the Tour de France wins €450,000. However, he will usually split this with his team-mates, or domestiques and the soigneurs. This is as a thank you for the collective effort of the team.

The word 'decathlon' was formed from the Greek word déka, meaning 'ten' and áthlon, meaning 'contest' or 'prize'.

Two runners are out training in the woods when one is bitten on the rear end by a rattlesnake. "I'll go into town for a doctor," the other says. He runs ten miles to a small town and finds the only doctor delivering a baby. "I can't leave," the doctor says. "But here's what to do. Take a knife, cut a little X where the bite is, suck out the poison and spit it on the ground." The guy runs back to his friend, who is in agony. "What did the doctor say?" the victim cries. "He says you're gonna die."

Singapore leads the world in medal rewards for Olympic golds in the 2016 Rio games. Singapore's swimmer Joseph Schooling won the countries first gold medal in 2016 and was rewarded with nearly three quarters of a million dollars! Below are amounts paid by countries to Olympic medallists.

	Gold	Silver	Bronze
Singapore	$741,000	$371,000	$185,000
Indonesia	$381,000	$152,000	$76,000
Kazakhstan	$250,000	$150,000	$75,000
Azerbaijan	$248,000	$124,000	$62,000
Italy	$166,000	$83,000	$55,000
Hungary	$125,000	$89,000	$71,000
Russia	$61,000	$38,000	$26,000
France	$55,000	$22,000	$14,000
South Africa	$37,000	$19,000	$7,000
USA	$25,000	$15,000	$10,000
Germany	$22,000	$17,000	$11,000
Canada	$15,000	$11,000	$8,000

Just imagine if Michael Phelps had been from Singapore. His total haul of Olympic medals is 28 with 23 gold, 3 silver and 2 bronze. Using the rewards listed above he would have been rewarded with the hypothetical number of $18,526,000!

In the 1920's, cyclists would often share cigarettes whilst riding. They were believed to help 'open the lungs' before big climbs.

Second most popular sport.

Table tennis is the most popular racquet sport in the world and ranked second overall in terms of participation of all sports. There are over 10 million players who compete in officially sanctioned table tennis tournaments each year.

The highest official attendance at a sporting event in England was 126,047 at Wembley Stadium on the 28th April, 1923. They were there to watch the FA cup final between Bolton Wanderers FC and West Ham United FC. Bolton won 2-0.

In 1969, during civil unrest in Addis Ababa, Ethiopia, 2-time Olympic marathon champion Abebe Bikila was driving his Volkswagen Beetle when he had to swerve to avoid a group of protesting students. He lost control of his car, which landed in a ditch, and he found himself trapped. The crash left him a quadriplegic. He was operated on at the Stoke Mandeville Hospital in England, after which his condition improved to paraplegic. He then started to compete in archery competitions for athletes in wheelchairs. Abebe joked that he would win the next Olympic marathon in a wheelchair.

I'm not a very muscular man; the strongest thing about me is my password.

Sports that are said to command the biggest television audiences are the summer Olympics, world cup football and Formula 1 motor racing.

The 'lanterne rouge' is the competitor in last place in a cycling race such as the Tour de France. The phrase comes from the French for 'red lantern' and refers to the red lantern hung on the caboose of a railway train. In the old days, the last rider would actually carry a red light to signify that the race had passed.

What do you call two Mexicans playing basketball? Juan on Juan. A bit like the two Spanish fireman Jose and Hose B.

'Plastic Brit' was applied to several athletes who chose to compete for Britain in the London Olympics, but they were able to do so because they had a British parent or partner, not because they were fast tracked into citizenship, as South Africa runner Zola Budd was in 1984. She became a British Citizen in just a matter of a few weeks.

In 2008 at the Chinese Open, Shaun Murphy and Dave Harold fought out the longest frame ever recorded in a snooker tournament, taking a yawn-some 93 minutes and 12 seconds to complete a single frame.

Did you hear about the race between the lettuce and the tomato? The lettuce was a "head" and the tomato was trying to "ketchup"!

The oldest stage winner of the Tour de France was Firmin Lambot. He won a single stage in 1922. He was 36 years old.

No space travel.

Stefan Schwarz arguably had the most bizarre clause to have ever been inserted into a player's contract. When signing for Sunderland in 1999, the Swede was banned from travelling into space!

On the professional circuit, players are allowed to throw darts that are up to 12-inches long.

Liechtenstein has competed in the most summer Olympics without winning any medal. They have travelled to 17 games without any medal success. Don't forget there are countries that don't participate in the Olympics such as the Vatican City.

A 'full in, full out' is a gymnastic move which is two somersaults and two twists with one twist performed on the first somersault and one twist performed on the second somersault.

Horizontal bar grips in gymnastics

- The overhand (regular) grip is the standard grip used for the horizontal bar. With this grip the hands circle the bar with the backs of the hands facing the gymnast.
- The reverse (underhand) grip is the opposite of the overhand grip. The palms of the hands face the gymnast. It is similar to the grip used in chin-ups.
- The elgrip (L-Grip or eagle grip) is also an underhand grip. In an elgrip gymnasts hands are turned 180 degrees outward from an over grip. Thumbs are turned out, but in the opposite direction of an under grip. This position requires very flexible shoulders.

Reggie Walker of South Africa won the 100 metres at the Olympic games in London in 1908. He is the only African to have won the Olympic 100 metre title.

The record for the most times being hit by a pitch in baseball is held by Hughie Jennings, who was hit an amazing 287 times before his retirement in 1918.

When Ronaldinho won the Copa Libertadores with Atlético Mineiro, he became one of only seven players to win both the Copa Libertadores and the UEFA Champions League. The other players who have completed this achievement are Dida, Cafu, Carlos Tevez, Roque Júnior, Juan Pablo Sorín and Walter Samuel.

Toronto Maple Leaf player, Tie Domi got into an unbelievable 333 fights in his career. That's (at least) 1,665 minutes spent in the penalty box for fighting.

Just three minutes to foul out!

Bubba Wells has the infamy of being the player quickest to foul out in the NBA. On December 29th, 1997, he took just three minutes to foul out of the game. He was playing for the Dallas mavericks against the Chicago Bulls. What makes this a little stranger, in all the other games he played for the Mavericks he'd never even recorded more than three personal fouls in a game.

I love the fall. It gives me a chance to sit at home and watch the World Series. Just like the Dodgers.

The first ever perfect score of 10 in Olympic female gymnastics was achieved at the 1976 Montreal Olympics by Romanian Nadia Comaneci. She went on to win three gold medals.

The Indianapolis 500 has an estimated crowd of 400,000 watching the race. There have been reports that it can take eight hours for cars to leave the car park after the race has finished.

Jonny Wilkinson kicked the 2003 World Cup winning drop goal with his wrong leg! True Legend.

A common misconception is that the word 'GOLF' is an acronym for 'Gentlemen Only Ladies Forbidden'. This is definitely not true. It is now accepted that the 'golf' is derived from an old word meaning 'club'. The first documented mention of the word 'golf' is in Edinburgh on 6th March 1457, when King James II banned 'ye golf', in an attempt to encourage archery practice, which was being neglected.

Azerbaijan is a country rich in oil but not athletes! Around half the 50 athletes who represented the country in the London 2012 games were naturalised citizens.

It is believed the Aboriginal game of Mangrook inspired many of the rules for AFL.

In the 1970's, Jack Nicklaus played all 40 of golf's majors and made the top 10 in 35.

Croquet was the first outdoor sport to embrace equality, allowing both sexes to play the game on an equal footing.

The bleep test.

David Beckham did not complete the multistage fitness test (bleep test). The record is level 17 shuttle 1. A few athletes share the record, and they are Sebastian (now Lord) Coe of athletics, football player Lee Gong Dook, Zain Wright from field hockey and basketball's Steve Nash.

In gymnastics, a double back is two back somersaults completed consecutively in the same skill movement.

Over the course of the 3-week event, the Tour de France cycle race has the highest number of spectators. In recent events, it has been estimated that up to 15 million spectators watch the race pass.

The record for the fastest 147 maximum break in snooker is held by Ronnie 'the Rocket' O'Sullivan, who made his clearance in just five minutes and 20 seconds at the World Championship in 1997. I did the maths on this one. In completing the maximum break he potted 36 balls in 320 seconds. That is under 9 seconds a shot on average!

Cornelius Horan, the idiot (imho) who attacked Vanderlei Cordeiro de Lima whilst he was leading the marathon in the 2004 Olympics was not imprisoned over the incident and only fined. He is also known for running onto the Silverstone racetrack at a Formula 1 event in 2003.

Fabio Casartelli died after crashing at 88kph whilst descending in 1995 and Tom Simpson died of a heart attack after taking amphetamines and attempting the climb up Mont Ventoux in 1967. In 1935, Francisco Cepeda crashed into a ravine, killing himself and in 1910, Adolphe Hélière managed to drown! These deaths all happened in the Tour de France.

Extreme sport.

Camping is the best extreme sport, It's in tents.

St Bernard of Montjoux became patron and protector of skiers through his four decades of missionary work in the Alps. He was paid a unique tribute when European dog breeders renamed their alpine herding and rescue dogs in his honour. The St Bernard.

Marathon des Sables run the equivalent of five and a half marathons in five or six days, a total distance of 156 miles. I also met the race organiser on Leith Hill a few years ago.

Edson Arantes do Nascimento's family originally gave him the nickname 'Dico'. His nickname Pelé was given at school where he used to pronounce the name of the local Vasco da Gama goalkeeper Bile as Pile. Legend has it that a classmate then gave him the name 'Pelé'.

France's Les Trois Vallées (3 valleys) is the largest ski resort in the world. It has 372 miles of pistes and trails, more than 180 ski lifts that can transport 260,000 skiers per hour, 1,920 snow cannons, 424 ski patrollers and 1,500 ski instructors.

In 2014/15, Leicester City football club spent 140 days at the bottom of the table without being relegated. This is longer than any other side in the history of the Premier League. They then went onto to become the 5000–1 winners of the next Premier League.

Unfortunately, water hardly contains any minerals and therefore isn't the best sports drink for performance. Sports drinks are ideal for returning to the body what it loses through sweat in training. They can contain calcium, potassium and magnesium and help prevent headaches and/or cramp as a result of dehydration. Water is important for other reasons though and it is quite a good idea to drink at least eight glasses a day.

The creator of Sherlock Holmes loved skiing in Norway and felt that Switzerland had the perfect terrain for it. It was pretty much unheard of in the country at the time. He wrote, 'the time will come when hundreds of Englishmen will come to Switzerland for the season'.

Black eyes are black lines painted onto face just below the eyes. The first person credited with using eye black at a major sporting event was Andy Farkas of the (then) Washington Redskins. He was photographed with it on in a game against the Philadelphia Eagles in 1942. Today, it's a common sight in sport and used by athletes trying to cut down on sun and light glare into their eyes.

Golfer: "You've got to be the worst caddy in the world." Caddy: "I don't think so sir. That would be too much of a coincidence."

Asmir Begovic, the goalkeeper for Stoke scored from 92 metres and it is officially named the 'longest goal scored in football.' Begovic scored after just 12 seconds against Southampton on the 2nd November 2013. This is unlikely to be beaten because he kicked the ball out of his hands (being a goalkeeper) in his own penalty area.

The chances of getting a full scholarship for sports in any American college is just 1%. The sports are really just restricted to American football, tennis, basketball, volleyball, gymnastics and track and field.

Number of sports in the world.

It is estimated there are in total about 8,000 indigenous sports and sporting games, currently in the world.

Mário Zagallo became the first footballer in history to win the world cup trophy as a player (1958, 1962) and then as coach (1970). Twenty years later, Franz Beckenbauer matched his feat to become the second player in the history of the world cup to win the title both as a player and coach with the 'Nationalmannschaft'. He led Germany to their second title in 1974 as a player, and 16 years later, he won it whilst managing them.

The longest surf ride ever recorded was 3 hours and 55 minutes, which must have been exhausting! The 13-time national Panamanian surfing champion Gary Saavedra took on the 2011 'Canal Cross' challenge and rode a 41.3-mile wave for nearly four hours. The artificial wave was created by a power boat.

The word 'snooker', is a slang military term referring to someone who is inexperienced and became tied to the game of snooker after Sir Neville Chamberlain (not the ex-prime minister of UK, but the inventor of the sport) called an opponent a 'snooker' after he missed a pot.

Bobby Zamora and Obafemi Martins are the only two players have scored Premier League football penalties with both feet.

The tolerances are so fine in a Formula 1 racing car that the engine cannot be turned over when it's cold. Warm oil and water need to be pumped through them to let the metals expand just a little, allowing things to rotate and for the engine to turn over.

How do baseball players stay cool? They sit next to their fans!

The 'full in, back out' is a gymnastic move that involves two somersaults with one full twist where the twist is executed during the first somersault

Cycling is the most efficient!

Walking takes six times more energy than cycling and running four times as much. On your bike then!

Table tennis was banned in the Soviet Union between 1930 and 1950. The sport was believed to be harmful to the eyes.

The sporting wave (known as the Mexican wave in many regions) was popularised at the University of Washington during Huskies games starting in 1981. This spread to Seattle Seahawks games, as well as the University of Michigan games. From the University of Michigan, it spread to the Detroit Tigers games in 1984, the year they won the World Series, which helped spread it nationally. It went international thanks to the 1986 FIFA World Cup in Mexico, which is why it's known as the 'Mexican wave'. All that said, contrary to popular belief, it was not invented at the University of Washington, but rather debuted during an Oakland Athletic/New York Yankees playoff game on 15th October 1981, it was led by professional cheerleader, 'Krazy' George Henderson. About two weeks later, it was borrowed by Robb Weller and Dave Hunter who led the wave at a Huskies football game on 31st October 1981.

Whilst playing for the New York Cosmos, Pelé would have to take about 25 shirts because everyone wanted to swap shirts with him and he found it the only way to stop the arguments!

The Australian rules season of 1916 had a team that came last in the league but also won it in the same season! This bizarrely happened because the league only had four competing teams. Fitzroy lost nine of their 12 league matches in the regular season being awarded the wooden spoon. All four teams qualified for the playoffs. They then went on to win their final three playoff matches, thus becoming champions.

Babe's trick.

Babe Ruth was quite good at 'homers' and was also famous for a trick. He was able to throw two baseballs simultaneously in such a way that the balls remained parallel to each other all the way from his hand to the catcher's glove.

The first president of the American Football League, which would later evolve into the NFL, was Jim Thorpe. Among his many achievements were college high jump, lacrosse, baseball and football (including leading his football team to the NCAA championship whilst playing running back, defensive back, placekicker and punter, all whilst scoring record 25 touchdowns that season). He even won an intercollegiate ballroom dancing championship. In the V Olympiad, he won gold in the pentathlon, winning four of the five events (long jump, discus throw, sprint and wrestling), but finishing third in javelin, an event he'd never done before arriving at the Olympics. He also finished fourth and seventh in the individual long jump and high jump, including competing with different sized shoes he found in a garbage bin (someone had stolen his shoes). He set the world record in the decathlon, with a total of 8,412 points, with second place being nearly 700 points behind him. He later went on to play in Major League Baseball and after that in the American Football League. In the American football seasons 1926 to 1928, he also played professional basketball. What a sportsman!

The biggest margin of victory in the Ryder Cup was the 23.5–8.5 win for the USA over Great Britain in 1967.

What do you call a cat with a sports car? A furr-ari...

The NFL league office is classified as a trade organisation whose primary purpose is to 'further the industry or profession it represents'. It is tax-exempt. This began in 1942 when the NFL was struggling to stay afloat and needed to find ways to save money wherever possible, so it filed an application for tax-exempt, non-profit status with the IRS. It was accepted and they've been tax-exempt ever since.

FC Barcelona is one of the only three teams who have held a record in La Liga in that they have never been relegated or played in anything but the top tier. The other teams are Real Madrid and the Basque club Athletic Bilbao.

Muhammad Ali travelled the world fighting. He won his heavyweight title bouts on three different continents. They were North America, Asia and Africa.

In 1869 Rutgers beat Princeton 6–4 in the first ever college football game. Touchdowns were only worth two points back in the early days.

St George, the patron saint.

You may well have wondered why there is the St Georges Cross on the logo of FC Barcelona? Well, the reason isn't that the English brothers Arthur and Ernest Witty were in the first side and indeed Arthur was one of the first captains of the side. The reason is that St George is both the patron saint of England and Catalonia (and a lot of other places). Even though he was actually a Greek soldier in the Roman army! It's all very complicated. What I do know is that St George killed the dragon in Medieval Mont Blanc, Tarragona which is about 100km south of Barcelona. I know this because I used to have a hotel there!

A single step takes 200 working muscles to complete the action.

Hacky sack was invented by an American football player in the mid-1970's who was injured and then used it to strengthen tendons he had torn in his knee.

In 1899, a Belgian driver named Jenatzy was the first to reach the speed of 62 miles (100km) an hour in his electric car 'La Jamais Contente'.

Eighteen men were killed in the 1905 American College football season, and there were another 159 who were permanently injured!

The Copa Libertadores de América is an annual international club football competition organised by CONMEBOL that started back in 1960. It is one of the most prestigious tournaments in the world and the most prestigious club competition in latin American football. The tournament is named in honour of the Libertadores (Spanish and Portuguese for liberators), the main leaders of the South American wars of independence so a literal translation of its name into English would be 'Liberators of America Cup'.

The Tour de France bikes are not the best available. Believe it or not, it's true. The bikes ridden in tour have to weigh 15.5 lbs. My local bike shop could (if I could afford it) sell me a lighter one. If the bike is underweight, they add lead weights to the frame. The UCI impose the limit so that manufacturers make reliable and safe bikes.

Humans are between 60 and 70% more economical when walking than when running.

Vaimonkanto

Every year, Finland holds the 'vaimonkanto' or 'wife carrying' championship. The objective is for the male to carry the female through a special obstacle course in the fastest time. The prize for winning is the winning wife's weight in beer!

A F1 engine usually revs up to 18000 rpm. This means that the pistons travel up and down 300 times a second. Road car engines rev up to 6000 rpm approximately.

The 'double double' is one of the hardest gymnastic skills performed on the floor exercise and usually performed in the layout or open tuck position. It involves two back somersaults with two twists.

In 1937, the Chicago White Sox's 'Bulldog Dietrich' was the first pitcher to throw a no-hitter whilst wearing glasses.

Where is the first tennis match mentioned in the Bible? When Joseph served in Pharaoh's court.

The much-loved Football Manager computer game was once banned in China because it 'threatened its content harmful to China's sovereignty and territorial integrity... (that) seriously violates Chinese law'. This was because the 2005 version included Taiwan and Tibet as separate countries and not as part of China.

Olympic badminton rules say that the shuttle has to have exactly fourteen feathers.

The five NFL teams that have bird nicknames are the Arizona Cardinals, the Philadelphia Eagles, the Atlanta Falcons, the Baltimore Ravens and the Seattle Seahawks.

During a marathon, the runner's heart beats about 175 times per minute during a race. Think of this compared to a typical adult's heart beating 72 times a minute at rest.

James Naismith the inventor of basketball in 1891 devised the game as a way to occupy students between the American football and baseball seasons.

Within the professional leagues of the MLB, NBA, NHL and NFL, the New York Yankees are by far the most successful and have won the most championships in their respected sport.

In the sport of professional boxing, over 80% of its fighters have suffered brain damage.

Real Madrid President Santiago Bernabeu's respect for Sir Matt Busby and his Manchester United team led to attempts to help rebuild the club following the Feb 6th, 1958 Munich air crash tragedy. They offered club staff holidays to Spain and even offered legend Alfredo Di Stéfano to Manchester United on loan.

A couple of oddish rules of truck racing, drivers must be at least 21 years old and that the extremely powerful trucks are limited to 100 miles an hour.

The dog isn't that clever.

In a park people come across a man playing chess against a dog. They were astonished and said: "What a clever dog!" But the man protested and replied: "No, no, he isn't that clever. I'm leading by three games to one!"

Rugby balls and footballs were made from pigs' bladders and had to be blown up by mouth, it was possible to become ill if blowing up a diseased bladder, the wife of a man who made balls for Rugby School in the 19th century, died after breathing in the toxic air from one of the balls.

Some crash helmets in cycling are designed to withstand impact only once. They are made of materials that absorb the force by disintegrating on impact.

Australian tennis champion Ken Rosewall didn't have to join the army in 1953. He had a medical skin condition that made it impossible for him to wear regulation army boots.

The Socceroo's have the world record for largest margin of victory in an international soccer match, beating American Samoa 31–0. That's around one goal every three minutes.

Scrambles was the original name of motocross in the UK.

The fastest ever Tour de France average was the 2005 edition which averaged 25.7mph. Don't forget this average includes going up the mountains as well! Originally, Lance Armstrong won this race, but I'm fairly sure you know what happened to him. The Italian Ivan Basso (originally 2nd) was subsequently awarded the win but later admitted drug use and was banned. The third cyclist to make the podium was the German Jan Ullrich. Any ideas what happened to him? You guessed it; he was disqualified for guess what? PEDS!

The Olympic rings.

The Olympic rings cover every flag in the world. Yellow, green, red, black, blue and white background were selected because at least one of those colours appears in every flag in the world. I spent hours going through every flag in the world trying to find one that doesn't contain at least one of the colours in the Olympic flag. I didn't find one.

In 1943, Barca won the first leg of the semi-final against Real Madrid in Copa del Generalísimo (which is now known as the Copa del Rey) 3-0, but in the second leg, Real beat Barca 11-1. There were significant reports of threats and intimidation, by the police and general Franco against the Barcelona players.

Croquet was a one-off Olympic sport in 1900, it was so poorly organised that one competitor went to his death without ever having known he was an Olympic medallist. Sadly, for croquet fans (and thankfully for the rest of us), there are not enough countries who play the game for it to be accepted back into Olympics.

Arsenal are the only team to have received a gold version of the Premier League trophy, when it was specially made to commemorate their 2004 'invincibles' season. This was instead of the silver trophy that every other title winning team have lifted. The Arsenal team went through the entire Premier League season without losing a single match.

National Association for Stock Car Racing was formed in 1948 and is the most popular motorsport in the USA.

The silhouette on the NBA logo is none other than hall of fame Laker Jerry West.

Bulls and White Sox owner Jerry Reinsdorf continued to pay Michael Jordan his reported $4 million basketball salary whilst he was experimenting with baseball.

If you want snooker notoriety, you could always try for the lowest possible clearance of 44. Just be warned that the lowest clearance is even more difficult (if not impossible) to achieve than the highest, since it requires potting all fifteen reds with the same single shot.

The word triathlon is of Greek origin, from treis (three) and áthlon, meaning 'contest' or 'prize'.

Sports longest win streak.

The longest ever sporting winning streak is in the America's Cup. It started in 1851, with Americans winning it for a straight 132 years until Australia took the Cup in 1983.

What's the difference between a teabag and England? The teabag stays in the cup longer!

Babe Ruth wore a cabbage leaf under his cap to keep him cool! He changed it every two innings!

Originally, the 500cc motocross classification was the blue riband event; however, the more manoeuvrable 250cc bikes became the premier class.

The youngest ever Olympian is Greek gymnast Dimitrios Loundras, who competed in the 1896 Athens Olympics. He was just 10 years old. There is less official talk of a Dutch 7-year-old at the 1900 Paris games winning gold as the cox of one of the rowing teams.

Pittsburgh is the only city where all its major sports teams (MLB, NHL, NFL) have the same colours. They all play in black and gold.

Arguably Finland's greatest ever footballer, Jari Litmanen holds an incredibly unique distinction. He is the only player to have played international football in four different decades. 'Kuningas' made his Finland debut in 1989 (the '80's), was a regular throughout the '90's and '00's, before making his final appearance in 2010 (the '10's). No surprise then that he is the nation's most capped player, representing Finland on 137 occasions.

Another one of Wilt Chamberlains amazing basketball records is that he leads the average minutes played per game stats. Throughout the 1961-1962 season with the Philadelphia Warriors, Wilt Chamberlain somehow managed to stay on the court for 48.5 minutes per game! A regular game of basketball is 4 quarters of 12 minutes. However, he was involved (through the season) in 8 games that either went to overtime, double overtime or triple overtime. Wilt would play all game and hence his amazing 48.5 average minutes played per game.

Why can't basketball players go on vacation? They aren't allowed to travel.

125,000 calories are burned by the average racer in the Tour de France.

- In Japan, it is customary for golfers who've hit a hole-in-one to throw a celebration for their closest companions, though this can also be as simple as buying them all a celebratory gift. Nearly four million Japanese golfers carry golf insurance, paying a $65 premium every year for $3500 worth of compensation.

- Up until 1936, the jump ball in basketball took place at centre court after every single made basket.

Slowing down.

- The velocity of a pitched baseball is about 8 mph faster as it leaves the pitcher's hand than when it reaches home plate.

- When volleyball was first devised in 1895, William G Morgan tried to use a basketball, but found it too heavy. So instead, he played with the basketball's inflatable rubber inside, this was until a custom ball was created just for the sport by AG Spalding in 1900.

- To wear a 'visor' on your helmet in the NFL, you have to have a doctor's medical note explaining the reason for the need of the visor.

- Golf balls can reach speeds of 170 miles per hour.

- Korfball is the only sport played with mixed teams, consisting of four men and four women.

- On average, it is estimated that females injure themselves ten times more than males do whilst playing sports.

- Kite flying is a professional sport in Thailand.

- If the air conditioning at the Astrodome in Houston were turned off, it would rain inside the stadium due to the humid air.

Type Federer

- 'Federer' can be typed entirely with the left hand using only one finger as all letters form a square next to each other.

- In cricket, a yorker is the king of all bowls. You have bowled a yorker when the ball lands directly at the batter's feet, making it extremely difficult to hit. There are two theories as to its origins. The Oxford dictionary suggests that the term was coined because players from York bowled them frequently. The second theory attributes the name to the other meaning of yorker which is a cheater. At the turn of the 20th century, the word 'york' was used to mean being sharp, or quick-witted. This then evolved over time to mean cheat. If you had just been swindled you may well have exclaimed, 'I've been yorked!'

There are just 18 minutes of total action in a baseball game.

Walt Bellamy, played 88 games of basketball in the 1968-1969 NBA season. Bellamy began the season with the New York Knicks playing 35 games. However, on December 19th, the team decided to trade Bellamy to the Detroit Pistons. At the time, the Pistons had played six less games than the Knicks. So instead of only 47 more opportunities with the Knicks, Bellamy had 53 with the Pistons. He played in everyone every one of the remaining games.

Contrary to popular belief, the Super Bowl is not 'watched by over a billion people per year'. This idea stems from the fact that when the myth started, if you added up the populations of all the countries where the Super Bowl was broadcast to, you'd get a total of about one billion people in those countries having access to the broadcast. But how many people actually watch the Super Bowl? In recent years, that amount has been around 110 million people, with an estimated 98% of those viewers being from North America, mostly from the United States.

Golfers use an estimated $800 million worth of golf balls annually.

Sumo wrestlers throw salt onto the floor of the dohyo (the area they fight) to ward off evil spirits. The whole ceremony surrounding sumo contests are based on Shinto religious practices. No women are permitted onto the dohyo. There was an outcry when a female paramedic entered once to tend to an injured wrestler!

How do hens encourage their baseball teams? They egg them on!

The origins of lacrosse date back to the mid-19th century. The name is from French (le jeu de) la crosse '(the game of) the hooked stick'.

The FIFA World Cup Trophy is about 14.5 inches tall and made entirely of gold. However, it isn't solid! This is for 2 reasons. The first is that it would be a waste of gold. The impressive looking trophy would appear no different if it was gold throughout. The second reason is that it would be too heavy and dangerous for the players to lift above their heads. The winners of the World Cup get to raise the real trophy but they get to take home a cheaper replica that is only gold plated. If you remember the Jules Rimet Trophy was stolen not once but twice and never recovered and so it is understandable that FIFA don't trust anyone with the real and very expensive trophy.

In 80AD, the colosseum in Rome held a hundred days of games. Over 5,000 animals were killed, including elks, elephants, tigers, lions, hyenas, hippopotamuses and giraffes.

Since the early noughties, professional bike riders have been linked up with communication devices. Some of us remember the exciting racing that took place before. Now it is very much a calculated and predictable sport. The purists say. "Get rid of them!"

First football tournament

The Youdan Cup was the first ever football tournament and it was held in the Sheffield area of England.

On 2nd March 1962, Philadelphia centre Wilt Chamberlain scored 100 points in one game against New York. That is the most one player has ever scored in one game.

In the 1930's, American track star Jesse Owens used to race against horses and dogs to earn a living.

1968 heralded the open era of tennis. This is when the sport allowed professionals to play in all tournaments.

What's the difference between ice hockey and boxing? In ice hockey, the fights are real.

Jimmy Connors has (and is the only person to have done so) won the US Open on three different surfaces. He first won on grass, then it went to clay and finally as it now played on a hardcourt.

In bowling, three strikes in a row were called a turkey. The term originated in the 1800's when at holiday time, the first member of a team to score three strikes in a row won a free turkey.

Richard Petty has the most career wins of any racer, with 200 wins. He is known as the 'king' of stock-car racing.

The Chinese characters that spell the word sumo 相撲 literally mean 'striking one another'.

Ban golf!

Golf was banned in England in 1457 because it was considered a distraction from the serious pursuit of archery.

The fastest serve in a game of tennis was in 1963 by Michael Sangster. It was clocked at 154 miles per hour.

A man walks into a bar with a dog. The bartender says, "You can't bring that dog in here." "You don't understand," says the man. "This is no regular dog, he can talk." "Listen, pal," says the bartender. "If that dog can talk, I'll give you a hundred bucks. "The man puts the dog on a stool, and asks him, "What's on top of a house?" "Roof!" "Right. And what's on the outside of a tree?" "Bark!" "And who's the greatest baseball player of all time?" "Ruth!" "I guess you've heard enough," says the man. "I'll take my hundred thankyou." The bartender is furious. "Listen, pal," he says, "get out of here before I belt you." As soon as they're on the street, the dog turns to the man and says, "Do you think I should have said 'DiMaggio'?"

Archery is the national sport in Bhutan, a Buddhist country in Asia.

The fastest human speed was set by Usain Bolt who was clocked at 27.79mph.

Europe was involved in the Ryder Cup from 1979 onwards. Ireland joined in 1973 and before that, it was just Great Britain against the USA.

The biggest ever 4th quarter comeback in basketball is from 29 points down. With just 8:43 remaining in the game, the Milwaukee Bucks managed this on November 25th, 1977 against the Atlanta Hawks.

Ferenc Szisz from Romania, driving a Renault, won the first ever Formula 1 Grand Prix held at Le Mans, France in 1906.

A perfect game.

A perfect game in baseball is one in which the same player pitches the entire game without allowing any player of the opposing team to reach first base.

The first modern Olympic games were held in Athens, Greece in 1896. There were 311 males but no female competitors.

Prior to 1900, prize fights lasted up to 100 rounds.

✝ Roger Bannister held the world record in the mile for just 46 days.

☡ If Michael Phelps were a country, let's call him 'Great Phelps'. Great Phelps with 23 gold medals would sit in equal 38th place with South Africa in the all-time medals table by countries.

⚖ Jordan Spieth won $61,867 less at the 2015 masters than Arnold Palmer won in his entire career.

⚽ In the second half of a 1986 World Cup soccer match against England, Argentina's Diego Maradona (RIP) performed perhaps the ballsiest act of cheating in the history of sports. Going up for a header, the player caught the ball in one hand and swiftly drove it straight into England's goal.

㊙ The first Olympic games were held in 776BC and then every four years until 339BC.

☺ Why did the chicken get sent off? For persistent fowl play!

㊙ The first Olympic race was won by Corubus, a chef. For many years, the Olympics consisted of only one race, a sprint of 192 metres.

🎾 The word 'tennis' is said come from medieval France. This is where the sport was first developed. Players shouted 'tenez!', which translates to 'take that!' as they hit the ball.

⚾ The Major League Baseball teams use about 850,000 balls per season.

㊙ Although his revolutionary technique struck gold in Mexico 1968, four years later, Dick Fosbury failed to qualify for the Munich games with the high jump he had invented!

🎾 The Grand Slam event, Roland Garros is named after Eugène Adrien Roland Georges Garros who was a great French man, amongst many interesting stories about him including war hero and multi sportsman was that he was the first person to fly across the Mediterranean. I love facts about everything, and the Mediterranean translates from its latin origins as sea at the centre of the world, which is what they thought it was in Roman times.

🏟 The word 'arena' derives from the Latin 'harena', which is a particularly fine/smooth sand that was used to absorb blood in ancient arenas such as the Colosseum in Rome.

☺ Did you hear the joke about the softball? It will leave you in stitches!

In fencing, points are signalled by a light that indicated weapon-to-body contact. Boris Onischenko's light went off without explanation during the fencing in modern pentathlon at the 1976 Games. It turned out the Soviet had modified his épée's grip to activate the light manually. You might find this strange but the Soviets have no recollection of the event.

The literal translation of taekwondo is 'way of the hand and foot'.

At the 1996 Atlanta Olympics, every softball game was sold out. However, it ceased to be an Olympic sport in 2008.

The first ever game of baseball took place in 1846 between the Knickerbockers and New York Nine.

The word 'gymnastics' is derived from a Greek word 'gymnos' which means 'naked'. In ancient Greece, most of the gymnastics competitions were done in the nude.

The basketball hall of fame was created in 1959 in Springfield, Massachusetts, where the game was created.

What should a soccer team do if the pitch is flooded? Bring on their subs!

Originally, when peach baskets were used as the hoop in basketball, every time someone scored, a referee had to fetch the ball by climbing a ladder.

The game of cricket itself dates as far back as the 13th century. A game called 'kreckett' was recorded in a 1598 court case. Cricket also used to be spelt 'creckett' and was played at the Royal Grammar School in England in 1550.

The centre court at Wimbledon wasn't always there. The previous one was a few miles away and it was moved in 1922 to its current position.

Tiger Woods first hole in one.

Tiger Woods was only eight years old when he made his first hole in one.

The 'doosra' is a bowling technique which takes its name from the Hindi word meaning 'other one'. The 'doosra' spins in the opposite direction to an off break, and can confuse the batsman.

English football side Derby County were placed under a curse by a group of Romani gypsies who were forced to move from a camp so that Derby could build their new stadium, the Baseball Ground. The curse was that Derby

County would never win the FA cup. A similar thing happened to another English football side, Birmingham City. They played 100 years under an alleged curse from 1906 to 2006. As the legend goes, the club moved from nearby Muntz Street into its current location at St Andrew's, building the stadium on land that was being used by the Romani people. After they were forced to move, the angry Romani people put a 100-year hex on the stadium. I can't imagine Birmingham City winning anything let alone the FA Cup even without the curse!

The largest golfing green is that of the 695-yard, 5th hole, a par 6 at the International Golf Club in Massachusetts. The green's area is in excess of 28,000 square feet.

The individual medley requires competitors to swim backstroke, butterfly and breaststroke. You then cannot repeat a stroke and must choose a fourth, unique stroke.

Golf has been banned three times in Scotland. The first time was in 1447, because it was interfering with military training. The second time it was banned was in 1471 and again in 1491.

The first organised ice hockey game played indoors occurred in 1875, in Montreal, Canada.

In recent Olympics, Team GB has performed with remarkable success finishing 2nd in Rio and 3rd in London but 1908 was the only time GB has ever won the medal table.

This is just wrong.

A group of totally healthy, non-handicapped Spanish basketball players participated in the 2000 Sydney Paralympics to win gold. Unfortunately for them, they were exposed and were stripped of the medals.

Why was the basketball player sitting on the sidelines drawing chickens? Coach told her to learn how to draw fouls.

Archery is considered to be one of the oldest sports in the world.

Originally, the football world cup was made of paper maché. The heavy rain in the 1950 competition ruined the cup and it had to be replaced.

Wimbledon is the only major tennis championship still being played on grass.

The founder of the modern Olympics Baron Pierre de Coubertin was a rower.

Figure skater Tonya Harding on the night before the 1994 US Figure Skating Championships in Detroit, hired someone to break rival Nancy Kerrigan's leg with a baton.

Average career of just 2 ½ years.

The average NFL career is about 3⅓ years. The running backs have the shortest careers lasting just 2½ years, wide receivers and cornerbacks play on average about three years. Quarterbacks have the longest careers lasting about five seasons.

'Nil', derives from the Latin word 'nihil', which actually means 'nothing'.

A cap is a metaphorical term for a player's appearance in a game at international level. In the early days of football, the concept of each team wearing a set of matching shirts had not been universally adopted, so each side would distinguish itself by wearing a specific sort of cap.

The phrase about winning something 'hands down' originally referred to a jockey who won a race without whipping his horse or pulling back the reins.

Derby County football club was formed in 1884, as an offshoot of the Derbyshire county cricket club. The football club played on a pitch that was part of the cricket ground. It gets a little more complicated because the cricket ground was in the middle of a racecourse! Industrialist and baseball fan Sir Francis Ley brought baseball to the UK and was instrumental in establishing the National League in 1890. Ley also built all the recreation and sport facilities as areas for relaxation for his company employees. After the swift demise of baseball, and with the football club's need for a stadium for spectators they were given the area to build their (now called) Baseball Ground.

Tiger Woods once made 142 straight cuts. This beat Jack Nicklaus' record by 37.

The sport lacrosse was initially played by native American Indians. They played the sport to prepare for war.

I used to play tennis, baseball, basketball and chess, but I stopped after my son broke my PlayStation.

William Dodd, who won an Olympic gold in archery, had a sister who only won an Olympic silver medal in archery. Her name was Charlotte "Lottie" Dodd, she was more known for winning the Wimbledon tennis title five times. The first of those titles she won as a 15-year-old.

Operación Puerto is the code name of a Spanish police investigation. Around 2006, they investigated doctor Eufemiano Fuentes and his doping of athletes. Numerous cyclists were involved and also there was a lot of talk of him doping La Liga football teams and also tennis players. The Spanish government ordered the destruction of all the samples!

John Isner and Nicholas Mahut (the 70–68 final set Wimbledon match) played 183 games over those three days, which beat the previous record of 112 games (set when there no tiebreaks for any set) by 71 (63% more) games, which is just insanity.

The Greeks threw diskos, while the Romans threw discus. Both diskos and discus referred to various 'round, flat objects' and also used to describe the 'face' of the sun. At the root of the Greek diskos is a verb meaning 'to throw' or 'cast.'

In the NFL, the average career is a bit over three years, in the NBA five years is the average, MLB and NHL have an average career of 5½ years. In the Premier League footballers have careers lasting eight seasons. Track and field athletes generally last about eight years, professional cyclists have race careers of nearly 10 years on average.

The 'quadricep' contains four muscles and their heads attach in four places. The quadriceps muscles are your;

- Rectus femoris,
- Vastus lateralis,
- Vastus medialis,
- Vastus intermedius.

The word 'sponsor' see its roots from sponsus, past participle of spondere 'meaning to give assurance or promise solemnly,'

In 1980, Rosie Ruiz won the Boston marathon in the female category in 2½ hours. It was later revealed that she disappeared into the crowd, then showed up on the course half a mile from the finish. She later admitted to taking the Metro.

The traditional distance of 26 miles was lengthened from and after the 1908 London Olympic games. The reason being to allow the royal family to watch the start from Windsor Castle's windows!

Fastest racquet sport.

The fastest racquet sport in the world is badminton, with shuttlecock speeds sometimes reaching more than 200 miles per hour.

Only 10 other quarterbacks in NFL history have thrown half as many touchdown passes as Peyton Manning!

Michael Jordan's nickname is high school was 'magic', after Magic Johnson.

In the Rome Olympic games, Lance Larson of the USA was in a close finish in the swimming with the Australian John Devitt. All three judges at Devitt's lane clocked him at 55.2 seconds. The three judges at Larson's lane clocked him at 55.1, 55.1 and 55.0. So, Larson won the race, right? Nope. After deliberation, a single Swiss judge inexplicably ruled Devitt the winner.

After a male boxer died in 1997, the governing Italian boxing association outlawed female boxing!

Astronaut Alan Shepard played golf on the Moon after he smuggled a golf ball and club on to the NASA Apollo 14 mission in 1971.

Regulation Major League baseballs should have exactly 108 stitches holding them together.

The tallest basketball players to ever play in the NBA were the Sudanese, Manute Bol and the Romanian, Gheorghe Muresan. They were both 7 ft 7 in tall (231 cm).

The dimples on a golf ball help reduce drag, allowing the ball to fly further than a ball without dimples.

What's the worst thing about being lonely? Playing frisbee.

The greatest batsman of all time, statistically, was Australian Don Bradman, who played professionally in the 1920's and 1930's. Bradman's career test batting average of 99.94 has been widely thought to be the greatest achievement in any major sport. The next best on the list of all-time batting averages is Dempster from New Zealand who averaged 65.72.

When 7–1 underdog Cassius Clay, (who would change his name to Muhammad Ali after converting to Islam just a few days later) defeated Sonny Liston in Miami beach in 1964, the 16,000-seat arena was half-empty. I'm sure the promotors would have put a spin on that fact that the stadium was 'half full'.

Why do football players like smart women? Well, you know opposites attract.

Béla Guttmann joined Portuguese club, Benfica in 1959 and coached them to two Primeira Liga titles, one Portuguese cup and two European cups. In 1962, after his second European cup title, he asked for a pay rise. This was turned down and he was also sacked for asking! Being quite annoyed he cursed the club and said, "Not in a hundred years from now will Benfica ever be European champion." That means the curse will be lifted in 2062, gets your bets on now. Unfortunately, I will be dead by then.

Cricket is originally thought to either have been derived from the old French 'criquet', meaning 'goal, post, or stick' or from the middle Dutch 'kricke', meaning 'stick' or 'staff'. The latter derivation from 'kricke' is generally considered more likely due to the strong medieval trade connections between south-east England and Flanders, which belonged to the Duchy of Burgundy.

First banned athlete.

The first athlete to be banned for the use of drugs was American swimmer Eleanor Holm, the 1932 Olympic 100m backstroke gold medallist. She was disqualified for being an alcoholic!

The difference between 'rugby' and 'football' is blatantly obvious nowadays. However, this wasn't always the case, one was originally known as 'rugby football', named after the public school where the sport was invented, whilst the other became known as 'association football'.

If you hear someone say the score in a football match is 'zero-zero', then they are being technically incorrect, it should be nil-nil. Tennis and squash start their matches love-all. Darts start theirs at 501 each!

At the time of Ayrton Senna's death, he had an Austrian flag in his car. Senna would normally fly a Brazilian 'Ordem e Progresso' flag when he won a F1 race. Just one day before Senna's death, Roland Ratzenberger, an Austrian died in a crash during qualifying for the same race. Ayrton had planned to win the race and fly the Austrian flag in memory of Ratzenberger.

The golfer asked his caddy, "Hey boy, do you think it is a sin to play golf on Sunday? Caddy replied, "The way you play, sir, it's a sin to play any day of the week!"

'Association football' gave rise to the term 'soccer', which is used more in the USA and Canada to distinguish it from American football, which itself developed from rugby.

Stimulants like caffeine, amphetamine and methamphetamine can enhance performance by enhancing focus and energy.

Why should you never date a tennis player, to them love means nothing. But according to etymologists, the word love is possibly derived from the French word l'oeuf which literally means egg. If we look at the shape of an 'egg' we can see it resembles zero and therefore came to be used when somebody has no score in tennis and other sports.

The ancient Olympic demise.

We always talk about 1896 being start of the modern Olympics but the ancient Olympics demised only once the Roman emperors became Christian. Pagan festivals were at first discouraged and then completely outlawed. The Olympic games were first and foremost a religious celebration in honour of Zeus, they held no place in the Christian empire. The Olympics were abolished by emperor Theodosius around 394 AD.

The gymnastics move the 'back in, full out' involves a double somersault with a full twist. The complete twist is performed during the second somersault.

To expel water from the body, diuretics are often used in sport. One of their illegal uses is by some fighters who need to meet weight restrictions.

We all assume the marathon is as old as the Olympic Games themselves. However, it is very much a modern Olympic sport. Its origins however, date back to the 5th century BC, when the Persians invaded Greece. They landed at Marathon which is a small town about 25 miles from the city of Athens. The Athenian army was badly outnumbered and quickly sent messengers to cities all over Greece including Sparta requesting support. Once the reinforcements arrived, they beat the Persians. One of the messengers called Pheidippides (who had run 150 miles in just 2 days prior to the battle) then ran from Marathon to Athens to announce the great Greek victory and once the message had been delivered, he collapsed and died. I checked the distance on Google Maps and not knowing exactly his starting finishing points it's difficult to confirm but by foot Google says it's about 35km. In 1896, the runners at the first modern Olympics raced from Marathon to Athens. The winner of the first Olympic marathon was the Greek Syridon Louis in a time of 2 hours, 58 minutes and 50 seconds.

Longest ever Tour de France.

🚴 The 1926 edition of 'le Tour de France' was its longest ever version and the total distance raced was 3570 miles in just 17 stages! That equates to 210 miles average per stage, the average length of a tour stage in the 2015 edition was just 160km (100 miles)!

🎽 The pagan festival of the Olympics was a tribute to Zeus and were one in a series of sporting events that happened each year. As well as the Olympic games at Olympia, there were the Isthmian games at Corinth, the Pythian games at Delphi and the Nemean games at Nemea. Several of the athletes were known to have competed with success at all four of the Athletic games.

☺ How did the basketball get wet? The players dribbled all over it.

🎽 The highest Olympics were held in Mexico City in 1968. Mexico City is 2300m above sea level. At that altitude, the atmospheric pressure is about 25% less than at sea level. Theoretically, we can throw and jump further with less air pressure, but the downside is the endurance athletes get less oxygen to the working muscles and fatigue quicker. There have been several Olympic games at sea level, Barcelona, London and Rio are a few.

🖳 The SI unit of pressure is the pascal, which is one newton per square inch. Pressure is defined as force per square unit area. One newton is about the force an apple or orange presses into your hand. Normal atmospheric pressure at sea level is about 100,000 pascals. The pressure inside a football is 180 thousand pascals. That's why the ball deflates once it's punctured!

Making the weight.

🎽 In the 1960 Rome games, Olympic weightlifter Charles Vinci had to lose 680 grams in two hours to compete at his official weight class. He managed this by running, sweating and also getting a haircut!

☺ Why are ice hockey rinks rounded? Because if they had 90 degrees, the ice would melt.

⚽ Manchester United's laundry bill in the original days of televised sport was bigger than the revenue gained from TV rights.

The 'Gaylord' is named after Mitch Gaylord who used this technique on the high bar in gymnastics. It involves a front giant arm-swing into a front one-and-one half somersault over the bar, before re-grabbing the bar at the end.

The 'clean and jerk' action lets the athlete raise more weight than with the snatch technique. Athletes generally lift at least twice their own body weight in this discipline of the weightlifting event.

In an 11 a side football match, there must be at least seven players per team on the pitch. If a team has a fifth player sent off or a player is injured and needs to leave the field of play and the team has used all their substitutes, the match is forfeited and 3–0 given.

An apartment building is on fire and people are at the window, screaming for help. "Just jump out the window," a man yells. "I'm a cricket player. I can catch you." One smart resident decided to first get a bit more information. "Wait," he said. "What team do you play for?" "I play for England" shouts the man. "Ehhhh," shrugs the resident. "I'll take my chances with the fire."

Coby Orr was five years old when he shot a 'hole in one.' He played the amazing shot on the 103 yd 5th at the Riverside Golf Course, San Antonio, in 1975. This it is thought to have made him the youngest player ever to have score a 'hole in one.'

Wide margins of pressure are allowed in different sports balls. The reason for this is that the pressure of air depends on its temperature. The temperature of a ball changes throughout a game. This might be affected by dropping the ball from warm hands into cold mud in a game of rugby for instance.

What time does Rafa Nadal go to his bed? Ten-ish.

'Diddle for the middle' is a slang expression used for the start of a darts game. Opposing players each throw a single dart at the bull's eye. The person who is closest or nearest to the bull (centre of the board) gets the choice of throwing first and, therefore, has an advantage in the match.

On rest days in the 'Tour de France', the racers don't rest. Instead, they ride their bikes for a couple of hours to rid the muscles of waste products such as lactic acid.

The fastest round of golf was completed by a team in just 9 minutes and 28 seconds. This amazing feat was set at the Tatnuck Country Club on 9th September 1996.

Frank Mahovlich played for three different teams during his NHL career: Toronto, Detroit and Montreal. For each of these teams he played for, his team number was 27.

The sweet spot.

Honey was used as a centre for golf balls. Some engineers used liquid cores in the design of balls to prevent them from spinning too much. Sounds a bit extreme using honey but there is some logic in that it never spoils and has all the physical properties necessary to make a great liquid-filled golf ball.

The last scoreless game in NFL history was in 1943 between the Detroit Lions and New York Giants.

In 1919, there were just 10 finishers in the Tour de France. The race started with 155 riders but the 3450 miles on roads ravaged by the first world war took its toll on the riders.

Canadian, Arthur Thompson completed a round of golf carding a 103 on the Uplands course of 6,215 yards. His age was 103!

The energy needed to slow a Formula 1 car from 315km/h to 185km/h is the same amount needed to make an elephant jump 10 metres in the air.

The broom wagon is the vehicle that used to follow the Tour de France metaphorically sweeping up riders as they abandoned the race.

The Chinese Nationalist Golf Association claims the game of golf is of Chinese origin in the 3rd or 2nd century BC and it was called ch'ui wan.

Ed and Dominic Joyce are brothers. Both are cricket players and both of them made their ODI debuts in the same year, 2007. They made their debuts on the same day and indeed in the same match but for different teams. Ed was playing for England and Dominic was playing for Ireland and they played against each other!

Extra long

XL on a golf ball means extra-long not extra-large!

Lean mass builders enhance muscle and lean body mass growth and are sometimes used by sportspersons to reduce body fat. They include anabolic steroids, xenoandrogens, beta-2 agonists, some androgen receptor modulators and various human hormones such as human growth hormone.

Cyclists whose cadence is about 90 revolutions per minute will perform about half a million-pedal strokes to complete the Tour de France. 'No chain' is the expression used by lance Armstrong when he was going well in the professional peloton. I wonder why he felt cycling was so easy?

Golfer: "My wife says if I don't stop playing golf, she's going to leave me!"
Caddy: "I'm sure you will miss her terribly, sir!"

The Foxberg Golf Club (1887) and St Andrews Golf Club of Yonkers (1888). Both claim to be the first established golf club in the United States.

In 1910, a baseball with a cork centre was used in a World Series game for the first time. The Philadelphia Athletics and the Chicago Cubs played for the championship. The Athletics must have found the new ball to their liking because they won the series in five games.

The Lancastrian businessman Samuel Ryder, who founded the Ryder Cup loved golf so much that when he was buried in 1936, he was buried with his favourite five iron!

African runners used to chew Khat to help them perform. Khat is a flowering evergreen shrub native to East Africa and the Arabian Peninsula. The plant (Catha Edulis) contains two alkaloids, cathinone and cathine, which both act as stimulants.

Unfortunately, in 1960, Danish cyclist Knut Jensen became infamous for dying in the Olympic road race. Ronicol (a stimulant that increases blood circulation) was found in his system and was given as the cause of his death. It was also 40 degrees that day and he crashed banging his head. The medical support entailed him being taken to a tent!

In the 1920 Antwerp Olympics, American sprinter and 100m gold medal winner Charlie Paddock drank sherry and ate raw eggs before the final.

The first documented doper in sport is the American, Tom Hicks. In the 1904 St Louis Games, he was given small amounts of strychnine and brandy. Although he was doped at the 22-mile mark, admitted to the doping, collapsed at the finish and nearly died. His gold medal was not taken away and he apparently showed no remorse! The marathon was held at the hottest part of the day and run in 90°F temperatures. The only water for the runners was a well at the 11-mile mark.

The Chicago Cubs were managed and owned by PK Wrigley. The baseball stadium was also named after him and his chewing gum business.

☺ Why are sports stadiums the coolest place to be? They are full of fans.

Adidas and Puma - The Dasslar brothers.

⌨ In the 1920s, the brothers started the Dassler Brothers Sports Shoe Company, Adolf ('Adi') Dassler was the quiet, thoughtful craftsman who designed and fabricated the shoes, Rudolph ('Rudi') was the elder and he was the frontman of the business. Both brothers joined the Nazi party when Hitler seized power in 1933, but this membership didn't stop them supplying legendary African-American track star Jesse Owens with track shoes. Jesse Owens won four gold medals in the 1936 Olympics and gave the Dassler's international exposure. The wives of the two brothers didn't get on and the tensions between the families increased during the war. When Rudi and his wife entered the same air raid shelter, Rudi heard Adi say, "The dirty bastards are back again." Adi says he made the comment about the Allied forces bombing above. Rudi was convinced it was made about him and his wife, the rivalry continued through the war, with Rudi being called up for service, convinced it was Adi who had tried to have him sent to the front line to get rid of him. Rudi was arrested twice for desertion and by the allies on suspicion of working for the Gestapo. Apparently, there was evidence that Adi had provided intelligence in both of these cases to the authorities. Rudi was sent to a prisoner of war camp and Adi took the opportunity to sell shoes to the American service men. The conflict escalated as the brothers split the company in two in 1948, dividing the assets and the employees between themselves. Adi named his company 'Adidas', a combination of his first and last names. Rudi attempted the same by first naming his company 'Ruda' but eventually changed it to the more athletic sounding 'Puma'. The two built competing factories on opposite sides of the river Aurach and quickly became responsible for much of Herzogenaurach's economy, with nearly everyone working for one company or the other. As the entire town got caught up in the Dassler family feud, the rivalry reached ridiculous proportions. There were local businesses that served only Adidas or only Puma people, dating or marrying across company lines was forbidden, and Herzogenaurach became known as 'the town of bent necks' since people first looked at which company's shoes you were wearing before deciding to talk to you. Whilst Rudi had the sales staff, and was better at moving product, Adi had the technical know-how and better relationships with athletes who could provide exposure, tipping the scales in favour of Adidas, with Puma constantly playing catch-up. However, in focusing so heavily on each other, both the companies were slow to react to the threat of Nike, which would come to dominate the athletic footwear industry, leaving them far behind. It wasn't until 2009 when employees of both companies symbolised the end of six decades of feuding by playing a friendly soccer match. By then, the Dassler brothers had both died, within four years of each other. Even in death, the animosity continued as the brothers were buried at opposite ends of the same cemetery, as far away from each other as possible.

Jesse Owens broke four world records in just 45 minutes at the 1935 Big Ten Track and Field Championships in Ann Arbor. His long jump mark of 8.13m would stand for 25 years! There were also rumours he had a back that day as well!

Soccer is surprisingly relevant to my life. Just consider its lack of goals.

Meaning of ambidextrous.

Ambidextrous doesn't mean 'someone who can use both hands', the word 'ambidextrous' is derived from the Latin roots ambi-, meaning 'both', and dexter, meaning 'right' or 'favourable'. Thus, 'ambidextrous' is literally 'both right' or 'both favourable'.

In the 2011 Women's football world cup held in Germany, eight Korean ladies tested positive for steroids.

When the Olympic and the other Panhellenic games introduced other sports events, the Stadion race was still seen as the blue riband event of the gymnikos agon (nude competition). It is of course still the most anticipated race (now the 100m sprint in track and field) in the modern Olympics and other rule changes include the wearing of sports kit by competitors.

The 'battle of the sexes' is a title given to three notable tennis matches. The first match was between Bobby Riggs and Margaret Court, over the best of three sets. The result saw Riggs beat Court convincingly in straight sets. The second was a nationally televised match between Riggs and Billie Jean King, over the best of five sets. Billie Jean King revenged Margaret Court's defeat and she won in straight sets. The final match was between Jimmy Connors and Martina Navratilova, over the best of three sets and a set of hybrid rules which favoured the female player, which was dubbed 'The battle of champions'. Despite the rules, which allowed Connors only a first serve and Navratilova being able to hit into some areas of the doubles, court Connors won the final battle of the sexes five and two in straight sets.

Before the start of the Ryder Cup each captain is required to put a name in an envelope. This player is the player that won't play in the singles should one of the opposition be sick. If that is the case, the match that didn't get played would be halved.

Francisco Lázaro was the first Portuguese Olympic marathon runner. He was also the standard bearer of the Portuguese team in the nation's first ever Olympic Games, the 1912 Summer Olympics, in Stockholm. Lázaro was an amateur sportsman, and his actual job was as a carpenter in an automobile factory in Lisbon. Lázaro was the first athlete to die during an Olympic event, after collapsing at the 30-kilometre mark of the marathon. The cause of death was thought to be severe dehydration due to the high temperature registered at the time of the race. It was later discovered that Lázaro had covered large areas of his body with wax to prevent sunburns. This wax prevented him sweating normally and led to the dehydration that killed him!

Golfer: "Well, I have never played this badly before! Caddy: "I didn't realise you had played before, sir."

The financial deal David Beckham was reported to have signed with LA Galaxy was worth £250 million over five years.

Adidas sponsored 33 countries totalling about 6000 athletes in the Atlanta Olympic games of 1996. Their athletes won 70 gold medals and Adidas saw their sales increase by 50%.

In 2009, Tiger Woods became sports first billionaire!

OBLA stands for 'onset of blood lactic acid'. It occurs when your body can't process lactic acid quickly enough and thus you begin to tire. It's a very small margin, as once you go beyond this level, the high lactic acid levels will make it impossible for your muscles to continue exercising efficiently.

I kept wondering why the football was getting bigger. Then it hit me!

In the 1964 Olympics, there were complaints from the Hungarian team that the pool was too shallow and gave an advantage to the taller Yugoslav team who could stand on the bottom of the pool with their heads out!

The gymnasium, in ancient Greece functioned as a training facility for competitors in public games. It was also a place for socialising and engaging in intellectual pursuits. That's why some German high schools are named gymnasiums. In most countries though, it is just used as an athletic area.

To hit an unreturnable serve in tennis is an 'ace'. The origin of the tennis meaning of this word dates back to around the 18th century where an ace in cards meant excellence. It was also a number 1 and so became synonymous with a single unplayable shot like a serve.

In the 1936 Berlin Olympics, Jesse Owens not only won four golds, but he equalled or broke the world record in each event. His events were the 100m, 200m, Long Jump and four x 100m. Also, not only did he record world records but he also broke nine Olympic records on route to the four golds! The relay team's world record would stand for 20 years!

The Bosman.

A Belgium man entered the European Court of Justice as a frustrated footballer at the end of his contract and left it as a noun. Jean-Marc Bosman was a football player for RFC Liège whose contract had expired in 1990. He wanted to change teams and move to Dunkerque, a French team. However, Dunkerque refused to meet his Belgian club's transfer fee demand, so Liège refused to let him go. In the meantime, Bosman's wages were reduced as he was no longer a first-team player. He took his case to the European Court of Justice in Luxembourg and sued for restraint of trade. On the 15th December 1995, the court ruled that the system, as it was constituted, placed a restriction on the free movement of workers and was prohibited by Article 39 of the European Community Treaty. Bosman and all other EU football players were given the right to a free transfer at the end of their contracts, with the provision that they were transferring from a club within one EU Association to a club within another EU Association.

The 'Curse of Ramsey', finds celebrities and famous people dying within hours of Welsh footballer Aaron Ramsey scoring. The curse has led to the death of Osama bin Laden, Muammar Gaddafi, Steve Jobs, Whitney Houston, Robin Williams, David Bowie, Alan Rickman and Nancy Reagan.

What's a ghost's favorite soccer position? Ghoul keeper.

Athletic sprinters have their own loudspeaker.

If the weather is nice, the speed of sound is about 343 metres per second at sea level, this means it takes a few hundredths of a second for the sound of a starting pistol to travel along the row of runners. The closer runner to the gun had the advantage. At big meets now, each athlete has a loudspeaker behind them to relay the sound simultaneously.

Peru beat Austria 4–2 all fair and square after extra time in the last eight of the 1936 Olympic games. Being good sports those Austrians, they appealed to the impartial German organisers. Their appeal was somewhat bizarrely based on the size of the pitch, the fact there some fans ran on the pitch celebrating Peru's goals and finally one of the Peruvian players had a gun and was pointing it at Austrian players whilst he was playing! Listening to all the absurd evidence, the organisers found in favour of the Austrians and ordered a rematch. Peru in protest withdrew from the tournament. Austria continued onto the final and I'm very pleased to say they lost to the Italians.

The first 'el Clasico' was on May 13th 1902 which Barcelona won 3-1, Real Madrid however were only formed on March 6th of the same year (which was about 2 months before!) Barcelona had been a competitive team for about 2 ½ years.

In 1974, the IOC removed from its charter the word 'amateurism' paving the way for the Olympics, as we know them today.

The International Olympic Committee banned doping in 1967. Today, the World Anti-Doping Agency (WADA) specifies which performance-enhancing drugs are banned. At present, there are over 300 different drugs on the list.

Basketball bans tall players!

During the 1936 Berlin Olympics, the International Basketball Federation imposed a ban on players taller than 6 ft 3 in (1.91m), The rule was later withdrawn following objections.

There have been five different recognised techniques for clearing the bar in the high jump.

- The highest 'scissor jump' was made by Barksdale who achieved an official clearance of 6 ft 9 in (2.05m) in early 1956.
- George Horine used the 'eastern cut' off to clear 6 ft 7 in (2.01 m) in 1912.
- The 'western roll' was the technique Walt Davis used to jump 6 ft 11.5 in (2.12 m) in 1953.
- Vladimir Yashchenko in 1978 'straddled' the bar 2.34 m (7 ft 8 in) high.
- The Cuban great Javier Sotomayor, 'fosbury flopped' 2.45 m (8 ft 1⁄2 in).

You might have heard the sports commentator identifying an 'Arabesque.' Well, they have just seen dance or gymnastics pose where the body is balanced on one leg and the other leg is extended up off the floor behind the gymnast's body.

Q: Why did the skydiving club disband? A: Because they had a falling out.

Coca Cola started its sponsorship of the Olympics by supplying the US team with 1000 cans of Coca Cola to aid them in the 1928 Amsterdam Summer games. To this day they are still sponsors of the organisation and the company with the longest association with the Olympic games.

From the years 776 to 724 BC, the stadion was the only event that took place at the Olympic games and the victor gave his name to the entire four-year Olympiad. It is well documented who the winner each race was.

- 1st   Olympiad 776 BC – Coroebus of Elis
- 2nd   Olympiad 772 BC – Antimachus of Elis
- 3rd   Olympiad 768 BC – Androclus of Messenia
- 4th   Olympiad 764 BC – Polychares of Messenia
- 5th   Olympiad 760 BC – Aeschines of Elis
- 6th   Olympiad 756 BC – Oebotas of Dyme
- 7th   Olympiad 752 BC – Diocles of Messenia
- 8th   Olympiad 748 BC – Anticles of Messenia
- 9th   Olympiad 744 BC – Xenocles of Messenia
- 10th   Olympiad 740 BC – Dotades of Messenia
- Beijing 2008 – Bolt of Jamaica
- London 2012 – Bolt of Jamaica
- Rio de Janeiro 2016 – Bolt of Jamaica
- Tokyo 2020 /2021?

The 100m sprint ends when a runner's torso reaches a point exactly over the finish line, the event is measured by an automatic 'slit-video' camera, which scans the finishing line up to 2000 times a second. Human judges then view the images to decide who wins.

London 2012 saw many Olympic records and personal bests, thanks in part to a new track design which featured revolutionary technology. In Beijing, the track was designed to maximise the rebound when runners pushed forward and backwards, but any sideways movement equalled lost energy. London's track had a special undelay comprising of rhombus-shaped ridges to increase the track's reaction to lateral movement so even if your little toe touched down first, it was rebounded in a forward motion. The top of the track had also been made softer than Beijing's to increase its ability to drive energy back into the athletes' feet. Even the roof of the stadium was designed to minimise wind on the track.

On his way home a man meets 2 men in masks.

A man leaves home, makes three left turns and is on his way back home when he notices two men in masks waiting for him. They're the catcher and umpire.

☺ Does running late count as exercise?

▨ "Stadium" is the Latin form of the Greek word "stadion" (στάδιον). The stadion was an Olympic sprint race named after the building in which it took place. There were other types of running events, but the stadion was the most prestigious. The winner was often considered to be the winner of an entire games. Though a separate event, the stadion was also part of the ancient pentathlon. The original stadion track in Olympia measures approximately 190 metres, a measure of length equalling the length of 600 human feet. As feet are of variable length, the exact length of a stadion would depend on the size of the foot used in measuring it! There was no starter's pistol with the race beginning with a trumpet blow. There were also officials at the end to decide on a winner and to make sure no one had cheated. If the officials decided there was a tie, the race would be re-run. Runners started the race from a standing position, oh and the athletes had to run naked!

🏸 Have you just broken the string on your squash, tennis or badminton racket? There are probably only two strings in your racket and you have probably only broken one of them, so stop saying you have broken your strings! Anyway, you'll need a restring. It might not seem logical but the lower the tension the more powerful the racket becomes. The lower tension strings stretch more during impact of the ball or shuttle, they are then able to store more energy and when the ball or shuttle rebounds from the racket, more energy is returned and it leaves at a higher speed. High tension on the strings gives more control of the object.

Perfect conditions for records.

▨ If you want to set your personal best sprint time, then the hotter the temperature and the better the tailwind, the better chance you have. Bolt's record-breaking 9.58, set in Berlin in 2009, was assisted by a 0.9m/s tail wind and an air temperature of just under 30 degrees. An increased tailwind reduces atmospheric drag, whilst thinner air and fewer molecules impeding athletes' paths result from hotter temperatures. The maximum tailwind allowed for world records is two metres a second.

🏅 Jesse Owens is known for his four gold medals in the 1936 Berlin games, this might not have happened were it not for a German. Carl Ludwig Long (Lutz) generously gave Owens advice on his technique as he was well on his way to not qualifying for the long jump final. Lutz was actually leading, having just set an Olympic record. Owens took his advice and went on to set a new Olympic record whilst winning Gold. Lutz was the first man to congratulate Owens and the two of them left the stadium arm in arm. This was right under the eye of none other than the Fuhrer himself!

The use of Anabolic steroids to gain lean muscle is proven. After 10 weeks of training, a group of steroid users who trained, gained an average 13 lbs of muscle, a group of clean athletes trained for 10 weeks and built on average 4 lbs of muscle and a third group who took steroids and didn't train at all gained 7 lbs of muscle each!

One of the runners in the 100m at the World Championships in Daegu 2011, finished 35 metres behind the heat winner. Sogelau Tuvalu, an American Samoan, failed to qualify for the shot put and decided to switch to the 100m. The 17-year-old was the only competitor not to have spikes on his shoes but still managed to beat his own personal best with a time of 15.66 seconds!

If a player, whilst running the bases runs past another player also rounding the bases, then the slower player is automatically called out. That in itself is quite logical but guess who gets the credit for this out? The closest fielder to the passed player!

Rowing is the only sport where competitors cross the finish line backwards!

By most people's admission, Pelé was quite good at football, however, he didn't manage to equal or beat a feat of his fathers and that was scoring five headed goals in a single game. Pelé (only) managed a mere four headed goals in a single game.

Sam Mussabini, the finest coach in the world.

Sam Mussabini was the coach of Reggie Walker, the first African winner of the Olympic 100m gold. He also went onto repeat the feat in coaching Harold Abrahams to the same title in 1924.

In 1926, before Armargh were due to play in a junior all-Ireland hurling final against the Dubs. The Dominican nuns of Omeath in Louth knitted them some orange and white kit. It would be shameful to ignore such a gift from these devout and holy women and they've dutifully worn them since. Armargh are a republican team from Ireland and the orange colour is associated with the unionist aligned to England. William of Orange is the reasoning behind the colour.

Golfer: "You've got to be the worst caddy in the world." Caddy: "I don't think so, sir. That would be too much of a coincidence."

We all love a national anthem and the most amazing one was the Brazilian one played and sang at their opening game of the 2014 football World Cup. However, the first time a national anthem was sung before a sporting event happened, spontaneously before a rugby match. On 16th November 1905 at Cardiff Arms Park. After New Zealand danced the Haka before the match, Wales responded by beginning to sing the Welsh national anthem, 'Hen Wlad Fy Nhadau'.

Would a cheetah beat Bolt over 100m?

An 11-year-old cheetah named Sarah, ran at 61mph at Cincinnati Zoo, covering 100m in 5.95 seconds, nearly 40% faster than Usain Bolt.

The Los Angeles games of 1984 were boycotted by 14 countries. Those boycotting were the communist countries including the USSR, Cuba, North Korea, East Germany etc. Their boycott was in retaliation to the U.S. led boycott of the Moscow 1980 games. The boycotting nations citing concerns over the safety of their athletes in what they considered a hostile and fiercely anti-communist environment.

Usain Bolt is 6 foot 5 inches tall, he has the leg speed of a 6-foot person and the stride of a seven footer!

We test for Performance Enhancing Drugs (PEDS) in sport in up to three different ways. Samples of urine or blood might be subjected to 'mass spectrometry' which involves vaporising and then ionising the samples. A magnet is then used, it sends the ions in different directions depending on their masses. They can be accurately identified by the final positions. This is a highly accurate but expensive process and might be used for the B sample test. 'Gas chromatography' is where the athlete's samples are vaporised and passed through a tube filled with a mixture of silicon grains and liquid. The different components of the sample will travel at different speeds through the tube and so arrive in turn at the final detector. This method is inexpensive, but its limitation is that it can't differentiate components with the same travel speed. The simplest but least accurate method is with the use of 'immuno-assays'. Here antibodies are introduced to the sample, and they react to the presence of the drug. The strength of the response is a measure of the amount of drug present.

Brazil are the only country to have attended every single FIFA world cup.

NASCAR racetrack Talladega Superspeedway has been said to have been cursed by a native American shaman. Some claim that it was built on a native American burial ground. The curse might explain the high number of unusual occurrences, accidents and deaths that have happened on the racetrack.

The UCI has a rule on minimum weight of all bikes. They must weigh 6.8kg or more. This was set to prevent flimsy and unsafe bikes being raced on. Manufacturers are saying they could make the bike just as reliable and weigh only 5kg. One unintended consequence of the rule is that riders are now able to race with expensive power meters, communication devices and deep section wheels. This is all adding weight to their bikes but not disadvantaging them against other riders.

Does EPO really work?

Oh yes, EPO use is known to improve somebody's time to exhaustion by more than 50% within four weeks of use! Not only does it improve cardiovascular endurance, but it is also able to improve peak power output by more than 10% in the first four weeks of its use.

A boxer goes to a doctor complaining of insomnia. 'Have you tried counting sheep?' asks the doctor. 'It doesn't work,' replies the boxer. 'Every time I get to nine, I stand up.'

To allow the sport to become professional, the Northern Rugby Football League was formed in 1922. To make the game more exciting with less breaks in play and to attract more spectators the RFL disposed of line outs and also rucks and mauls. All were replaced with the 'play the ball'.

Mexico have hosted the FIFA world cup twice (1970 and 1986) and are to be joint hosts of the 2026 tournament along with the USA and Canada.

London hosted the 1908 games, but they were not originally awarded the games. They had been awarded to Rome but in 1906 Mount Vesuvius erupted and sent the Italian economy into chaos. The Italian government appealed to the IOC for a change of city and London was chosen as a replacement.

Why do runners faint at the end of races?

The answer to this question is actually very interesting. When people are involved in high intensity exercise over prolonged periods, the working muscles require a lot of blood flow. The blood vessels in our muscles, especially the legs, dilate (get bigger) to accommodate all this increased blood. Now, our body depends on contraction of our leg muscles to push blood from the legs back up to the heart. During intense exercise, our ability to maintain adequate blood pressure depends on this pumping of blood back to our heart by our legs. If you suddenly stop running, the blood return from your legs to your heart suddenly drops and so you don't have enough blood to pump to your brain. This might in actual fact cause you to faint and fall. Sometimes this is called the 'second heart theory', where our leg muscles act as sort of a second heart pumping blood back up to the real heart. At the end of long distances races, you will often see 'hot walkers', volunteers or medical staff keeping finishers walking after crossing the line. By continuing to walk after you finish, you keep using those leg muscles to pump blood back up until your cardiovascular system recovers from the effort. I could run a marathon tomorrow. It would be slow and painful, but I could run it none the less. However, I can't go shopping with my wife and that is only for a couple of hours. All the standing still, choosing a dress (she will probably return) stops my calf muscles contracting and helping return the blood back up to the heart.

How did the pirate become a boxing champion so fast? Nobody was ready to take on his right hook.

Harold Abrahams won the 100m Gold at the 1924 Paris Olympic games. The 100m final was held on the 7th July at 7pm. Abrahams won, Jackson Schulz was second and lesser known is that New Zealand's Arthur Porritt was third. Abrahams and Porritt were friends and dined together every year on the 7th July at the same time of 7pm. This tradition carried on for more than 50 years until Abraham's death in 1978.

After being signed by Santos, Pelé made his debut against Corinthians on 7th September 1956. Maybe at the time they didn't realise it was a sign of things to come, but he scored four goals on his debut!

In the 1932 Olympic games in Los Angeles, Bob Tidsall from Ireland was first over the line in the 400m hurdles and won the gold medal. Not only had he won the race, he thought he had also set a new world record in a time of 51.7 seconds. However, the strict rules of the day say if a hurdle is hit then no record can be validated. He won the gold medal but was not given the world record time.

To check if your basketball is inflated correctly, drop the ball naturally from 6-foot-high and the return bounce should see it up to four foot.

The 'snatch' is a lift whereby the athlete raises the bar with an explosive action directly above their heads with straight arms.

Do you drink enough water?

The American Council on Exercise recommends drinking 17 to 20 ounces of water two to three hours before exercising and seven to ten ounces of water every 10 to 20 minutes during a workout.

Golfer: The doctor says I can't play golf. Caddy: O! So, he too has played with you?

Forrest Smithson set a world record running the 110m hurdles in the 1908 London Olympics holding a bible because the race was run on the Sabbath (Sunday).

Stay in shape.

You have to stay in shape. My mother started walking five miles a day when she was 60. She's 95 now and we have no idea where she is.

Sweating is the important and necessary process that cools the body down. When your body starts to overheat, the nervous system stimulates sweat glands to release perspiration. As the droplets evaporate off your skin, they take some body heat into the atmosphere. Sweating might simply be a sign that you're in shape. Trained endurance athletes sweat sooner and produce more perspiration compared to untrained people. The fitter you are, you often find your body becomes more efficient in producing sweat. Since sweating helps cool you down, you will be able to compete or train at a higher intensity for longer. To further complicate things, a few more factors impact how much you sweat and they are;

- Your gender. Men perspire more than women.
- Your body mass. Big people with more muscle mass, and the higher a person's body mass index (BMI), the more they sweat.
- Drinking hot drinks increase your body temperature, which in turn encourages sweating.
- Alcohol increases your heart rate and dilates blood vessels in your skin, bringing blood to your skin's surface. This in turn raises your body temp, which can cause you to sweat more
- Eating spicy foods also triggers your body temperature to go up, so your body produces sweat to help cool itself down
- Warmer days raise your body temperature, increasing heart rate and blood flow in an effort to cool down the core.
- As a footnote, our bodies have a critical core temperature of 104 degrees Fahrenheit or 40 degrees Celsius. At this temperature, we humans tend to pass out from heat stroke.

Popping noises from your knees and cracking your knuckles is most likely caused by cavitation. Cavitation results from a change in joint pressure that allows carbon dioxide, which is normally dissolved in your joint fluid (synovial fluid) to come out of the solution and form gas bubbles within the joint. When the joint closes quickly around these bubbles, they pop giving us the cracking noise.

How does Lionel Messi change a light bulb? He holds it in the air, and the world revolves around him.

Approximate 80,000 components come together to make an F1 car. If it were assembled 99% correctly, it would go onto the track with 800 faults.

In ice hockey, if you are the instigator of a fight in a match, you will not only receive a penalty for starting the fight, if you are wearing your face shield, you will also receive a second penalty. If you take the face shield off, the second unsportsmanlike penalty won't apply!

The distinctive white with red dots (polka dot) jersey is given to the Tour de France rider with the most mountains points. Mountains points are awarded to a certain number of riders who crest the Tour de France's climbs at the head of the race. The number of points awarded depends on the severity or 'category' of the mountain. The bigger it is, the more points are on offer to more riders. The toughest 'hors catégorie' climb first placed rider will gain 20 points, points are awarded down to the eighth placed rider who will get 4 points. On the much easier fourth category climb only the first rider over gets anything and that is only a single point. The rider must complete the tour to be eligible to win the coveted jersey.

Try to picture the American football scene. The opposition punts the ball and it's about to bounce close to the touchline and then who knows where it might go? The defending player sticks one of their feet out of bounds, catches the ball and the ball is then deemed out of play on the full. That I understand, it happens in rugby as well in a similar manor. What is strange is the ball gets returned to the 40-yard line for a 1st down. This all from a situation where if you hadn't interfered, the ball would have landed in play.

Coach - There were twenty teams in the league and we are in the last place? Player -Well, it could have been worse. How? There could have been more teams in the league!

In basketball, the game clock must indicate 0:00.3s (three tenths of a second), in order for a chance of making a basket. This is the amount of time it is thought a player needs to gain control of the ball on a throw in. If the game clock indicates 0:00.2 or 0:00.1, the only type of a valid field goal made is by tapping or directly dunking the ball. This is because the clock only starts again once the ball is touched. This rule was introduced as a result of a game between the Knicks and the Bulls in 1990. The scores were tied at 106 each and 0.1 seconds was remaining on the clock. Mark Jackson in-bounded to

Trent Tucker who turned and hit a 3-point basket. Everyone agreed it was impossible to do it in 0.1 seconds and a committee decided that 0.3 was the minimum it would take a player to score from free play. However, the result stood, even after an appeal from the Bulls.

Severity of strain

A muscle strain, or pulled muscle, normally occurs when the muscle is overstretched or torn. This usually occurs as a result of fatigue, overuse or improper use of a muscle maybe due to poor technique. No muscles are immune, but strains are most common in your lower back, neck, shoulder and hamstrings. These strains can cause pain and may limit movement within the affected muscle group. Mild and moderate muscle strains can be successfully treated at home with ice, heat and anti-inflammatory medications. Grade 3 tears may require medical treatment. Depending on their severity, muscle strains are categorised into Grades 1, 2 or 3:

- Grade 1 strain

    - There is damage to individual muscle fibres (less than 5% of fibres). This is classified as a mild strain which requires two to three weeks rest.

- Grade 2 strain

    - There is more extensive damage, with more muscle fibres involved, but the muscle is not completely ruptured. The rest period required is usually between three and six weeks.

- Grade 3 strain

    - Grade 3's are a complete rupture of a muscle. And they will require surgery to repair the muscle. The rehabilitation time is around three months.

An MRI (Magnetic Resonance Image) can identify the severity of the muscle strain quite simply by seeing the amount of redness and swelling around the affected area.

NHL player Bill Barilko, of the Toronto Maple Leafs, scored the Stanley Cup winning goal in the 1951 season in overtime against the Montreal Canadians. In the off-season, he went on a fishing trip. Tragically, his plane crashed and he was killed. The Maple Leafs did not win another cup until 1962, that was

11 years after the crash. It was also the same year that they found Barilko's body.

⊘ Putting spit, sweat, grease and other things onto a baseball lets it pitch in an atypical way due to its new weight distribution and aerodynamics. To prevent a pitcher throwing the illegal spit-ball, they cannot lick their hand, wipe their brow, or adjust their waistline and then directly touch the ball. The pitcher must first wipe their hand on the outside of his uniform and only then proceed to grip the baseball.

☺ What season is it when you are on a trampoline? Spring time.

⊘ In 1890, Aston Villa won the first and only National League of Baseball in the UK.

How to become an Olympic sport.

❀ So you want your sport to be one of the 26 Olympic sports? First, you must put aside all the politics of the more than 200 Olympic nations and then one of the existing sports needs to go, or you might be involved as an invitation sport. However, the key factors in determining a sport's suitability for the Olympics include its youth appeal, its universality, its popularity, its excellent governance and its respect for athletes and respect for the Olympic values. In total, there are 33 criteria that must be met under eight categories that include the sports history, its image, its health and safety record and the costs to host the sport. It makes you wonder how on earth Rio de Janeiro, 2016 managed to have both golf and rugby sevens included? Tokyo's new sports are skateboarding, surfing and sport climbing. Paris 2024 has included breakdancing for the first time.

⊕ I'm sure you are wondering why body quivers sometimes whilst performing or after some exercise. It is all to do with the relationship between your nerve cells and muscle fibres. Vigorous exercise depletes the chemical messengers that carry the signals between nerves and muscle cells. This causes some of the nerves and their corresponding fibres to stop working temporarily. Because your cells don't all fire at once, some are contracting as others are relaxing, resulting in the muscle and body shaking. Exercises such as planks and the dreaded wall sits are especially likely to trigger the shaking because your muscles must generate a lot of force to hold your body in one position thus depleting the chemicals and starting the process off.

⊕ Arsenal were founded as Dial Square in 1886 by a group of workers employed by the Dial Square workshop at the Royal Arsenal, an armaments factory in Woolwich, Kent.

Originally, there were just eight weight classes in boxing with up to 15lb between the classifications. The professional women have 13 classes. Listed are the current 17 weight divisions of men's professional boxing and a few notable champions (past and present) of those divisions. (lbs to kg divide by 2.2)

Minimum weight	105 lbs	Ricardo Lopez
Light Flyweight	108 lbs	Eric Ortiz
Flyweight	112 lbs	Charlie Magri
Super Flyweight	115 lbs	Román González
Bantamweight	118 lbs	Eder Jofre
Super Bantamweight	122 lbs	Hozumi Hasegawa
Featherweight	126 lbs	Erik Morales
Super Featherweight	130 lbs	Manny Pacquiao
Lightweight	135 lbs	Roberto Durán
Super Lightweight	140 lbs	Julio Cesar Chavez
Welterweight	147 lbs	Oscar De La Hoya
Super Welterweight	154 lbs	Floyd Mayweather, Jr.
Middleweight	160 lbs	Thomas Hearns
Super Middleweight	168 lbs	Sugar Ray Leonard
Light Heavyweight	175 lbs	Roy Jones Jr.
Cruiserweight	200 lbs	Evander Holyfield
Heavyweight	>200 lb	Muhammad Ali, Mike Tyson, Anthony Joshua, Tyson Fury

I wonder why there is as little as 3lbs between weights and as much as 8lbs between the classifications? It would seem logical that the distribution would be even?

What's the hardest thing about learning to ice skate?

The ice.

If the fans of the ice hockey home team throw objects on to the ice that delay the start of the game, then then a penalty will be awarded against the home team. However, this rule is waived if they throw hats on to the rink when a 'hat-trick' is scored.

The first NASCAR race was held on 19th June 1949 in North Carolina at the Charlotte Speedway. The circuit isn't as we see today, back then it was a ¾ mile dirt track.

- The terms pugilism derives from the Latin pugil, 'a boxer', and related to the Latin word 'pugnus', 'fist,' this in turn derives from the Greek word pyx, 'with clenched fist'.

- 3 Strikes and you're out! That's how the saying goes but it isn't true. If the catcher drops or fumbles the ball on the 3rd strike, the batter can attempt to run to first base before the catcher recovers the ball and tries to throw out the batter at first base. All this is unless someone is already standing on first base. Then the player is straight 'out'.

Shortest managerial job.

- Leroy Rosenoir manager of Torquay United, lasted just 10 minutes in the position, a new board took control straight after his appointment and sacked him in 2007.

- Team USA was beaten in the 1908 tug of war by Great Britain. They were beaten by a team of Liverpudlian police officers complete with hobnail boots! Even though the United States team were massive men, made up of shot putters and discus throwers, the contest was a one-sided affair. The well-trained and experienced police team pulling the American athletes who had little technique and were also wearing a variety of footwear. They were said to have pulled the big Americans over the line like schoolboys much to the delight of the hysterical crowd. The Liverpool police were beaten in the final by the London police.

- The 'delayed onset of muscle soreness' is often the effect of hard or new training. The main cause of the DOMS is microscopic tears in the muscle fibres. Post exercise, the muscles damaged set off an inflammatory response, resulting in swelling and tenderness in the area. Most of the symptoms of the DOMS are a result of the inflammatory response, not the actual muscle damage itself. Muscle soreness lasts two days or so after heavy training or sport with the second day after being more painful than the first. There are no easy fixes for DOMS. You can try ice, compression, non-steroid anti-inflammatory drugs, massage or the dreaded active recovery to speed things up. However, 'rest' is your best weapon. You have to question your training if you are experiencing DOMS and whether prevention is a better cure and back of the intensity.

- I think that it is better to give that to get. You have a very generous thinking. Are you a humanitarian? No, I'm a boxer.

- Arsenal football club were originally led by a Scotsman, David Danskin, he even bought the club its first football. One of the original players included the former Nottingham Forest goalkeeper Fred Beardsley, who managed to get a set of red kits from his old club, the rest as they say is history and Arsenal play in red.

During a game of tennis, if you somehow injure your opponent and it wasn't intentional, you win the game or maybe the match if your opponent can't continue.

If a baseball player has been announced by the public address (PA) system, that announced player must then either bat to remain in the game or is then made ineligible to play for the remainder of the game!

Tennis has 30 rules and the USTA have a 324-page book explaining them. Why use one word when ten will do!

When I worked in a ski resort in the late 1980's I was told snow cannons needed -2 degrees to work. Now they can work from freezing downwards and indeed -10 is perfect for the machines.

If a player in baseball attempts to use his face-mask or hat to either catch the ball or change the trajectory of the ball, then a three base hit is awarded.

This flag dips to no earthly king.

The arrogant tradition of the Team USA captain not lowering the stars and stripes during the opening ceremonies of Olympic games started back in 1908. They refused to lower their standard as they paraded past King Edward. The USA captain Martin Sheridan said about the stars and stripes, "This flag dips to no earthly king."

Why did the man keep doing the backstroke? He'd just had lunch and didn't want to swim on a full stomach!

In cricket, you are out LBW (leg before wicket), if the ball hits your legs and would (if it hadn't hit you) have continued on to hit the stumps. If you are kneeling or crouching down and the ball hits you on any part of the body not with a bat in it, this also includes your head, and would have continued onto hit the stumps, you can still be out LBW.

Javelin throwing was one of the events of the original pentathlon at the ancient Greek Olympics. The historic Hellenes didn't call it the javelin, they called it akon or akontion.

- In American football, if the team plays its third string quarterback before the end of the third quarter, then it immediately disqualifies its starting quarterback and the backup second QB for the rest of the game.

- If the ball pitches outside of the leg stump, you cannot be out LBW. Don't be afraid to kick it away if you want. If you don't understand what I'm saying, just move on and read about the Honey Bears.

- The Chicago Bears owner, George Halas hired 'the Honey Bears', a cheerleading squad in 1977. Unfortunately, George died in 1983, and the team was left to his daughter, Virginia Halas McCaskey. She tried to have the Honey Bears disbanded because she saw them as 'sex objects'. The Honey Bears had a contract up to and including the 1985 season. In their final season, the Bears lost only one regular season game that year and won Super Bowl XX. The following season the Honey Bears contract was not renewed, and the Bears have not won the Super Bowl since!

Change ends.

- In polo after every goal is scored, the teams change ends! The reason for this originated in the days when many polo fields ran from east to west and neither team wanted to play for extended periods of time with the sun and/or wind in their faces.

- What would you get if you crossed a pitcher and the invisible man? Pitching like no one has ever seen.

- Joe Louis and challenger Billy Conn fought in the first televised heavyweight championship on 19th June 1946. The famous quote 'He can run, but he can't hide' was said by Louis pre-fight because of Conn's fast feet. 146,000 people watched on TV as Joe Louis won in the 8th.

- The Kolman is a release move performed on the men's high bar where the gymnast leaves the bar. He then performs two back somersaults and one full twist over the bar and then re-catches the bar at the end. Named after Yugoslavian gymnast Alajz Kolman.

- Golfer: "Please stop checking your watch all the time, caddy. It's distracting!" Caddy: "This isn't a watch, sir, it's a compass!"

- The 2-phase action of the clean and jerk will see the weightlifter raise the bar to their chest and then in the second phase above their heads.

First base player Lizzie Murphy, also known as 'Spike', was described as the Queen of baseball. She started her career at age 15, and eventually played semi-professional for the Boston All-Stars. She was that good that in 1922, she became the first woman to play for a major-league team in an exhibition match. The Boston Red Sox sponsored a charity game against a team of male All-Stars. Lizzie was chosen to play first base. Not content with being to be the best female player, the first female player to play in an All-Star game she also played a game in the Negro League, for the Cleveland Coloured Giants.

Are you bowling or throwing?

When bowling in cricket you might be considered to have thrown the ball instead of bowling it. The correct bowling technique should have the ball leave from a near straight arm. If you bend your arm more than 15 degrees, then you are deemed to be throwing. Video analysis is used to determine if indeed the ball is being bowled or thrown.

The Olympic torch on route to its host city has travelled in many ways, it is usually carried by runners, I have even carried one! It has also travelled on boats, airplanes (including the now obsolete Concorde), on horseback, on the back of a camel, via radio signal, underwater, in a canoe, it has also been into space!

Golfer: "Do you think my game is improving?" Caddy: "Yes sir, you miss the ball much closer now."

In tennis, if the ball is hit and it lands on the opponent's side of the net and then either blows or spins back on to the side it has just been hit from, the other player must attempt to hit it without touching either the opponent's side of the court or the net. A shot they could play if they could manage it is to reach over and smash it back into the net to win the point.

In football, you can't be offside in your own half or from a throw in.

A Chinaman bowler is basically a left arm spin bowler who brings the ball into a right-handed batsman using his wrist as the source of spin. Usually, a left arm spin bowler spins the ball away from a right-handed batsman, called orthodox left arm spin. The term Chinaman was first introduced in 1930. Ellis Achong of the West Indies, with Chinese ancestry, was a left-handed spinner. He was playing against England in 1930 and one of his balls to Walter Robbins surprised everyone. Achong bowled the ball from the wrist, which went through to the right-hand batsman's off-stump. As Robins, took the walk of shame back to the pavilion a spectator was heard to say. 'Fancy being done by a bloody Chinaman.'

ⓣ A few average speeds for top athletes, skiers and drivers.

🏃 100m	Track and Field	37 km/h
🏃 200m	Track and Field	37.5 km/h
🏃 400m	Track and Field	33.5 km/h
🏃 800m	Track and Field	28.5 km/h
🏃 1500m	Track and Field	26.5 km/h
🏊 1500m	Freestyle swimmer	6 km/h
🏊 50m	Freestyle swimmer	8.2 km/h
🚶 50km	Race walker	13.7 km/h
🚶 Marathon		19.6km/h
🚴 1 km	Cycling time trial	60 km/h
🚴 Sprint cycling		71 km/h
⛷ Downhill Skiing		80km/h
🏎 Formula 1 car in Barcelona		182 km/h

Do you know the difference between bat, paddle, stick and a racket?

🖥 Generally, bats feature a long solid striking surface. Just like a baseball bat or cricket bat, whilst rackets feature a hoop with crossed strings as the striking surface, which is attached to a handle. Somewhere in between is a paddle, which usually has a rounded solid, non-elastic striking surface. Don't forget we also have sticks in sports like hockey and lacrosse.

🏎 Horsepower is a measurement of the rate at which work is done, and differs from torque, which is a measurement of the amount of force applied to do that work. In motorsport, engines, you can think of higher horsepower being the specification that will sustain a higher rate of work once moving, while torque is the figure that gets a car moving quickly. In other words, engines high in horsepower but low in torque will feel less powerful from a stop and initial acceleration than engines lower in horsepower but higher in torque.

🖥 To finish the argument about what constitutes sport, here is the definition of a sport: A game, competition or activity needing physical effort and skill that is played or done according to rules, for enjoyment and/or as a job.

☺ How do you make a fruit punch? Give it boxing lessons.

🖥 The Olympics get their name from the ancient Greek city of Olympia where the first ancient games were held in 776BC. Every Olympics was held in Olympia until 394AD. They were held every four years in honour of the mythical Greek God Zeus.

In doubles tennis, if either you or your doubles partner get hit by a serve on the full you lose the point.

If a football player takes their shirt off whilst the game is playing, they will receive a yellow card. Get two of these and they send you off. I presume the players know this, they score, take their shirt off, showing off, receive a second yellow, get sent off. I wonder what is more stupid the rule or the players?

Optionals are a category of gymnastics competition where the gymnasts and coaches create their own routines with individual skills and the required elements that are determined by the International Federation of Gymnastics. Optional gymnasts are ranked higher than compulsory gymnasts. Compulsory elements are usually in lower-level competitions.

I'm in shape. Round is a shape.

Wildcard entry wins Wimbledon.

In 2001, Goran Ivanisevic won Wimbledon. Amazingly he didn't qualify but was given a wildcard entry and thought to have no chance of winning.

The competition order for international gymnastic competitions for women are the vault, the uneven (asymmetric) bars, the balance beam and the floor. The men participate on the floor first, then the pommel horse, the still rings, the vault, the parallel bars and lastly the horizontal (high) bar. The order for rhythmic gymnastics is the rope, hoop, ball, clubs and finishing with the ribbon.

In 1954, the actor Robert Redford attended the University of Colorado on a baseball scholarship.

Since 1948, the Colombian football team América de Cali was under a curse. There was a discussion that year, in a meeting held by team owners, about moving América into the professional league. Benjamín Urrea, one of the owners, was opposed to the idea, so he said famously, "They can do whatever they want with the team, but I swear to God they will never be champions." He left the room in a rage, whilst the other owners laughed at him. He never returned to the team. The team had to wait for 31 years to get its first professional title, in 1979. In trying to overcome the curse in the Copa Libertadores, journalist Rafael Medina and singer Antonio del Vivar performed an exorcising ritual on América's home field in 1980 to help the team. At present, they are still waiting for the Copa Libertadores success.

In 1992, the Champions League replaced the European Champion Clubs' Cup, or simply European Cup, which had run since 1955. The pre-1992 competition was initially a straight knockout tournament open only to the club champions of each country. During the 1990's, the format was expanded, incorporating a group stage to include clubs that finished runner-up of some nations' top-level league. This expansion continued and now sees some countries eligible to enter five teams! There are also now 55 countries involved in the Champions League.

No ball warm up needed in squash.

A top fact, I was having dinner with an ex-Dunlop (historically, the number one squash ball manufacturer) employee at a good friend's unbelievable farmhouse. (www.farmhouseinwales.com) and was told that Dunlop had developed a ball that had all the characteristics of a championship ball without the need for it to be warmed up. They didn't produce it because it was thought that the players enjoyed the procedure of warming the ball up.

Originally, both men and women competed in parallel bars. In 1936, the uneven bars debuted at the Olympics as a female event. The women had the choice of competing on uneven or parallel bars because the event was so new. Only the Czechoslovakian gymnasts opted for the uneven bars. By 1954, the parallel bars for women as an event finished, leaving them just the uneven bars.

Before the NFL mandated the use of helmets in 1943, Chicago Bears lineman Dick Plasman was the last player not to use one.

In 1987–88, PSV Eindhoven won the European Cup, on route they only won three games, and also they didn't win a single game from the quarter-final onwards. They won in the last eight and last four on the away goals rule, and the final on penalties.

I'm not into working out. My philosophy is no pain, no pain.

The Brawn team went from previous mediocrity in Formula 1 to have Jenson Button win and become world champion. It was the first time any team had ever won the Formula 1 championship in its début season.

Mesomorphs physically have hard and muscular bodies, and overly mature appearance, they have thick skin and an upright posture. Their personality traits are that they are adventurous, they have a desire for power and dominance, they are courageous, indifferent to what others think or want, they are assertive and bold. They have a zest for physical activity, they are competitive, and they love risk and taking chances.

Betty Okino gave her name to the gymnastics move performed on a balance beam. It is a skill where the gymnast performs a triple pirouette (turn).

A coin toss decides to decide the winner.

Unfortunately, there have been seven European Cup ties have been decided by a coin toss, the last one in 1969–70. The games included Anderlecht winning the toss against Bologna in 1964 and Liverpool won the toss in 1965 against Cologne after both home and away games resulted in 0–0 draws and a neutral venue playoff provided a 2–2 result.

El Clásico (the Classic) is the game between the Spanish club giants Real Madrid and Barcelona. Historically they haven't got on very well with each other. Franco and civil war had a lot to do with it.

The author of Sherlock Holmes, Sir Arthur Conan Doyle, was the first keeper for AFC Portsmouth in the English football league.

The button-down collar that comes and goes in high street fashion was developed by the Brooks brothers. They designed the button-down collar specifically for polo players so things didn't flap around whilst they were playing.

Major League Baseball requires players who were not in the major leagues before 1983 to wear a batting helmet with at least one earflap. The last player to wear a flapless helmet was the Florida Marlins' Tim Raines who continued until 2002. Raines started his career in 1979. Julio Franco was the last player who was eligible to use the old-style helmet because he turned pro in 1982; however, he saw sense and used the much safer and newer helmet which included an earflap.

In 1967, the NFL Championship game between the Dallas Cowboys and the Green Bay Packers played in Green Bay up on the Great Lakes of North America. The game was played in temperatures as low as –13 degrees.

Milan in 1993–94 were the only team that has won the Champions League after losing the previous year's final until Liverpool repeated the feat. In 2018 Liverpool lost to Real Madrid in the final, the next year they won the competition by beating Tottenham Hotspur in that final.

Why did the skydiving club disband? Because they had a falling out.

- At 120 miles per hour, a Formula 1 car generates so much downforce that it can drive upside down on the roof of a tunnel.

- The Brooklyn Dodgers vs Philadelphia Eagles on 22nd October 1939 became the first baseball game televised. The match was broadcast by NBC and it was only to 500 television sets!

- Brazil has hosted the football world cup twice (1950 and 2014) and didn't win the tournament on either of those occasions. However, they are the only country to have won the competition five times. Winning in Sweden (1958), Chile (1962), Mexico (1970), United States (1994) and Japan/ Korea (2002).

- Mark Spitz is well known for winning seven gold medals at the 1972 Olympics but what is less well known is that he set world records in all the events as well.

- In the sport of snowboarding, the terms 'stale fish' and 'mule kick' are used to describe techniques.

Right handers only.

- Due to safety reasons, no players are allowed to play left-handed in polo. Lefties were banned from polo in the 1930's, but the restriction was relaxed after World War II when getting people to play polo was difficult. The ban was reinstated in 1974 and it still stands to this day.

- To keep up morale, George Washington was known to have played cricket with his troops.

- A 'yankee' is a bet made up of 11 individual bets in horseracing.

- Russia first competed in the modern Olympics in 1908.

- The Arizona Cardinals National Football League franchise is suffering a curse put on them by the citizens of Pottsville, Pennsylvania for undeservedly claiming the 1925 NFL championship from the Pottsville Maroons. Potsville were stripped of their title by the NFL in one of the greatest controversies in sports history. They were stripped of the title by the NFL after they played an unauthorised exhibition game in Philadelphia. The problem was that they had violated the territorial rights of the Frankford Yellow Jackets. The curse will supposedly only be lifted when the championship is returned to the Maroons. The Cardinals team holds the NFL record for the longest championship drought.

In golf, the maximum time limit allowed to look for a lost ball is five minutes. This time only starts when you start looking for it. If the ball is lost, then the shot must be replayed from the original position and the player will incur a one-shot penalty.

In 1950, India withdrew from the football world cup because FIFA refused to let them play barefooted!

Who was the last person to box Rocky Marciano? His undertaker.

A long time before South Africa's first democratic elections in 1994, Errol Tobias became part of South African rugby history by becoming the first black player to start a test match for the Springboks. His first match was against Ireland at Newlands on 30th May 1981. He played 15 times for the Springboks, which including in six tests. Errol Tobias and the Springboks were undefeated in all those matches!

Alberto (Baby) Arizmendi holds the record of being the youngest ever professional boxer. It was thought he turned professional at just 10 years old!

The Americas Cup yachting race was called the Hundred-Guinea Cup. This was until a team from the United States of America won the race in 1851.

Celtic won the European Cup in 1967 with all of their players being born within a 30-mile radius of their home ground in Scotland.

Mary Queen of Scots, the first known female golfer, coined the term 'caddy' in 1552, calling her assistants cadets. Derived from the French word, 'le cadet.' This term means, 'the boy,' or, 'youngest of the family.' It was also during her reign that the famous golf course at St Andrews was built.

Baseball was the first sport televised in the United States.

Fewest shots to win a tennis set.

Twelve strokes are the minimum needed to win a set of tennis by one player. If they serve aces on all their serves and their opponent double faults every serve, then the set winning player will only have played 12 strokes!

Harold Grange was the Chicago Bears running back and his nickname was 'The Galloping Ghost'.

The Olympic motto is 'Citius Altius Fortius' and it translates to 'Faster, Higher, Stronger'.

Polo is played on the largest sports pitch in the world. A full-size polo field is 300 yards by 160 yards, this is about the size of three football pitches. The goal posts are eight yards across and designed to collapse on impact to prevent injuries to both players and horses.

The men's champion at the French Open (Roland Garros) in tennis is awarded the 'Coupe des Mousquetaires' (the Musketeer's Trophy). The trophy is named after the four French tennis greats of Rene Lacoste, Henri Cochet, Jean Borata and Jacques Bragnan.

The Cape Argus 'Pick n Pay' Cycle Tour is the world's largest individually timed cycling event. Fields as large as 40,000 competitors have been known to ride. The London Prudential ride in 2016 had about 27,000 riders in it. There are some unconfirmed reports that on a sunny day in the UK, 100,000 cyclists completed the London to Brighton ride.

Dopey lives.

The seven dwarves are down in the mines when there is a cave-in. Snow White runs to the entrance and yells down to them. In the distance a voice shouts out "Aston Villa are good enough to win the Champions League" Snow White says, "Well at least Dopey's alive!"

In the opening ceremony of the 1908 games in London, the Australian swimming team paraded in their swimming kit and even walked around the arena in bare feet!

When a football club wins the European Cup or UEFA Champions league title three years in a row or five times overall, they are allowed to keep the cup and a new one is commissioned. Only five clubs own a Champions League trophy and they are Real Madrid, Bayern Munich, Liverpool, Barcelona and AC Milan.

The sport of baseball is the most common cause of eye injuries in the USA.

A 'squidger' is used in tiddlywinks and is the thing you press down to make your tiddly wink jump!

Archie Griffin was the only college football player to win the Heisman Trophy twice.

The football world cup of 1990 attracted a television audience of more than one billion people.

The team to have won the Champions League with the fewest games won is Manchester United (1998–99) with just five wins out of nine. However, they went through the competition unbeaten with the other games all being draws.

Last bare knuckle championship.

The last bare-knuckle championship fight took place 8th July 1889 in Richburg, Mississippi. The fight was between reigning champion John L Sullivan and the contender Jake Kilrane. It took Sullivan 75 rounds to defend his title by stopping Kilrane.

Wrestler Hulk Hogan's real name is Terry Gene Bollea.

Martin Luther is credited with inventing nine-pin bowling!

Drew Bledsoe threw 70 passes in a single game of American football.

William Shakespeare refers to tennis in Henry V.

Bob and Tom both like to play golf. One-day Bob went to Tom and said, "Hey look at this great ball!" Tom replied, "What's so great about it?" Bob said, "Well if you lose it, it will beep until you find it, and if it goes into the water it will float. This ball is impossible to lose!" "Wow!" said Tom, "Where did you get that from?" Bob replied, "I found it."

American football was played by Harvard teams from 1871 onwards and was commonly referred to as the 'Boston game'.

Sex tests were first used in the 1968 Olympics in Mexico City.

Did you know that eyebrows help keep moisture out of our eyes when we sweat, play sport or walk around in the rain? The arch shape diverts the rain or sweat around to the sides of our face, keeping our eyes relatively dry.

The word 'fan' means 'enthusiast, supporter' is a shortened form of 'fanatic.' Its etymology lies in the Latin word 'fanaticus' means 'inspired by god' and come from 'Fanum' meaning 'a temple'.

History has it that the steeplechase event began on horseback in Ireland, where riders once raced through the countryside, using steeples as distance markers/finish lines and negotiating stone walls and streams along their way. This event made itself onto the athletics track and is the 3000m race we know now with water jumps and large hurdles.

If the quarterback lines up under the centre and misses the snap of the ball with it travelling between his legs untouched, the ball can't be recovered by the opposing team. However, if the ball travels past his hip or over his head then its game on. Between the legs seems to be a sacred place in football as it should be everywhere.

F1 carbon brakes need to be at least 500 degrees Celsius before they will work effectively and will top 1,000 degrees under braking. If the pace (safety) car is out then the driver will brake frequently to try and keep them working properly, otherwise the driver will have (what is referred to as) a dead pedal when the race restarts.

The rower closest to the stern (back) of the boat, responsible for the stroke rate and rhythm. This will be in fact be the front of the boat whilst it is moving because rowers row backwards!

Arnold Palmer won the 'Athlete of the Decade' honours for the 1960's.

Mexico became the first non-US country to win the Little League baseball world series.

No Olympic nations.

In the first four modern Olympics, athletes competed for themselves as members of nations. From 1908 onwards, athletes represented their nations.

Although Spain has produced most winners in Champions League (European Cup) history only Real Madrid and Barcelona have won the Champions League. England, however, has produced five winners, Liverpool, Manchester United, Nottingham Forest, Aston Villa and Chelsea all having lifted the trophy.

In 1894, the Paris – Rouen race was held. This was the first time that motor cars were raced city to city. The race not only included cars but motorbikes as well.

Arsenal football club was the first to field a team without any English players in the Premier league.

At the Indianapolis Motor Speedway track, seven Formula 1 drivers have been killed since 1950.

The real McCoy is a term used all over the world as something genuine. The boxer Norman Selby changed his name to Charles 'Kid' McCoy in 1873. He went on to become welterweight champion of the world. Selby changed his name because Irish boxers were popular in the USA at the time. Selby adopted the name 'the Real McCoy' to make sure there was no confusing him with another fighter whose name was Al McCoy. The phrase itself comes from Scotland where the real McKay was used to describe grade A whiskies.

Yo momma's so stupid she thinks a quarterback is a refund!

Only three clubs have won the UEFA Champions League fielding teams made up entirely from their birth town. Celtic in 1967, Real Madrid in 1966 and FC Steaua Bucureşti last did it in1986.

As one of the most eligible bachelors of his time, Fred Perry dated a string of famous women including actress Marlene Dietrich. He was ranked world No 1 tennis player for four years.

Charles Burgess Fry was the greatest all-round sportsman of his time. Fry took a scholarship to Oxford, where he won blues for cricket, association football and athletics, and would have had a rugby blue as well except for an injury. Not content with these achievements in 1893, he equalled the world record for the long jump after a good lunch and a cigar. Between 1894 and 1908, he was opening batsman for Sussex on tour to South Africa. He was also capped twenty-six times for England in cricket. He was also a super interesting and enigmatic man and I would urge you to read more about him.

Horses don't have hands.

Horses don't have 'hands' but they are measured in them. A human hand when clenched is about four inches from the little finger up to the medial part of the flexed thumb. Horses are measured from the ground up to the top of the withers (an area on their back at the base of their neck). The horse's height is referred to as the number of HH, hands high.

Over his career, Valentino Rossi has won championships in Moto GP at all levels. He has won the 125, 250 and the 500cc world championships. However, he didn't win any of those titles on the first attempt. They were all in his second year in that championship.

In 1943, both the Philadelphia Eagles and the Pittsburgh Steelers had lost so many players to military service during WWII, that they were forced to temporarily merge. The resulting team formed from the merger were known as the Steagles.

Shuttlecock derives from 'shuttle' (from the back-and-forth sense of the word that originated with loom weaving) + 'cock' (from its resemblance to a male bird's plume of tail feathers) which dates way back to 1522.

Golfer: "I think I'm going to drown myself in the lake." Caddy: "I don't think you can keep your head down that long."

A boxer's reach is measured from the tip of the longest finger (thumbs pointing down) to the tip of the longest finger on the other hand whilst the arms are spread and raised horizontal to the side of the fighter's body.

Nadia Comăneci scored the first female perfect 10 and this was the level that all gymnasts hoped to achieve. However, it all changed in 2006 when a two-part system for scoring was introduced. The first score is the difficulty score and is called the A score. It is based on the various elements in a routine and how hard they are to perform. The B score is the execution score and is awarded based on performance of the skills. The B score is similar to the previous scoring method, with a top score of 10. With the relatively new method of scoring, a perfect 10 is a thing of the past.

During the 2006 Champions League competition, Arsenal went more than 900 minutes (10 matches) without conceding a goal. They beat Sparta Prague twice and then drew with Ajax in the group stage. In the last 16 beat and drew with Real Madrid, in the last eight they beat and drew with Juventus and in the semi-final they beat and drew with Villarreal. In the final, they lost to Barcelona 2–1 after leading 1–0. It was a case of what might have been as after just 18 minutes in the final, their goalkeeper Jens Lehmann became the first person to be sent off in a European Cup final.

In the late 19th century, table tennis was called whiff whaff.

Three teams in the Champions League.

Athens is the only city to have been represented by three teams in the Champions League. Those teams were Olympiacos, Panathinaikos and AEK Athens.

Just 23% of golfers are women.

Fred Perry of tennis fame also won a gold at the 1929 world table tennis championships in Budapest.

Newcastle United in 2002 progressed out of the group stages of the Champions League after losing their first three matches.

Max Woosnam was an extraordinary sportsman, not only did he captain Manchester City and England at football, he was also Olympic champion at tennis, won Wimbledon, scored a Lord's century in cricket, made a maximum 147 break in snooker and just to round things off he was a scratch golfer!

The only heavyweight boxing champion to finish his career undefeated was nicknamed 'The Brockton Blockbuster'. Rocky Marciano defended his title six times and finished his career with a record of 49 wins and no defeats.

Individual trampolining was added to the series of gymnastics events at the Sydney Olympics in 2000. Trampolining involves a series of ten jumps and aerial skills (a routine) performed without a break.

My new job.

I told my girlfriend I had a new job in a bowling alley. She said "Tenpin?" I said, "No, it's permanent."

English teams were banned from the European Cup (latterly the Champions League) between 1986 and 1991 following a series of stadium disasters and hooliganism problems.

We all know about Nadia Comăneci and Nellie Kim who both received perfect scores at the 1976 Summer Olympics held in Montreal, Canada. However, they were not really the first gymnasts to complete the perfect event. Several men scored 10's in 1924 at the Paris Olympic games. However, these 10's were scored in the now obsolete Olympic event of rope climbing!

Nottingham Forest is the only club to have won the European Cup more times than they have won their domestic league. They were twice European Champions and only won the league once.

The 1904 summer Olympics were held in St Louis. This was the first time the United States had athletes competing in the gymnastics. Travel wasn't as easy back then and of the 119 gymnasts competing that year, 111 of them were American. In those days, there were no female competitors!

Between them, the following clubs share more than 85% of the European championships. They are Real Madrid, AC Milan, Bayern Munich, Barcelona, Ajax, Liverpool, Manchester United, Internazionale, Juventus, Benfica, Porto, Nottingham Forest.

The Mayo Curse of '51 prevents Mayo from winning the Sam Maguire Cup (the trophy awarded to All Ireland Football champions) until the death of every member of the last winning team from 1951. The Mayo Curse remains unbroken, this is despite the team reaching the final numerous times since, either they completely collapsed on the day or they have been undone by other unfortunate events. The legend tells us that whilst the boisterous Mayo team were passing through Foxford on the victorious journey home, the team failed to respect a funeral ceremony. The residing priest consequently put a curse on Mayo football to never win the All-Ireland Final.

Tour de France climb categories.

- There are five categories of climbs used in the Grand Tours

  - Category 4 – These climbs will have up to 2km @ 6% or up to 4km @ < 4%
  - Category 3 – Ascents that 2–3km long @ 8% (or less on average, but with very steep pitches), 2–4km @ 6% or 4–6km @ 4%
  - Category 2 – Getting a bit longer now. Between 5–10km @ 5–7% or more than 10km @ 3–5%
  - Category 1 – Between 5–10km @ >8% or between 10–15km @ 6%
  - HC (Hors Catégorie) – These are the biggest and toughest and involve more than 15km @ 8% or greater or quite simply climbs more than 20 km long.

- It should be called the technical jump, not the long jump. In the old days, measurements were more difficult to make and therefore a line was used. For sure, athletes could jump further if they were measured from where they take off to where they land. There have also been numerous cases of top jumpers not making a distance because of no jumps on three occasions.

- Celtic was the first British side to win the European Cup in 1967. The same year, they also completed the 'quadruple' winning their domestic league and both Scottish cup tournaments.

- Unlike the modern Olympics with its 1000's of officials from all four corners of the world, the judges in the ancient Olympics didn't even come from all over Greece but they were all residents of Elis and called Eleans. The region that included Olympia. The Eleans had a reputation for their honesty and the notion of cheating was unthinkable, because of this honesty, the local Eleans were allowed to compete in the games.

- John L Sullivan, who was a bare-knuckle boxer, was the first sportsman to earn $1 million. Unfortunately, he was also the first sportsman to lose a million as well!

☺ What do you call a lady in goal? Annette!

▢ The baseball team named 'The LA Angels' has their name directly translate to 'The The Angels Angels'.

🏋 10,000 spectators saw the Fitzsimmons v Sharkey title fight in 1896. Fearing a fix, Wyatt Earp the gunslinger famous from the 'OK Corral' was persuaded to officiate. Before the bout started, Wyatt was drinking in a nearby bar and had his gun taken from him. Unfortunately, the match ended in controversy when Earp declared Tom Sharkey winner after a low blow from Bob Fitzsimmons crumpled Sharkey in the eighth round. There had been low blows throughout the fight from both fighters!

Richest sportsperson ever.

▢ The highest earning athlete ever was a Roman charioteer named Gaius Diocles. His total career earnings totalled 35,863,120 sestertii. When we adjust this to a modern-day figure, he would have had a net worth of 15 billion dollars!

✵ Up until the mid-seventies the Pittsburgh Penguins wore blue, they had to ask the league to change their colours to black and gold to match the other Pittsburgh teams

⚽ Juventus could be the most unfortunate football team in the Champions League history. During the 1970's and '80's, they were very successful but only won the trophy once. That year was 1985 and the victory was marred by the Heysel stadium disaster tragedy in which 39 Juventus supporters died due to fan hooliganism.

☺ I've got nothing against watching a darts match. I just wish my IQ were low enough to enjoy it.

⚾ The Pittsburgh Pirates fielded the first American baseball with no white players in the line-up.

🏈 The first professional American football player was William 'Pudge' Hefflefinger. In 1892, he was paid $500 (about $15,000 adjusted with inflation) for a game he played representing the Allegheny Athletic Association (nicknamed the 3A's) in Pittsburgh.

🚲 Throughout his career in the Tour de France, Eddy Merckx spent a record total of 96 days in 'yellow' which means he nearly rode five complete tours in the coveted 'Yellow Jersey'. He actually only rode seven tours and there were

151 stages in total, and so in the seven tours he rode in 'yellow' 64% of the days!

☐ We know that some sports are fast moving with plenty of exciting action. The following tells you just how fast something moves after being hit in sport.

- Malaysia's Tan Boon Hoeng hit a badminton shuttle 493 km/h
- American Maurice Allen drove a golf ball 339.6 km/h
- The jai alai pelota is 3/4 the size of a baseball and harder than a golf ball and has been recorded at 302 km/h
- Australian Cameron Pilley has hit a squash ball 281.6 km/h
- Samuel Groth from Australia hit a 263.4 km/h tennis serve.
- Ronny Heberson the Brazilian football player hit a rocket of a free kick at 131 mph (210.8 km/h)
- New Zealander, Lark Brandt a table tennis player hit a smash at 112.km/h
- Not quite hitting but Nolan Ryan threw the fastest ever recorded pitch at 108.1 mph (174.0 km/h)
- Shoaib Akhtar in 2003 recorded the fastest bowl of a cricket ball. His bowl reached 161.3 km/h.

The stake.

☐ The prize money won in sport became known as 'the stake' because the bag it was in was literally staked into the ground to prevent people running off with it!

Cricket was played as part of the 1900 Summer Olympics. Four teams entered the competition, Belgium, France, Great Britain and the Netherlands. However, Belgium and the Netherlands pulled out, leaving Great Britain to play France in a straight 2-day final. Neither team was nationally selected. The British side was a touring club, the Devon and Somerset and the French team represented by the French Athletic Club Union who spectators said somewhat bizarrely were the most British of the two teams. Great Britain bowled France out in the second innings for just 26 to win the match by 158 runs. However, if France had managed to put a flat bat on the ball for just five more minutes, the match would have been drawn!

Ectomorphs are thin, flat chested, delicately built, young in appearance, tall, lightly muscled, stoop shouldered and have a large brain. Their personality traits include self-consciousness, a preference for privacy, they are introverted, inhibited, socially anxious, artistic, mentally intense and emotionally restrained.

If a pitcher drops the ball whilst on the mound, it is deemed a 'balk' or hesitation and any player already on base gets a walk to the next one. Once the pitcher winds up and starts the pitching action, they are not allowed to interrupt this action and it is then the ball cannot be dropped.

In 1984, the longest recorded point in tennis history took 29 minutes and featured the ball crossing the net 643 times in a match between Vicki Nelson and Jean Hepner. The rally wasn't the most competitive and was mostly both players stood on the baseline lobbing ball back to each other. Eventually, Nelson went for a winner and was successful. At the end of the rally, Nelson collapsed with cramps in her legs. The umpire had no sympathy for her and hit her with a time violation warning!

Why are baseball umpires fat? They always clean their plate!

Fined for cowardice.

Any athletes caught violating the rules of the ancient Olympics were fined by the judges. Any money collected as punishments was then then used to carve statues of Zeus, the god of the games at Olympia. One wrestler was fined for breaking the rules, and his crime was being scared to fight! He was fined for cowardice!

The first ever winner of the Tour de France was Maurice Green in 1903. He went on to win it again but was later disqualified for cheating. He was caught taking a train!

If you spend all afternoon or evening at the ballpark, watching the whole game of baseball's nine innings. On average, you will have watched less than 18 minutes of action!

Bob Beamon's 1968 Olympic record in the long jump wasn't just good. Forty-four years later in London 2012, it would have beaten Greg Rutherford's gold medal jump by nearly two feet!

The 1947 winner of the Tour de France would take lead bidons (bottles) on-board at the top of climbs before descending. Jean Robic realised the extra weight would help him descend quicker. But if all things fall at the same rate due to gravity, that shouldn't really be the case. What Newton's law of universal gravitation states is that 'every mass attracts every other mass in the universe, and the gravitational force between two bodies is proportional to the product of their masses, and inversely proportional to the square of the distance between them'. For the items to fall at the same speed, they must fall in a vacuum. The tour mountains are anything but vacuums and because the Bidon doesn't add to the aerodynamic drag of the rider, it means that he can descend quicker with more weight on board.

During the 1936 world table tennis championships, which took place in Prague, Alojzy 'Alex' Ehrlich became famous after a record-breaking one-point exchange with Romanian player Paneth Farkas. The exchange lasted two hours and 12 minutes and the ball crossed the net more than 12,000 times. After two hours, Farkas' arm began to fatigue, and he lost the first point. The point was so long that the referee had to be replaced during the match, because his neck was so sore. The rally for the second point started going the same way and after 20 minutes Ehrlich thought it was time for some gamesmanship. Whilst playing, he instructed his Polish teammates to set up a chess board on the side table and then proceeded in calling out the chess moves whilst playing the point. The gamesmanship worked and his opponent became frustrated and lost the point!

Obesity runs in the family.

Guy: "You see doctor, the problem is obesity runs in the family." Doctor: "No, the problem is no one runs in your family."

Eddie Gaedel had his American League contract annulled after playing one game in 1951, what was his crime? He was just 3 foot 7 inches tall (short!) Because of his height, the strike zone was so small he was walked on his only ever bat. Not wanting to turn the game into a mockery, little Eddie was prevented playing. The strike zone is defined as the volume of space above home plate and between the batter's knees and the midpoint of their torso. Maybe we should give the very tall hitters an extra strike just to make things a little fairer?

In American football, you are not allowed to get a boost from any other player on your team in an attempt to gain more height on the field. If caught, you are punished with an automatic 15-yard penalty.

Most of us know the summer and winter Olympic games alternate and are staged every two years. This hasn't always been the case. Up until 1994, the Winter Olympics were held a few months before the Summer Olympics in the same year.

Spartak is the Russian name of Spartacus. Originally, Spartak Moscow was originally known as MKS (Moscow Sports Circle). The name Spartak was adopted in 1935. The story of Spartacus was popular in the pre-war Soviet Union.

In early editions of the 'Le Tour', there were 14 rest days instead of the two we have currently. Stages would often go on through the night and the racers needed the next day to recover.

The Marquess of Queensbury gave his name to the standardised rules of boxing in 1866, not because he devised them but because he was the chairman of the committee who devised them.

I have flabby thighs, but fortunately my stomach covers them.

No professional sport in the USA.

There are only two days a year in the United States where there are no professional games played in the MLB, NBA, NHL or NFL. These are the day before and the day after the Major League All-Star baseball game.

Danny Heep became the first player in a World Series to be a designated hitter (DH) with the initials 'DH'. He was on the winning side as the New York Mets of the National League beat the American League champions the Boston Red Sox.

There are only seven teams whose nicknames do not end with an 'S' in major US professional sports. In basketball, there are the Miami Heat, the Utah Jazz and the Orlando Magic. Baseball has the Boston Red Sox and the Chicago White Sox. Ice hockey has the Colorado Avalanche and the Tampa Bay Lightning. In American football, there aren't any!

What is a boxer's favourite part of a joke? The punch line!

Baseball pitcher Gaylord Perry remarked tongue in cheek in 1963, "They'll put a man on the moon before I hit a home run." On 20ᵗʰ July 1969, a few hours after Neil Armstrong set foot on the moon. Guess what? Gaylord Perry hit a homer and it was the only home run he hit in his entire professional career.

The NASCAR acronym stands for the 'National Association for Stock Car Auto Racing'.

When the University of Nebraska Cornhuskers play football at home to a sell-out crowd of 90,000. The stadium is classified as the third largest city in the state.

In the USA alone, there are 300 million golf balls lost or discarded every year.

Closest Tour de France win.

The smallest winning margin in the Tour de France's history is just eight seconds. After 21 stages and 3,285 km of racing the American Greg LeMond beat Laurent Fignon of France by this narrow margin in the 1989 edition of the race.

The first female gold medallist of the modern Olympics was a British lady. Her name was Charlotte Cooper and she won the ladies tennis singles gold in the 1900 Paris games.

The first Kentucky Derby was run at Churchill Downs in 1875 and it was won by Aristides.

The first modern Olympiad was held in Athens in 1896. Four hundred and eighty-four contestants from 13 nations participated. The 2016 Rio games had 11,000 competitors from more than 200 countries.

Golfer: "Well, I have never played this badly before!" Caddy: "I didn't realize you had played before, sir!"

Tradition has it that in the opening procession of the Olympics, the team representing the host nation always marches last.

Gatorade was developed in Florida and was named after the University of Florida Gators.

A baseball batter is not allowed more than 18 inches of pine tar on their bat. If the other team or umpire suspects they do, then that batsman is automatically declared out. The pine tar gives extra grip to the wooden bat.

Celery was awarded to winners of sports events by the ancient Greeks.

In 1935, Jesse Owens put a handkerchief 26 feet 2½ inches past the take-off board. The marker for the existing world record. He proceeded to jump almost six inches past it. His mark of 26' 8.1" wouldn't be beaten for 25 years.

Juventus just finished playing Manchester United in the Champions League, a little fan runs up to Ronaldo after the match waving a piece of paper to get an autograph. CR says, "Sure, do you have a pen?" The kid says, "I'll get one." He throws himself on the ground and starts rolling around, holding his knee and crying. Cristiano says, "You said you were getting a pen." The kid replies, "Well, it works for you."

In the 650 matches that are played in grand slam event of Wimbledon, there are on average 42,000 balls are used. New balls are introduced every seven games within a match. The seven game old balls are given to local clubs, coaches and schools.

Left handers are better.

Compared to right-handers those who are left-handed are better at sports that require good spatial judgment and fast reactions.

In major sports, both cricket and baseball are unique because it is the defence that controls the ball.

Eric Liddell was devout Christian and was selected to represent GB in the Paris 1924 games, he was informed months before that the qualifiers would be held on the Sabbath (Sunday) and that was a day of rest for him. He refused to run the 100m and instead moved up successfully to the 400m winning the gold. In the classic film 'Chariots of Fire', a bit of artistic licence is used and it appears he only finds out about the itinerary on the journey to the games.

FIFA (Fédération Internationale de Football Association) is the world governing body of football. They have 6 regional confederations who govern their federations. In total there are 211 federations of football around the world.

- UEFA - Union of European Football Associations – 55 federations
- CONMEBOL - CONfederación SudaMEricana de FútBOL – 10 federations
- CONCACAF - Confederation of North, Central America and Caribbean Association Football – 35 federations
- CAF- Confederation of African Football – 54 federations
- AFC - Asian Football Confederation – 46 federations
- OFC - Oceania Football Confederation – 11 federations

Before George Patton became the famous World War ll General, he competed and came 5th in the pentathlon in the Stockholm 1912 Olympic games.

Le Tour de France is nicknamed 'La Grade Bouche', and this translates to the big loop.

The 1900 Paris games had a 'holding your breath underwater event', and also a 'swimming obstacle race'.

No high jumper has ever been able to stay off the ground for more than one second.

Sorcery in baseball!

A man was imprisoned in Mississippi in 1884. Nothing special about that apart from his crime was throwing a curveball and the charge he was found guilty of was sorcery!

The official budget for the 1908 London games was £15,000, just over a century later the budget for the London 2012 games was £9.29 billion. The organisers were very proud of the fact they came in under budget. They spent £528m less than expected, and the final figure was a mere £8.77 billion!

It is just before Scotland v Brazil match at the football world cup. Ronaldo goes into the Brazilian changing room to find all his teammates looking a bit glum. "What's up?" he asks. "Well, we're having trouble getting motivated for this game. We know it's important but it's only Scotland. They're 'merda' and we can't be bothered." Ronaldo looks at them and says, "Well, I reckon I can beat these by myself, you lads go down the local barzinho." So, Ronaldo goes out to play Scotland by himself and the rest of the Brazilian team go off for a few caipirinhas. After a few drinks, they wonder how the game is going, so they get the landlord to put the tele on. A big cheer goes up as the screen reads 'Brazil 1–Scotland 0 (Ronaldo 10 minutes)'. He is beating Scotland all by himself! Anyway, a few more drinks later and the game is forgotten until someone remembers 'It must be full time now, let's see how he got on'. They put the scores back on. "Result from the Stadium 'Brazil 1 (Ronaldo 10 minutes)–Scotland 1 (Angus 89 minutes)'. They can't believe it; he has single handedly got a draw against Scotland! They rush back to the stadium to congratulate him. They find him in the dressing room, still in his gear, sat with his head in his hands. He refuses to look at them. "I've let you down, I've let you down." "Don't be daft, you got a draw against Scotland, all by yourself. And they only scored at the very, very end!" "No, No, I have, I've let you down... I got sent off after 12 minutes."

The term birdie (might) come from an American, Ab Smith. In 1899, he played what he described as a 'bird of a shot', which over time became known as a 'birdie'.

Major League Baseball's Harry Chiti was not the first player to be traded but he was the first player to be traded for himself! The Cleveland Indians traded him to the New York Mets for a 'player to be named later'. After an unsuccessful period at the Mets, he was shipped back to Cleveland as the trade for himself.

The national sport of Japan is Sumo wrestling.

Hitler refused to attend any medal ceremonies.

Hitler's Olympics in 1936 were the perfect opportunity for him to showcase to the world his master race. He only shook hands with two gold medallists on the first day, a German and a Finn. He soon realised what Jesse Owens and company were doing and what was happening, maybe his team weren't the master race after all. He left after the first day and refused to attend any more medal ceremonies or congratulate any more winners.

In the sport of hurling, there are no international fixtures at all. The sport is nearly all played in Ireland.

Irrelevant on how much they won, it was customary for jockeys to be paid in coins.

What is the difference between a golfer and a fisherman? "When a golfer lies, he doesn't have to bring anything home to prove it!

The original multi-sport event in the Olympics for men was known as the pentathlon and included wrestling. The other four events being the long jump, discus, javelin and the sprint.

The chances of making two holes-in-one in a round of golf are one in 67 million.

In decathlon, the rules stated that athletes get a minimum of 30 minutes rest in between events. This rule is sometimes implemented, imagine as an athlete, warming down, warming back up, refuelling and possibly having to use the bathroom. It doesn't leave a lot of time.

Before his NASCAR days, Lee Petty once left a pit stop and did a full lap with a pit crew member still on the hood of the car!

Two surfers are getting ready to paddle out. Surfer one: "Hey, guess what! I got a new longboard for my wife!" Surfer two: "Great trade!"

In decathlon competitions, it is the score that matters the most. Decathletes are actually competing against a scoring table not just winning events. The object is to accumulate as many points and at the end of all events, the athlete with the highest score wins.

Morihei Ueshiba, founder of Aikido, once pinned an opponent using only a single finger.

Jan Mashiani and Len Tau were in St Louis in 1904 as part of the exhibition about the Boer War at the Worlds Trade Fair. They both entered the men's marathon. Tau finished ninth and Mashiani twelfth. Both of them were the first African athletes to compete in the modern Olympics.

Tiger Woods is the first athlete to have been named 'Sportsman of the Year' twice by the Sports Illustrated magazine.

The slowest Tour de France.

The slowest Tour de France was straight after the World War I, in 1919 and it averaged just 14.9 mph. Don't be too hard on the cyclist though, the roads were in a terrible state of disrepair.

The average height of an NBA basketball player is 6 feet 7 inches.

I phoned the local gym and I asked if they could teach me how to do the splits. He said, "How flexible are you?" I said, "I can't make Tuesdays or Thursdays."

Professional volleyball players can spike the ball at 80 miles per hour. Have a look at how many taped their fingers for the game. The most injuries occur when blocking a spiked ball.

Unfortunately for the Dodgers in 1948, Jackie Robinson picked up a hamstring injury and would be out for two weeks. The Dodgers solution to keep the spectators coming was to replace him in the line-up with a white man named Herschel Morowitz and paint his face black!

Sharunas Marchulenis was the first Soviet basketball player to join the NBA. The Lithuanian played for the Golden State Warriors in 1989 and his NBA career lasted eight years, playing also for the Seattle Super Sonics, Sacramento Kings and the Denver Nuggets.

The best strings used in tennis are made from animal intestines. Sheep, cow or goat used to be the most commonly used. The strings were so good because of the intestine's softness and resilience. The natural strings are produced by drying fibres extracted from part of the intestine which contains collagen and it is the collagen that gives then their elasticity.

In the decathlon or the heptathlon, failing in one event could easily ruin your whole competition. In 1992, Dan O'Brien was a favourite for the Barcelona

Olympics, however he missed his opening height in the pole vault three times in a row, meaning zero points for the event, his Olympics and chance of gold finished on the pole vault run up.

Give a man a fish and he will eat for a day. Teach him how to fish and he will sit in a boat all day and drink beer!

The Indianapolis 500 is run on Memorial Day which is the day for remembering the people who died whilst serving in the country's armed forces.

In 1970, just 127 runners ran the New York marathon. By 1998, this number had risen to 32,000 competing each year.

In 1870, British boxing champion Jim Mace and American boxer Joe Coburn fought for three hours and 48 minutes without landing one punch.

The most favoured badminton shuttles are made from 16 goose feathers.

First ever football team.

Founded in 1857, Sheffield FC is officially recognised by FIFA as being the oldest association football club in the world.

A perfect score in the decathlon is 1,000 points in each event for a cumulative score of 10,000 points. It has never been done, but decathletes have scored more than 1000 points in individual events within the competition. No decathlete has ever scored a 1000 points in either the discus or 1500m events.

In rugby union, the scrum half is the ½ and the outside centre the ¾, thus, the players in between them had to be something else, namely the 5/8's.

The striped billiard balls weigh 0.1 ounces or so more than the solids.

The Greeks measured time in various ways and the Olympiad was one of those. The Olympic games were used as a starting point, year one of the cycle of four years. The Nemean and Isthmian games were both held in year two of the cycle, followed by the Pythian games in year three. Year four would see the return of the Nemean and Isthmian games. The cycle would then start again with the Olympic games. The Nemean and Isthmian games although held in the same year were held in different months. They were structured this way so that individual athletes could participate in all of the games.

Is sweating it out a good way of recovering after a party night or celebration?

Sweating does not detox your body after alcohol or food consumption excesses. More than 99% of sweat is water, along with trace amounts of electrolytes like salt. Only small amounts of toxic substances can find their way out of the body through perspiration, detoxification primarily occurs in the liver, kidneys and lungs, not through the skin. Instead of the sauna, drink lots of water.

In 1912, the USA's Jim Thorpe became the first winner of the Olympic decathlon and was declared the greatest athlete in the world by King Gustav V of Sweden. The Olympics were wholly amateur in those days and he was disqualified for playing professional baseball. It was only after his death that his Olympic titles were reinstated.

Two into one goes.

Two basketballs should fit through the hoop because the diameter of a full-sized basketball is half the diameter of a basketball hoop. The rim inside diameter is 18 inches and ball diameter is 9 inches.

Five times winner of the football world cup, Brazil played their first ever international game in Rio De Janeiro against another powerhouse of the game, Exeter United! Brazil won the game 2–0 but there is a rumour that the Exeter team (from south west England) left the pitch early because it was too hot to play.

"Help!" screamed the hunter into his cell phone, "I was trying to shoot a deer and by mistake I killed my partner." "OK," said the ranger into the phone, "try to calm yourself down. First, I would like you to make sure he's dead." "OK," said the hunter, "hold on one second." Suddenly, BOOM, then the hunter came back on, "Yeah he's dead."

Up until the 1870's, baseball was played without the use of gloves or mitts.

Walter Hagan winner of 45 PGA Tour events, 11 majors and the Ryder Cup as both player and captain cancelled a 1914 try-out for the Philadelphia Phillies Baseball team in order to play in golf's US Open. He won it and never looked back. He became the first professional golfer to make his living playing the game as opposed to teaching it. Walter also became the first American golfer to earn more than a million dollars in his career. Adjusted for inflation that would be about $40 million.

The five Olympic rings represent the continents of the world. By accepted convention, there are seven continents: Asia, Africa, North America, South America, Europe, Australia and Antarctica. Go figure IOC!

I prefer golf.

Golfer: "Well caddy, do you like my game?" Caddy: "Very good, sir! But personally, I prefer golf."

The theme song of the Harlem Globetrotters is 'Sweet Georgia Brown'.

In the 1949 world ice hockey championships, Canada thrashed Denmark 47–0. The ice hockey game is split into 3, 20-minute thirds. The score by third was 13–0, 16–0 and 18–0. Not quite a goal a minute but not bad. Imagine what Czechoslovakia (the team that beat Canada in the final) would have done to Denmark.

Boxing is considered and has always been the easiest sport for gamblers to fix. In years gone by, many fights were controlled by the Mafia.

Professional sumo wrestlers, called rikishi, must be quick on their feet and supple, but weight is vital to success as they hurl themselves at their opponents, aiming to floor them or push them outside the 15-foot fighting circle. To bulk up, rikishi eat huge portions of protein-rich stews called chankonabe, packed with fish or meat and vegetables, plus vast quantities of less healthy foods, including fast food. They often force themselves to eat when they are full, and they have a nap after lunch, thus acquiring flab on top of their strong muscles, which helps to keep their centre of gravity low. The average rikishi tips the scales at about 280 pounds, but the heaviest sumo wrestler ever recorded is Manny Yarbrough (aka Tiny) an American who weighed in at a thundering 828 lbs.

It is thought the 'huddle' in American football was formed due a deaf football player who needed to hide the signals he was communicating in sign language to his teammates.

The Los Angeles games of 1932 were the first to feature the three-level winner's stand (podium) that has now become the normal way the top three athletes or teams are awarded their medals. In earlier games such as London 1908, all the winners were given their medals on the last day of the games in one big awards ceremony.

What goes all the way around the baseball field but never moves? The fence.

The Miami Dolphins were the last NFL team to go through a season unbeaten.

21 to win.

In the first rules of baseball, a team was required to score 21 runs to win the game.

The city of Denver was chosen to host and then refused the 1976 Winter Olympics because of the cost of hosting. Innsbruck stepped in and saved the day as they had previously hosted the games 12 years before and still had the infrastructure and were ready to go almost immediately.

The world's biggest bunker in golf is known as 'Hell's Half Acre' on the 585 yd seventh hole of the Pine Valley course, Clementon, New Jersey.

All competitors at the Ancient Olympics were required to train at Olympia for a month before the games started. Any athletes who didn't take part in this training were fined. A fine was given to an athlete who claimed he was stuck on a ship unable to dock. The real reason he wasn't at the training camp was that he had been travelling around Greece entering different sports competitions!

Sumo wrestlers cannot wipe their own backsides, their wives traditionally do it for them! After training sessions, it is tradition that the younger sumo wrestlers clean ALL areas of the older sumo wrestler's body!

Baseball's home plate is 17 inches wide. Originally, it was one-foot square. In 1874, it was rotated so that point faced forward, now making it 17 inches wide. It became a pentagon following the 1899 season.

In gambling language, for a gambling house a 'sure-thing' is a wager that a player has little chance of winning; 'easy money' is their profit from an inexperienced bettor, an unlucky player is called a 'stiff'.

Kresimir Cosic, a 6 ft 11 in (2.11 m) Croatian is only non-American player in NBA Hall of Fame. He played for the Los Angeles Lakers.

Japans deadly martial art of Tessenjutsu is based on the use of a fan to kill.

The State of Nevada first legalised gambling in 1931. At the same time, the Hoover Dam was being built and the federal government did not want its workers (who earned 50 cents an hour) to be involved with gambling, so they built the town of Boulder City to house the dam workers. To this day, Boulder City is the only city in Nevada where gambling is illegal.

What's a dominatrix's favorite sport?

Kickball

The Boston Red Sox's Mike Greenwell holds the major league record for the most 'runs batted in', that accounted for all of his team's runs. The game was against the Seattle Mariners and Greenwell batted in nine runs in a game.

A few miles away from me is world's oldest real tennis court. It was built at Hampton Court in 1530 for Henry VIII.

To save you checking what US patent number 638,920 is, I can help you. It was filed on 12th December 1899 and the invention was the golf tee. It was designed to stop Dr George Grant getting his hands dirty whilst building a pile of sand which was normally what the players drove off.

Two not very clever runners were out training in the countryside and they noticed some tracks. The first said, "Deer tracks?" "No," replied the second, "Bear tracks?" The conversation ended abruptly when the train hit them.

The original name for basketball, as invented by Dr James Naismith, was indoor rugby. It was one of the game's first players that started calling it basketball because of the peach baskets that acted as the original goals.

The winners of the Super Bowl in American football are awarded The Vince Lombardi Trophy.

Baseball rules were codified in 1846 by Alexander Cartwright of the Knickerbocker Baseball Club.

'Checkmate' the expression used to signify the end of a match in chess comes from the Persian phrase 'shah mat' which means, 'The king is dead'.

The visionary of the modern Olympic games, Baron Pierre de Coubertin was like most men in those days, very sexist. He was not in favour of women's participation in either the Olympic games or in sports in general. He believed that a woman's greatest achievement would be to encourage her sons to be distinguished in sports and to applaud a man's effort!

In Clearwater, Florida at the Jack Russell Stadium, on 26th June 1985, the Philadelphia Phillies team's organist Wilbur Snapp played 'Three Blind Mice' following a call by umpire Keith O'Connor. The umpire was having none of it and ejected the organist from the game!

The word 'karate' means 'empty hand'.

In 1925, the 'Four Horsemen' of the 'Fighting Irish of Notre Dame' played together for the last time. Their last game was the Rose Bowl Victory against Stanford, the 'Four Horsemen' were Elmer Layden, Don Miller, Jim Crowley and Harry Stuhldreher.

Princess Anne, the daughter of Queen Elizabeth II, was the only female competitor who did not have to undergo a sex test during the 1976 Olympics. She competed on the British equestrian team.

In 1976, the IOC started testing athletes for anabolic steroids.

A pole vaulter, when landing, may absorb up to 20,000 lbs of pressure per square inch on joints in their legs.

In Portsmouth, Ohio, they have a law that ranks baseball players in the same class as vagrants, thieves and other suspicious characters!

Banned for his tattoo.

Josef Craig was banned from a S8, 100m freestyle swimming final for having an Olympic logo tattooed on his chest. This constituted advertising, as he is a Paralympian and not an Olympian. Had he the Paralympic logo of the three agitos, I presume he would have been OK?

Who was the poet of basketball? Longfellow.

In 1957, two men scored holes in one on the same golf course. What was unique is that both men had the same name, Edward Chapman got a hole in one on the eighth hole. Later that day, Edward Chapman hit one from the sixth tee.

Uruguay refused to enter the 1934 World Cup hosted in Italy making them the only World Cup champions not to attempt to defend their title four years later. Italy had refused to make the trip to Uruguay four years prior. Uruguay's nonattendance in Italy was in revenge to this snub.

That famous sea-going nation of Switzerland won the Americas Cup in 2003. The Alinghi team, owned by Ernesto Bertarelli, flew a huge banner pronouncing 'We did it' and depicting the cup at the top of the Matterhorn. The winners were accused of buying success and employing the best sailors. Makes you wonder how they could have won the trophy any other way. Switzerland is completely land locked!

Diane Leather was the first woman to break five minutes for a mile with a time of 4:59.6 seconds. This feat was achieved in Birmingham, England. The world record was broken on 29th May 1954 just 23 days after Bannister' first 4-minute mile.

Joe Nuxhall of the Cincinnati Reds was the youngest pitcher in major league baseball. He was only 15 years, 10 months and 11 days old when he pitched in the game against the St Louis Cardinals. There was a player shortage during WW II and he pitched two thirds of an innings.

At one point during a game, the coach said to one of his young players, "Do you understand what co-operation is? What a team is?" The little boy nodded in the affirmative. "Do you understand that what matters is whether we win together as a team?" The little boy nodded yes. "So," the coach continued, "when a strike is called, or you're out at first, you don't argue or curse or attack the umpire. Do you understand all that?" Again the little boy nodded. "Good," said the coach, "now go over there and explain it to your mother."

Why West Ham play in claret and blue.

West Ham and Aston Villa both play in claret and blue because Villa gave them a kit as payment for a bet in 1899. The bet was made by four Aston Villa players who thought they could outsprint William Dove. The Villa players lost and as they couldn't afford to pay the money originally wagered, they instead offered William Dove who played for the Thames Ironworks (now West Ham United) a full kit as payment.

In 1743 boxing with gloves, rules and a roped ring were all introduced by Jack Broughton. He was a British fighter who was known as 'the father of boxing'. He was British champion for 21 years. The reason gloves were introduced, and bare-knuckle fighting finished was because some of the aristocracy were boxing fans and wanted to spar with professional boxers. To prevent them from being injured, gloves called 'feather bedders' were used.

During the football world cup in Brazil, the England team visited an orphanage. "It was heart breaking to see their sad little faces with no hope," said Fernando, age 6.

A regulation football match games is 90 minutes, but the ball is in play on average for only 62 minutes. The clock runs continually, and the 28 minutes is lost to such things as throw ins, free kicks, penalties, time wasting, substitutions and injuries.

The billiards master, Walter 'Wally' Lindrum, OBE (29 August 1898 – 30 July 1960) was an Australian professional player who held the World Professional Billiards Championship from 1933 until his retirement in 1950. He made a world record break of 4,137 in a match against Joe Davis on 19th January 1932. Wally occupied the table for 2 hours 55 minutes and made about 1,900 consecutive scoring shots!

In 1998, Mark McGwire hit a record 70 home runs. If the total of all these hits are added together the balls will have travelled a total of 29,598 feet. Mount Everest is only 29,029 ft high! That's nearly six miles!

It's a terrible statistic, but between two and three jockeys die each year in horseracing. Just putting that into context, in baseball's entire history only three players have died whilst playing!

Who is the silhouette on the NBA logo?

Standing 6ft 9in and weighing 220lb, Bill Russell earned the reputation as one of, if not the greatest basketball's greatest player. In a 13-year career which saw him help Boston Celtics to 11 NBA Championships. Known as 'the Ghost' for his uncanny ability to rise up and block his opponents' shots. He is the silhouette on the NBA logo as well.

I'll never understand how you can come up second in a biathlon. I mean – you've got a gun, haven't you?

Bulgaria played a game in the 1994 world cup finals with the entire team having a surname ending in the letter 'V'. The team was Stoichkov, Penev, Kostadinov, Balakov, Letchkov, Yankov, Kiriakov, Hubchev, Tzvetanov, Ivanov and Mihailov. Indeed, in the entire 22-man squad there was only Petar Mihtarski without the surname ending in a V. It wasn't a bad team, Stoichkov won the Golden Boot, for the most goals scored in the tournament and they went on to finish in fourth place after losing to Italy and Sweden, in the semi-finals and third-place game, respectively.

Mickey Mantle for the 10th time in his career did something quite unusual. He hit home runs from both sides of the plate in the same game!

The Athens Olympics of 1896 was opened by the British King George 1st. In total, 241 male athletes competed from 14 countries. The USA narrowly beat Greece in the medals table winning 11 golds to Greece's 10.

Golfers use an estimated $800 million worth of golf balls annually.

What's the difference between a Celtic fan and a coconut? You can get a drink out of a coconut!

The sport of gossima (table tennis, as we know it now) was originally played with balls made from champagne corks. The corks were rounded off and the paddle bats were fabricated from cigar-box lids. James Gibb created it in the 1880's. Gibb was a British engineer who wanted a fun and invigorating game that could play indoors especially when it was raining. Gibb's cork balls were replaced with celluloid ones and the manufacturer of these new balls renamed the game 'Ping-Pong' in 1901. The rest as they say is history.

What is the name of the small Chinese sportsman? Knee High

Due to the lesser air pressure, it is estimated a fly ball in baseball will travel about seven feet further for every 1,000 feet of altitude the game is played.

Regulation bowling balls have a maximum of five finger grip holes, although three holes is the most often used.

Kangaroo's nose.

In Australia's aboriginal language, tennis professional Evonne Goolagong's last name means 'kangaroo's nose'.

In July 1934, Babe Ruth hit his 700th home run in baseball. The fan that catches or retrieves the ball normally keeps it. Babe Ruth, however, paid the fan $20 dollars for the return of the baseball. Imagine what that would be worth now?

How many golfers does it take to change a lightbulb? Fore!

10 was the name of Pearl Jam's first album and it was named in tribute of basketball player Mookie Blaylock whose number was 10. Pearl Jam were originally called 'Mookie Blaylock' until they were forced to change their name. Mookie spent 13 years in the National Basketball Association playing for three different teams, the New Jersey Nets, Atlanta Hawks and the Golden State Warriors.

On 6th May 1954, Roger Bannister became the first man to break the four-minute mile, this was a staged event and not really a race. He ran 3:59.4 whilst being paced by other runners including Chris Chataway and Chris Brasher. Bannister's 400m splits were 57.5s, 60.7s, 62.3s and 58.9s.

The decathlon perfect score for each event is 1000 points (you can score more though). This is what you'd need to do in order to score the 10,000 mark.

Event	Performance	Score
100m	10.395s	1000
Long Jump	7.76m	1000
Shot	18.4m	1000
High Jump	2.208m	1000
400m	46.16s	1000
110M hurdles	13.8s	1000
Discus	56.2m	1000
Pole Vault	5.287m	1000
Javelin	77.2m	1000
1500m	3min 53.7s	1000

We get the word 'coach' from the village of Kocs in Hungary, where sports coaches were first used.

Struck twice by lightning.

Green Bay Packers backup quarterback, Matt Hasselbeck, has been struck by lightning twice in his life.

I remember the classic rivalry between Seb Coe (now Lord Coe) and Steve Ovett. In the 1980 Moscow games, they both became Olympic champions. Coe in the 1500m and Ovett in the 800m. What was interesting about this is that neither won at their preferred distance.

What runs along the edge of the pitch but never moves? The side-line.

The whole of Malaysia's Nike factory workers annual wages combined do not equal Michael Jordan's remuneration from the company!

In the 1886 Baseball World Series, there were a total of 63 errors made. On average, there is less than one error made per game nowadays.

Paralympic medals have small balls in them so that the visually impaired competitors can hear them.

Fuzzy Zoeller defeated Tom Watson and Ed Sneed in the first ever sudden-death playoff at the Masters in 1979.

The traditional route into the NBA is via the Collegiate system, Moses Malone was the first basketball player to go directly from high school to a professional American team. The Utah Stars signed him in 1974.

'The Sultan of Swat', Babe Ruth hit his first major-league home run on 6th May 1915. This was for the Boston Red Sox, he went on to hit 714 homers before he retired as a New York Yankee in 1935.

Should have sold more coffee.

Brazil sent 69 athletes to the 1932 LA Olympic games but unfortunately only 24 competed. The athletes travelled on a coffee boat hoping to sell coffee to raise funds to enter. The entry fee was $1 each. They only sold enough coffee for 24 to enter. The Brazilian government sent more money to cover the shortfall but the Brazilian cruzeiro had devalued so much that if the cheque was cashed it still wouldn't have been enough. However, just to finish off the debacle, the cheque bounced!

The Paralympic games weren't always called that. Up until 1960, they were known as 'the Stoke Mandeville games,' and were a competition for wheelchair athletes only. The logo is made of three Agitos with the Latin meaning 'I move'.

The great Joe Namath became the highest paid rookie (at the time) when he signed a $400,000 contract with the New York Jets in January 1965.

An Aston Villa fan walks into a pub with his dog just as the football scores come on the TV. The announcer says that Aston Villa has lost 3-0 and the dog immediately rolls over on its back, sticks its paws in the air and plays dead. "That's amazing," says the barman, "what does he do when they win? "The Aston Villa Fan scratches his head for a couple of minutes and finally replies, "I dunno... I've only had the dog for eight months."

Hoyt Wilhelm, a baseball hall of famer hit a home run with his first ever attempt in the professional game. Nothing fantastically unique about this but in the next 20 years of playing professionally, he never hit another one!

They reckon that grunting whilst hitting a tennis ball gives the player 5% more ball speed.

As Leprosos (lepers) is a name that Newell's Old Boys is often called. The reason for this being that they were invited to play a charity game in the 1920's to raise money for leprosy sufferers. Their fierce rivals Rosario Central were due to be their opponents, but they pulled out at the last moment, resulting in the match being cancelled.

Dimples on their balls.

Books like these will have you believe that golf balls have 360 dimples. However, some balls have as many as 420. Also, for those of you interested, there are also different dimple patterns on the balls!

The Jules Rimet (football world cup) trophy was stolen in 1966 and was found wrapped in newspaper by a dog named Pickles. Brazil were awarded the Jules Rimet Trophy in perpetuity after winning the world cup for a third time. Unfortunately, the trophy was stolen again in 1983 from a display case in Rio de Janeiro. The display case was thought to be unbreakable, with its bulletproof glass. However, it had a flimsy wooden frame and was easily broken into. The trophy was never recovered but they did find its original base.

Gary Lineker who played professional football for 16 years at clubs such as Leicester City, Tottenham Hotspur and Barcelona was never cautioned by a referee for foul play. He never once received a yellow or a red card. He was also the world cup Golden Boot winner in the Mexico world cup 1986.

In dressage and equestrian events, the uniform for the rider has been known to cost nearly £10,000! Sport for all!

A single cowhide makes 10 American footballs. All the cows come from Kansas, Iowa or Nebraska.

Difference between walking and running.

In the sport of walking, competitors must always have at least one foot in contact with the ground. To enable this, race walkers rotate their hips about 20 degrees, this enables them to reach extraordinary walking speeds. Normal walking sees the person rotate their hips about four degrees.

Why was Cinderella kicked off the basketball team? She ran away from the ball.

Not so long ago in 1995, a Manchester City fan was banned from Maine Road (Manchester City's old stadium). The offence was bringing dead chickens into the ground and swinging them around his head when City scored.

American footballers' knees have greatest risk of injury.

The ancient sport of hammer throwing has a legend that says the Celtic hero "Cu Chulainn" picked up a chariot by its axle, spun it around his head and threw it further than any mortal could. I wonder if there was any drug testing back then?

The penalty spot in football was invented as a time and cost saving measure in the late 1800's. Originally, the penalty line was drawn completely across the whole pitch.

The patent for the baseball catcher's mask was awarded to Frederick Winthrop Thayer of Massachusetts in 1878. He was also the captain of the Harvard University Baseball Club.

Smallest world cup crowd.

The smallest attendance at a football world cup finals match was just 300. The infamous match was between Romania and Peru during the 1930 World Cup in Uruguay.

When Henry Aaron hit his 715th home run and broke Babe Ruth's record. both Aaron and Al Downing (the pitcher) were wearing number 44 shirts!

If one athlete on an Olympic team is found guilty of taking performance enhancing drugs, the entire team may be disqualified and forced to return any medals they may have won. This has happened quite a few times. Both the US team, which had Tyson Gay was a part of in London 2012 and the 2008 games and the Russian Sprint team which included Yuliya Chermoshanskaya had to all return their medals.

In American football, the oldest stadium used in the NFL is Soldier Field in Chicago.

Up until 1859, baseball umpires used to sit in padded chairs behind home plate and give their decisions in comfort.

It was only after 1917 that goalkeepers in ice hockey were allowed to drop to the ice to make saves, prior to that they had to stay on their feet!

In the sport of chess, the number of possible ways of playing just the first four moves on each side is 318,979,564,000.

The New York Giants baseball catcher Roger Bresnahan introduced shin guard's way back in 1907.

What do you call an Englishman in the knockout stages of the football world cup? A referee.

The penalty arc is marked alongside the penalty area. Its purpose is only to keep the players 10 yards from the penalty spot when a penalty is being taken. It serves no other purpose. Goal keepers are not allowed to handle the ball in this area.

Baseball player Mike Schmidt earned the first $500,000 salary in 1977.

The Chinese often call American football 'olive ball', because of a football's resemblance to an olive.

What kind of stories are told by basketball players? Tall tales!

Anabolic steroids work by helping the body's muscle cells produce more protein which leads to increased muscle size and strength and, at the same time, also allows the body to produce more ATP, the 'fuel' muscles need to move. We synthesise more protein from the food we consume. In eating protein rich steak, the body might normally absorb about 2% or 3% of the protein goodness, the rest of the protein is excreted out of the body in your number 2's. Athletes taking anabolic steroids are able to absorb more than 90% of the protein eaten.

The taxonomy of somatotyping was developed in the 1940's by American psychologist William Herbert Sheldon. He named the three body types after the three germ layers of embryonic development. The Endomorph (fat person) after the endoderm, (develops into the digestive tract). The Mesomorph is muscular and named after the mesoderm, (becomes muscle, heart and blood vessels), and finally the Ectomorph (tall and thin person) is named after the ectoderm (forms the skin and nervous system).

Presidential decree.

US president, Richard Nixon is thought to have once offered tactics to the Redskins vs. 49ers. The tactic involved a trick play. The 49ers defence read the play at the snap of the ball and turned it into a 13-yard loss. The subsequent field goal was blocked and Washington went on to lose 24–20. In the postgame analysis, one player claimed that the coach had received 'executive orders' to call the play.

The first black professional football player was Arthur Wharton. He was born on the Gold Coast, now Ghana. He was Rotherham United's goalkeeper way back in 1889.

The golf cart was invented the in the 1940's for players with disabilities as a way of getting around the course.

The super bowl trophy costs $25,000 to manufacture.

In Uruguay, July 31st is a national holiday. The reason for the holiday is a celebration of them winning the inaugural football world cup in 1930.

Can throwing a round heavy object as far as you can be classed as a sport? Discus.

1000 year wait.

The current waiting list for a Green Bay Packers season ticket is about 1000 years!

In the sports of running, swimming, motorsports and cycling, slipstreaming can give you a valuable advantage. By cycling in somebody's slipstream, you use about 30% less energy than the person in front.

Baseball's National League was born in 1876. Eight competing baseball teams met in New York City's Grand Central hotel. The original eight cities with teams were: Boston, Chicago, Cincinnati, New York, Philadelphia, St Louis, Louisville and Hartford. Only two of the original teams currently play in the American League and they are Boston and New York.

President Dwight D. Eisenhower was a massive golf enthusiast, so much so that he had a putting green installed on the White House lawn.

Edson Arantes do Nascimento's nickname is Pelé. Some say he got this from the skill he had at Pelada. Which is a street game of football played in Brazil.

In 1978, Bucky Cox ran the marathon in 5 hours and 29 minutes. What's so special about that? Well, he was only five years old!

Aston Villa was founded by cricketers. It was in 1874 that players from Villa Cross Wesleyan Chapel cricket team discussed how to keep fit during the winter months. They saw a football game being played and decided it was the perfect solution.

Football is often called soccer around the world. This was coined by Charles Wreford Brown way back in 1863. At the time in Oxford University, students made names for lots of things such as 'rugger' for rugby and 'soccer' for association football.

☺ If horse racing is the "sport of kings", is drag racing the sport of queens?

⚒ JFK's golf clubs sold for an incredible $772,500 at a 1996 auction. The person who won the auction was none other than Arnold Schwarzenegger.

You're going home in a horse drawn ambulance.

⚽ England is often credited for hooligans in the football game. Indeed, English clubs were banned from European competitions for 5 years because of it. However, in 1AD, the crowd was fighting each other in Pompeii's amphitheatre. The locals and visitors from Nuceria started with verbal abuse of each other, then stone throwing started and eventually they were fighting each other with weapons. As a result of the violence, Emperor Nero banned sports gatherings for 10 years.

⚛ The custom of carrying the Olympic flame from Greece to the host city started in 1936 when Adolf Hitler's Berlin Olympics were the first to do so.

✂ There are two types of rowing. They are sculling and sweeping. In sculling, the rowers have an oar in each hand, whilst in sweep rowing, they have both hands on a single oar.

⚛ In the ancient Olympics, there were no photo finishes or timekeeping devices to record the winner and so a group of judges were used. They would deliberate on who was the winner and then cast a secret vote to determine the winner. There were cases of the wrong athlete being awarded the win.

♔ Combining professional football and cricket hardly distinguishes Chris Balderstone. What does make him unique is that on one day in September 1975 he turned out for Leicestershire (in cricket) during the day and in the evening played for Doncaster Rovers. The next day he returned to the crease to score a century against Derbyshire and take three for 28 in a match his team won with five minutes to spare. After celebrating Leicestershire's first county championship title, he ran out for Doncaster again the following Saturday. Balderstone became a first-class umpire on retirement.

⊘ JPR Williams was one of rugby unions greatest full back's, he was also a Wimbledon junior champion in 1966. He was a trained surgeon, he once stitched up a hole in his own cheek before returning to the field against New Zealand. I lived on the same street as him in Teddington.

⚛ In the ancient Olympics, women were not allowed to compete. Indeed, they were not even allowed to watch! It was thought that their presence would defile Olympia's oldest shrine to Rhea, the mother of Zeus. Any women found attending would be thrown off a cliff! The only exception to this was the mother of an athlete named Pisodorus. She snuck in wearing men's clothes and pretended to be one of the judges, when her son won and she jumped up excitably and the men's clothing fell off. She was pardoned because her son had won in such style. To prevent a reoccurrence, the judges from then on were required by law to judge the event naked!

Tennis great, Bjorn Borg won a table tennis tournament at the age of nine and he was given a tennis racket by his father as a reward. It was only after this, the Borg lost interest in his favourite sport of ice hockey.

Frisbee gets its name after William Russell Frisbee opened 'the Frisbee Pie Factory' in 1871. Yale students adopted the name for the lid of the pie tin that was then thrown to each other after the pie was eaten.

Sugar Ray Robinson, the five times world middleweight champion acquired his name by accident. His first amateur fight was as a last-minute replacement for another boxer. At the time, he had no official registration card and used the card of a previously retired boxer Ray Robinson. He won and never changed his registration card. His real name was Walker Smith! It doesn't quite sound as good, 'Sugar Walker Smith.'

What do you call someone who is bad at sports but likes to participate? A try athlete.

Fosbury flopped.

Dick Fosbury invented the highest high jumping technique 'the Fosbury Flop'. However, he never set a world record using his own technique!

In the 1974 football world cup hosted by Germany, Zaire somewhat abused the transport privilege when they were caught trying to use the official bus to take them all the way back to Zaire!

Whilst playing for the New York Yankees, Babe Ruth won 4 out of 15 World Series. A return of about 25%. The Yankees have won a total of 27 championships in 113 years. A return of about 25%! Yogi Berra, however, won 72% of the World Series he played in, winning 13 in 18 seasons.

William Webb Ellis (aged 15) invented rugby at Rugby school in 1823 when he picked up the ball in a game of football and ran with it. There is an eyewitness to the event who wrote about in the school magazine. Webb Ellis went on to become a vicar and died in 1872 without ever laying claim to being the inventor of the game!

Club Atlético Newell's Old Boys was established in 1903. The name 'old boys' is often used to describe graduates of a school. Newell's was a school in Argentina. The original first team was made of graduates of Newell's School. Lionel Messi was not an old boy of the school!

Last night on ESPN I was watching women's beach volleyball. About three minutes into the game, there was a really bad wrist injury. The doctor said I should be fine in a few days though.

In the 2010 Winter Olympics, cross country skier and favourite for gold, Odd-Bjoern Hjelmeset delivered an under-par performance and when asked for a reason why, he replied he had been watching too much porn!

Less than 100 NBA players have attempted more free throws than basketball legends, Wilt Chamberlain and Shaquille O'Neil both have missed in their careers! Both missed more than 5000 free throws each and only averaged 51.1% and 52.7% success from the line respectively.

Roger Maris hit 61 homers in a season and the pitchers never thought to walk him. Not even once! The reason for this is that Mickey Mantle followed him in the batting line up.

Bob Beamon in the 1968 Mexico games jumped nearly 10% more than the second placed German Klaus Beer, beating him by a massive 71cm! At the height of his long jump, Bob was six feet up in the air!

The first Asian team to take part in the football world cup finals were the Dutch East Indies in 1938.

Don't mess with Elvis.

Elvis Presley was a black belt in karate.

Michael Chang had the audacity to underarm serve in his victory over Ivan Lendl in the 1989 French Open. He isn't the only player to have pulled off this cheeky serve, Martina Hingis did the same to Steffi Graff in 1989. (By the way, Ivan, if you ever read this, I collected you and a couple of others in a TESLA from the Langham in 2015 and took you to the Roehampton club). Also, Australian, Nick Kyrgios likes to sometimes use the serve and some consider he does it to wind his opponent up.

In the 1970 Mexico football world cup, Pelé was about to kick off with the eyes of the world upon him when he signalled to the referee that he needed to tie his laces. The cameras panned in on him and his Puma boots. This exposure saw sales of Puma boots increase significantly.

Unfortunately for the Boston Bruins, somehow, they had their name incorrectly spelt on the Stanley Cup after winning it. Instead of O's, Q's were used and so their name reads BQSTQN BRUINS.

Tennis legend Chris Evert was the top money earner in 1974, there was also a horse named after her who was also top money earner in the horse-racing world.

In the football world cup, the most common score is 1–0, whereas in the English top division (Premier league and its predecessors) it is 1:1!

A man comes into library and asks where he could find books about Everton in the Champions League. "Fairy tales and fantasy are on the second floor, sir."

Everyone knows the great Wilt Chamberlain for his 100-point game and string of basketball records, but less well known is his volleyball ability and he is also inducted into their hall of fame.

Wheelchair tennis great, Esther Vergeer went on a win streak of 470 matches. She finished her career with 700 wins which included four Paralympic golds and 21 Grand Slams. She only ever lost 25 matches in her life!

A 'spitball' is an illegal baseball pitch in which the ball has either saliva, petroleum jelly or some other product that alters the balls original aerodynamics.

Super Bowl XV was a matchup between the American Football Conference champions, the Oakland Raiders and the National Football Conference champions, the Philadelphia Eagles to decide the National Football League champions for the 1980 season. The Raiders defeated the Eagles by the score of 27–10. The Oakland Raiders became the first wild card playoff team to win a Super Bowl.

Kobe Bryant was named by his parents and they named him after the famous beef of Kobe, Japan. His middle name is Bean, and this is after his father's nickname of Jellybean.

A perfect game is the highest score possible of 300 in a game of 10-pin bowling, this is achieved by rolling a strike during every frame. To achieve the perfect score, the player must make 12 strikes in a row. Normally, there are only ten frames in a game. In the tenth frame, the player would be able to make three more strikes. 30 points are possible in a given frame multiplied by 10 frames equals 300.

Why are frogs so good at basketball? They always make the jump shots.

The monkey hangers.

Hartlepool football club are based in the UK and their fans are known as the 'Monkey Hangers', the reason being that during the Napoleonic wars of the early 19th century, a shipwrecked monkey was questioned and suspected of being a French spy! The monkey refused to speak and defend himself and so was hanged by the people of Hartlepool.

In the UK, Olympic podium funding competitors are banded into three categories. They are as follows.

- Band A are medallists at Olympic games or senior world championships or gold medallists at Paralympic games or senior world championships. These sportspersons are awarded up to £28,000 a year.
- Band B must have a minimum of a top eight finish at Olympic games or senior world championships or medallists at Paralympic games or senior world championships. They are eligible for up to £21,500 from the lottery.
- Band C sportspersons have up to £15,000 a year if they are likely to be major championship performers and those who demonstrate the capacity to achieve a medal result at World or Olympic level within four years, but flexibility given to individual sports to set their own criteria.

All the athletes awarded lottery funding are means tested on their incomes and so the well paid and endorsed athletes like Mo Farrah and Andy Murray would not receive any funding.

What's the easiest sport to get into?

Limbo. They don't set the bar very high.

Moses Fleetwood Walker was the first black baseball player to play in the Major League. Walker played one season in 1884 as the catcher of the Toledo Blue Stockings. He then played in the minor leagues until 1889, when professional baseball banned black players. The ban on black players lasted for nearly 60 years! After leaving baseball, Walker became a businessman. A super interesting man with a story, he received a patent in 1891, for an exploding artillery shell.

Whilst playing tennis, if an item of your clothing or the second ball falls to the ground during a rally, a point may be awarded to your opponent or the umpire may rule that the point must be replayed.

Portugal's prolific goal scorer Cristiano Ronaldo has scored at 11 times in the 68th minute of games making this his most productive minute, just beating the 23rd minute where he only managed 10. Don't be fooled by the stats that show his 45th and 90th minutes as the most successful. These minutes include extra time. Over his entire career he has netted in every minute of the 90-minute game.

10 pin bowling techniques include the cranker, who spins the ball using as much wrist as possible, the stroker who lets the ball go smoothly and the helicopter (or UFO), who releases a ball such that it is rotating along a horizontal axis in a counterclockwise motion (for a right-hander) as it moves down the lane.

Argentine Guillermo Stábile represented his country in the 1930 World Cup and ended up with the Golden Boot scoring eight goals in four matches. With this type of goal ratio, you would have thought his international playing days were far from over. However, he was dropped after the tournament and never played for Argentina again. He did though, go on to manage the national team and win six South American titles.

Karate is from India

Karate origins first started in India before spreading to China and then Japan.

A South African referee shot dead a coach and wounded two players who challenged a decision he had made. The incident started with a yellow card being given to a player during a match between two local teams in Kenton-on-Sea on the Eastern Cape in 2004. The yellow card was met with protests from both the coach and the players of the team whose player had just been cautioned. The protests turned into a fight and this in turn led to the referee settling the argument once and for all by killing the coach and shooting two players. As the saying goes, "The referee is always right!"

On June 15th, 1996 Roy Jones Jr beat Eric Lucas in 11 rounds but only after he had played a game of basketball for the Jacksonville Barracudas in the morning, winning 107-94 against the Treasure Coast Tropics. It was reported he made $1.7 million for the fight and $300 from the basketball match.

☺ I'm 45 years old and I just bought my very first sports car. My girlfriend thinks I'm going through a midlife crisis. But what would she know? She's only 18.

ॐ Olga Korbut, the Russian gymnast was 17 years old and only stood 4ft 11in tall (1.49 metres), when she was competing in the 1972 Munich games.

⚽ The 'Golden Boot' awarded to the football world cup highest scorer has never been made of gold. It is just gold coloured. It would be too expensive said the multibillion-pound organisation FIFA.

🚲 The prologue in the Tour de France is a short stage of under 10km. Bradley Wiggins used to smash out 550 watts in what he called 'Prologue Power' in these stages.

ॐ Simone Manuel became the first black female swimmer to win an Olympic title as she shared the women's 100m freestyle gold with Canada's Penny Oleksiak, after a dead heat. In Rio de Janeiro, she not only won the 100m freestyle but also won gold as a member of the 4 x 100m US freestyle relay team.

The French love their wine.

ॐ Prohibition (a ban on alcohol) was in place in the USA in 1932. The French athletes were a bit naughty in the 1932 Los Angeles Games and drank wine with their meals.

⚽ Pelé was named after the American inventor Thomas Edison who was famous for inventing the light bulb. Pelé's real name being Edson Arantes do Nascimento and he did light up the football world.

🚲 The tour rider loses an amazing 5% of their power output overcoming the drag from their helmet. The more aerodynamic tear drop shaped ones are better, but not by much.

∅ In rugby union, if a ball falls off the kicking tee, part of 'Rule 9' states that a player cannot return and put it back on but must first ask permission from the referee.

☺ There is only one sport in which I can get a high score. It's golf.

🎾 Most tennis racquets are strung to between 50 and 70 lbs. Racquets with lower tensions give more power to the racquet and less control. The opposite is found for higher tensioned racquets with are characterised by more control and less power.

When Garrincha and Pelé played together for Brazil, they never lost a game.

Sawgrass has the deadly 17th hole on the Stadium Course. It's estimated that 125,000 balls a year find the water here.

IOC members get paid $7,650 for the three weeks of the Olympic games. Most athletes get paid nothing!

A first-grade teacher can't believe her student isn't super excited about the Super Bowl. "It's a huge event. Why aren't you excited?" "Because I'm not a football fan. My parents love basketball, so I do too," says the student. "Well, that's a lousy reason," says the teacher. "What if your parents were morons? What would you be then?" "Then I'd be a football fan."

Midgets were hired to serve food in the stands to the Chicago Cubs fans. The reason behind the appointments was that no fans would have their views of the field blocked by tall people walking around the stands.

I bet you didn't know that injuries to cheerleaders' heads and spines are more common than all other high school and college sports combined.

In just 60 minutes batting training, Babe Ruth once hit 125 home runs!

The modern pentathlon was based on the skills required of a cavalry courier.

Why did the golfer wear two pairs of pants? A. In case he got a hole in one.

Fastest Illinois Agility Test.

The fastest ever Illinois Agility Test was by Nick Wald. He holds the world record with a time of 10.28 seconds. He ran it on 9th December 2011.

A massive 70% of a cyclist's power output goes into pushing themselves and the bike through the air.

Estádio do Maracanã, is a football stadium in Rio de Janeiro, Brazil. The stadium was used for final game the 1950 world cup final where Uruguay beat Brazil 2–1 and more recently in the Rio de Janeiro Olympics for the opening and closing ceremonies. The stadium is part of a complex that includes an arena known by the name of Maracanãzinho, which means 'The Little Maracanã' in Portuguese. Owned by the Rio de Janeiro state government, it is in the Maracanã neighbourhood where it is located and named after the Rio Maracanã, a now canalised river in Rio de Janeiro.

Craig MacTavish was the tough guy who is known not only just as a St Louis Blues ice hockey player but as the last professional player to play without a helmet during the 1996–97 season. The use of helmets became mandatory in 1979 but players (including Craig) who had signed contracts before this year were allowed to play bare headed under a grandfather clause. A grandfather clause allows people and companies to continue to use or do what they had done before a new rule or regulation has been brought in.

One day, a man came home and was greeted by his wife dressed in stunningly sexy lingerie. "Tie me up," she purred, "And you can do anything you want." So he tied her up and went to watch a football match.

Grandfather clauses in sport include both Bayer Leverkusen and PSV Eindhoven, both the Bundesliga and the Royal Dutch Football Association prohibit corporate ownership of more than 49% of football clubs. The two corporations of Bayer and Philips can maintain their football clubs as their property and names as they were founded before the rules were introduced.

In 1920, Major League baseball prohibited the spitball, at the time there were some professional pitchers who had built their careers on using the spitball, and so the league made an exception for 17 named players, who were permitted to throw spitballs for the rest of their careers. Burleigh Grimes continued throwing legally the outlawed spitball for another 14 years and finally threw the last legal spitball in 1934.

There are two types of wrestling. Freestyle and greco-roman. Both types involve grappling. The key difference though is that in greco-roman wrestlers aren't allowed to grapple below the waist. Also, only men are allowed to participate in the greco-roman events.

The NFL outlawed the one-bar facemask from the 2004 season onwards but allowed existing users to continue to wear them. It was only really kickers that used them, Scott Player was the last player to wear the one-bar facemask and he retired after the 2009 season.

I decided to jump on the treadmill.

I was in the gym earlier and decided to jump on the treadmill. People were giving me weird looks, so I started jogging instead.

The OJ in OJ Simpson stands for Orenthal James.

Real Madrid were defending La Liga champions and signed David Beckham to strengthen for the 2003/04 season. Things were going well but inexplicably they lost every single one of their last five games dropping from first to fourth, behind Valencia, Barcelona and Deportivo de La Coruña.

Do you know how easy it is to fail the pre-fight weigh in? Piece of cake.

To complete the multistage fitness test, you must run an accumulative 4920m and it will take you 21:56 minutes to do so. You will also complete 247 laps and reach a speed of 18.5km per hour or 11.5 miles per hour.

Canoeing is when the person sits or kneels in a central and forward-facing position. They use a single or double-bladed paddle. Kayaking is when the canoeist sits and uses only a double-bladed paddle.

The word 'decathlon' comes from Greek and means 'ten prizes'. It includes four track events and six field ones.

The custom that has become known as spring training isn't called spring training because of the time of year it takes place as you might imagine. It came about when in 1885 the White Sox decided to practice in Hot Springs, Arkansas before the start of the season.

Swimmers find their bodies drag through the water and create drag. Bodysuits reduce drag resistance by 7%, technologies in swimsuit design led to faster times and it is for that reason they were banned.

Club Atlético Huracán from Buenos Aires have the nickname 'Globo', which literally translates to "Balloon". The reason for the nickname is from the Huracán ('Hurricane') balloon flown by Jorge Newbery in 1909. The team's supporters are called "los Quemeros" or translated "the Burners" because the stadium was built on a garbage burning area.

In basketball, if a player breaks the sheet of plexiglass that forms the backboard, the player is given a 'non-unsportsmanlike' conduct technical foul". I'm no expert in English but don't the 'non' and the 'un' cancel each other out? Then we would be left with 'sportsmanlike conduct'?

A sheer coincidence that an American 'FOOTball is about a foot long!

The official name of the Maracanã stadium is the Mário Filho.

Send the Guinea Pig out.

Before a kitesurfing competition, a person is sent out to see if the wind is suitable. This person is known as the 'Guinea Pig' or 'Wind-Dummy'.

A home run is often the result of hitting the ball out of the park, the rule states that the player still has to round the bases. Also, they must keep to their batting order. If the runner on first, passes the second base runner in this ceremony the home run is nullified. This is still case even if a player is injured whilst running.

In the 1912 Stockholm Olympics, boxing was not one of the sports contested. The reason, boxing was then illegal in Sweden.

The "oche" is the line from which a darts player must stand behind when throwing. It is 7ft 9¼in (2.37m) from the front of the board. The quickest way of scoring points is to hit the triple 20, however this area worth 60, only measures 259mm² and is less than 1% of the dartboard itself. The origin of the word 'oche', is thought to have come into use in the 1920's. It was originally spelled 'hockey', only becoming 'oche' in the late 1970's when excitable TV commentators from the north of England would pronounce it this way. The reason it was the word "hockey" was that the News of the World (an English newspaper) held and reported on darts tournaments. This newspaper used the word "hockey" for the throwing line in their tournament rules. "Hockey" might be derived from the old English word of "hocken" meaning "to spit". In the bars of English public houses (pubs), spitting competitions were held, and that the "hockey line" was how far a competitor could spit with their back against the wall.

Why can't orphans play baseball? They don't know where home is.

The Socceroos (the Australian football/ soccer team) were playing Rhodesia, in the 1970 Mexico World Cup qualifiers in Mozambique, some of the team asked for help from a witch doctor before the game. The witch doctor put a curse on the opposition and buried bones near the goal-posts. Australia went on to beat Rhodesia 3–1. Everything was going fine until the witch doctor demanded £1000 for his services. The team couldn't come up with the money and so the witch doctor subsequently cursed the Australian team. Afterwards, the Socceroos failed to beat Israel and did not qualify for the world cup.

Between 1928 and up to Rome 1960, India won a record six field hockey Olympic golds. The team to finally end their remarkable win streak was none other than their bitterest rivals. Pakistan!

Why can't you play soccer in the jungle? There're too many cheetahs!

Harold Abrahams famously won the Paris 1924 blue riband event of the 100m. However, he wasn't the first athlete in his family. His elder brother,

Sidney Abrahams, competed without success in the 1906 Intercalated games of 1906 and in Stockholm six years later.

The blue ribband (sometimes called the blue ribbon) is a symbol of high quality. It is a prize awarded for the fastest crossing of the Atlantic Ocean by a passenger liner. Prior to that from Cordon Bleu, which referred to the blue ribbon worn by French exceptional chefs. It has transferred into sport meaning the most prestigious or important event.

The great Arnold Palmer was the last Ryder Cup player-captain, he led the USA to victory both on and off the course in 1963. Something a bit more interesting was that he picked himself for every session. He won 3½ out of a possible five points that year.

The bull's eye target wasn't originally used in archery, traditionally archers would aim at trees! The bull's eye was first used in shooting as targets for rifle and handgun competitions.

In the NHL, teams are allowed to hire a temporary player, provided he plays for free!

Whilst cycling, your wheels contribute just about 4% of total drag. This figure reduces to 2% if the wheels are solid carbon disks. There are no spokes in these wheels and, therefore, less air turbulence is created.

American football teams can play with just 8 players.

In American football, a team's offensive line up can have no more than 11 players at the snap, but the offense can play with as little as eight players if they want.

Squash ball colours explained – the hotter the temperature the faster the ball will travel.

- Double yellow dot – slowest ball and used in competitions
- White ball – used on a glass exhibition court in competitions
- Single yellow dot – a bit slower than the red dot.
- Red – fastest ball, used by beginners.

I was at a party last night and got talking to a leading expert in the use of drugs in sport. He told me about a female Bulgarian athlete who had used so much steroids in the 70's that she started to grow the beginnings of a penis. "Anabolics?" I asked. "No," he said, "Just a penis."

Originally, a furlong represented the distance that a team of oxen could plough a furrow, (which is a long shallow trench in a field ready for planting) before they had to rest. It became standardised to an eighth of a mile. It is thought that the word furlong started to be used in horse racing because races were run alongside ploughed fields and therefore distance were assessed by measuring the number of furlongs run past in those neighbouring ploughed fields.

Vanderlei de Lima was given the honour of lighting the Olympic cauldron at the opening ceremony of the 2016 Rio de Janeiro Olympics. He is best known for winning a bronze medal at the 2004 Olympics. Vanderlei was attacked by a spectator, Cornelius Horan, whilst he was leading the race by nearly a minute at the 35K mark of the marathon. His momentum was ruined, and he started to suffer leg cramps. He struggled to the finish line in 3rd place. De Lima danced across the finish line and congratulated the winner and silver medallist. De Lima was praised after the race for his demeanour and awarded the Pierre de Coubertin prize for sportsmanship. The Brazilian federation filed an appeal to name Vanderlei Cordeiro de Lima as a co-winner of the race due to the circumstances, but the appeal was denied.

Argentina shouldn't be called the Pumas.

The Argentina rugby union team is nicknamed Los Pumas because of the animal used as the team's emblem. That animal, however, is a jaguar and not a puma!

The rule in volleyball states that if the volleyball hits any permanent part of the ceiling, then it is deemed to be out. Should it hit a temporary object such a flag hanging from the ceiling then the point is void and the referee will give the two thumbs up replay the point signal.

Tyrone Bogues, better known as Muggsy Bogues, played for Washington Bullets, Charlotte Hornets, Golden State Warriors and finally the Toronto Raptors. His height in a sport of giants was just 1.6m.

On Nov 20th, 1977, the day Walter Payton broke OJ Simpson's record for most rushing yards in a single game, Walter was suffering from the flu. He said afterwards, "I had hot and cold flashes on Wednesday and felt weak," he continued, "I didn't even think I was going to play. You put your faith in God and he'll take care of you. I was hoping he would do so today, and he did." He ran for 275 yards on 40 carries in a game that helped Chicago advance to the playoffs. He was also asked after the game how the defence might best have stopped him. His advice to them was to have kidnapped him the night before!

Catch a crab.

A crab is the term rowers use when the oar blade gets "caught" in the water. It is caused by a poor oar technique. Anyone who has rowed competitively will have experienced one. The result of catching a crab could be severe enough to break the nose of the rower and be so forceful that the rower is thrown from the boat. It is often the case that crews must cease rowing for the rower to regain control of the oar.

Which goalie can jump higher than the crossbars? All of them. Crossbars can't jump.

The golden goal is a possible way that overtime in a football match could be finished. The first team to score wins the game immediately. This method has been tried in major tournaments and is not liked by the media because of the uncertainty of the finish time. It lost favour and most tournament football now has 30 minutes extra time and possibility of penalties as a final determiner.

An Ippon, (一本), is the highest score a fighter can achieve in a Japanese martial arts ippon-wazari contest. It means 'one full point'. Ippons are usually found in the kendo, judo, karate and jujutsu martial arts.

What's the difference between a pickpocket and an umpire? One steals watches and one watches steals.

Former England football manager Sven Goran Eriksson had a passion for ski jumping. As a teenager, his best leap of 75 metres is four metres further than Great Britain's most famous ski jumper, Eddie the Eagle. Eddie made his British record jump at the winter Olympics in 1988. Eriksson was the first foreign manager to be appointed coach of the England national team. He led England to the quarterfinals in the 2002 World Cup where they lost to Brazil, 2-1.

The "Curse of Billy Penn" is probably the reason the Philadelphia 76ers failed to win a basketball championship after beating the LA Lakers in the 1983 NBA finals. There are some that believe that the city's breaking of a gentlemen's agreement in 1987, that buildings could not be higher than the statue of William Penn on the top of the spire of City Hall. William Penn was an English real estate entrepreneur, philosopher, early Quaker and founder of the Province of Pennsylvania. Because buildings were built higher than the statue, the curse was put on the team. Builders of the Comcast Centre which finished construction in 2007 and became Philadelphia's tallest building managed to remove the curse put on the city by attaching a small figure of

William Penn to top of the building. The following season, the Philadelphia Phillies won the 2008 World Series.

Nike is the name for the Greek goddess of victory.

The worst penalty taker?

Despite missing 2 penalties in Spain's draw against Switzerland in 2020. Sergio Ramos isn't the worst for missing penalties. Martin Palermo infamously missed three penalties for Argentina against Colombia in 1999. Incidentally, Ramos scored his 25 previous consecutive attempts.

A man went to the doctor one day and said: "I've just been playing rugby and when I got back I found that when I touched my legs, my arms, my head, my tummy and everywhere else, it really hurt." The doctor gave him the once over and told him, "You've broken your finger."

The Unlawful Games Act 1541, was an Act of the Parliament of England, designed to prohibit 'Several new devised games' such as football and tennis that caused as the government said, 'the decay of archery'. It stated that all men under the age of sixty years 'shall have bows and arrows for shooting'. Children between seven and seventeen were required to have a bow and two arrows. Men seventeen years and older were forced to keep a bow and four arrows. The penalty for breaking the law was a fine of 6s.8d. The Act was replaced by the Betting and Gaming Act 1960. This new Act (amongst several other things) forbade all sport on Christmas Day with the exception of archery.

After Nigeria was unable to win any medals in Rio Olympics, the Nigerian Sports Minister personally offered to refund all the expenses of fans that traveled to Brazil. He said he just needs their bank details and pin numbers to complete the transaction.

Sports minister is sorry.

The word 'doping' which we now associate with cheating in sport comes from the early 19th century in Holland where doop is a 'sauce', and from doopen which is 'to dip or mix'.

The much-feared 'burpee' got its name in the 1930's. The exercise was named after Royal H Burpee, who was an American psychologist. The original usage was the 'burpee test', which was designed to measure agility and coordination.

Around 50 competitors remained in Australia illegally after going missing during the Melbourne 2006 Commonwealth games. Additionally, nearly 200 others applied for refugee status. During the Gold Coast games of 2018, 11 athletes disappeared!

If you are seven-foot-tall and live in the USA, you have a one in seven chance of becoming an NBA player!

What is the noisiest sport? Racquetball

The first known use of the expression 'Grand Prix' was the French Grand Prix de Paris, an international horse race established in 1863. Literally it translates to the grand prize of Paris. Now it is used in numerous sports around the globe.

You cannot replace football goal keepers during a penalty shootout unless the keeper is injured. There have been instances of goalkeepers being substituted in the last minute of regulation or extra time in preparation of the shootout.

A golf club's shaft length must be greater than 18 inches but not more than 48 inches.

The reason Uruguay held the first football world cup was that they were the only country not to withdraw from the bidding process. Italy, Sweden, Spain, Hungary and the Netherlands all wanted to host the 1930 world cup but withdrew due to economic reasons. There was a stock market crash in 1929. For political reasons England had resigned from FIFA and weren't eligible to play or host, even though they were the inventors of the game. Uruguay who had great economic prosperity at the time offered to pay the travel expenses of European teams, despite this generosity only 4 teams travelled. They were France, Romania, Yugoslavia and Belgium.

Where referees came from.

The word 'referee' originated in association football. In the old days the sport of football was played by gentlemen, any disputes would be resolved by the two captains on the pitch. As the sport evolved, the captains had to concentrate on playing and they were replaced by umpires. Each team would bring their own. Sometimes these two partisan umpires couldn't agree on a decision and so (later) a third neutral official was introduced. This official would be 'referred to' if the umpires could not resolve a dispute, and so the referee was born. The referee did not take his place on the pitch until 1891, and the two club supplied umpires became linesmen, now assistant referees.

- The 'Panenka' is a technique used while taking a penalty kick in which the taker, instead of kicking the ball with force or precision to the left or right of the goalkeeper gently lobs the ball straight down the centre. Goal keepers normally commit to one side or another when attempting a penalty save and so would be unable to adjust quick enough to save the penalty. It was first believed to have been used by Czech player Antonín Panenka, in the 1976 UEFA European Championship final, when he beat West German goalkeeper Sepp Maier to win the championship for the Czechoslovakian national team. However, it really should be called the 'Meredith' because Billy Meredith used the technique about 70 years earlier whilst playing for Manchester City.

- The Panenka penalty kick is also called:

  - Il cucchiaio 'the spoon' in the Italy
  - Cavadinha 'little dig' in Brazil
  - Penal picado 'poked penalty kick' in Argentina.

- The first ever volleyball was made from the bladder of a basketball.

- The Ballon d'Or, the award for the world's best football player could only be won by a European player until 1995.

Air dribbling

- Back in the olden days of basketball, people could air dribble. Instead of regular dribbling (bouncing the ball on the ground), players would bounce the ball up in the air with their hands and move.

- In race-walking, the rules state that you are supposed to keep one foot on the ground at all times. But this rule is commonly broken because the rule is so hard to implement. A warning system is put in place and competitors are given 3 warning before disqualification.

- A woman goes into a sporting goods store to buy a shotgun. "It's for my husband," she tells the clerk "Did he tell you what gauge to get?" asked the clerk. "Are you kidding?" she says. "He doesn't even know that I'm going to shoot him!"

- If you injure yourself rounding the bases after a home run in baseball or softball you are not allowed to receive assistance from your own teammates and must get round anyway. There is a story of a collegiate softball player who tore her ACL (anterior cruciate ligament) while rounding the bases and wasn't allowed any assistance by her own team. In an excellent example of sportsmanship, the other team's players helped her touch all the bases.

Golfers have to sign their scorecards, or else they are disqualified.

In show jumping, horses cannot have cuts on their legs. There is a belief that the possible pain from hitting the cuts helps the horse jump higher.

Leave your opponent's balls alone.

There is only one ball allowed to be touched in water polo! Any touching or grabbing of the opponent's groin is grounds for removal. Another rule is that you cannot splash water in your opponent's face.

In the unlikely event a pitched baseball is lodged into the umpire's mask, all runners advance one base.

Patient: Doctor, please, please help me. I keep thinking I'm John McEnroe! Doctor: You cannot be serious!

In gymnastics, competitors bras and underwear have to either be nude-coloured or the same colour as their leotard. If not, fractions of a point may be deducted.

A college freshman decided to try out for the football team. "Can you tackle?" asked the coach. "Watch this," said the freshman, who proceeded to run smack into a telephone pole, shattering it to splinters. "Wow," said the coach. "I'm impressed. Can you run?" "Of course, I can run," said the freshman. He was off like a shot, and, in just over nine seconds, he had run a hundred-yard dash. "Great!" enthused the coach. "But can you pass a football?" The freshman hesitated for a few seconds. "Well, sir," he said, "if I can swallow it, I can probably pass it."

In chess there is a rule that says you must wear undistracting clothes and a female can lose a chess match should she show too much cleavage. Judges are tasked with deciding whether amount of cleavage is distracting to the opponent.

After a fair catch in American football, your team can opt to try an uncontested field goal. This option isn't taken often as most catches happen deep in their own half.

In tennis, if you were wearing a hat and it falls off, your opponent can say that it was a distraction and negate the point.

There's something called the ground-rule triple in baseball. If someone tries to catch the ball with their hat, the batter is awarded third base.

☺ Jose Mourinho was caught speeding on his way to the Tottenham Hotspur stadium today. "I'll do anything for three points," he said when questioned.

⊛ If you were to take your football boot off and hit the football with it then that is considered to be a handball.

🚲 A women's one-day cycle race in Belgium was temporarily halted after breakaway leader Nicole Hanselmann just about caught the men's race. The men's Omloop Het Nieuwsblad race started 10 minutes before the women but Hanselmann started to catch the back of the men's support vehicles after just 35km due to her breakaway. Unfortunately for her, the race organisers "neutralised" the women's race to recreate a gap between the men's and women's races.

Longest football club name.

⊛ The longest football club name in the world is: Nooit opgeven altijd doorgan, Aangenaam door vermaak en nuttig door ontspanning, Combinatie Breda. Luckily the Dutch Eerste Divisie side is more commonly known as NAC Breda.

⊛ Dundee united have an 100% record against Barcelona. They have won all four games against the giants.

☺ What's the difference between basketball players and soccer players? Basketball players get actual injuries.

⊛ Nawaaf Al-Abed scored after just 2.4 seconds, making it the fastest football goal ever recorded. Nawaaf was playing for Al Hilal v Al Shoulla in the Saudi Arabian Prince Faisal u21 Cup. Unfortunately, his spectacular halfway strike was for nothing because Al Hilal fielded more than 6 over aged players and the match was cancelled!

☺ Sarah was reading a newspaper whilst her husband was engrossed in a magazine. Suddenly, she burst out laughing. "Listen to this," she said. "There's a classified ad here where a guy is offering to swap his wife for a season ticket to the stadium." "Hmmm," her husband said, not looking up from his magazine. Teasing him, Sarah said, "Would you swap me for a season ticket?" "Absolutely not," he said. "How sweet," Sarah said. "Tell me why not." "Season's more than half over," he said.

✗ Flamengo from Rio de Janiero, Brazil is actually a rowing club!

⊕ The oxygen levels are 15% less at 1800m than they are at sea level. This makes any physical effort more difficult.

The world toughest 2-day race.

The Barkley Marathons is certainly the world's toughest 2 ½ day race. It was inspired by the failed jail break by James Earl Ray, the man convicted of the assassination of civil rights activist Martin Luther King. In the 55 hours whilst on the run Ray only covered 8 miles (13 km). Ultra-runner Cantrell believed he could cover at least 100 miles in the time it took Ray to be found. The Barkley Marathons are held in Frozen Head State Park, Tennessee. Runners can opt for the 60-mile (97 km) fun run or attempt the full course which is approximately 100 miles (160 km). The race is limited to a 60-hour period. Only 15 runners have ever completed the course and some years there isn't a single finisher!

What would you call one of the world's greatest ice hockey players if he'd decided not to play hockey? Wayne Regretsky.

The law regarding running out a batsman backing up at the non-striker's end is known as 'Mankading'. This is where the bowler stumps the non-striking batsman (who often stray out of their crease) out whilst they are in the process of bowling. The controversial dismissal method is known as a 'Mankad' after India bowler Vinoo Mankad who ran out Australia batsman Bill Brown in 1947.

The Greek word for prize.

The word athlete derives Greek athlein meaning to 'compete for a prize', and from athlon meaning 'prize'. Athletes in ancient Greece were 'prizefighters, contestants in the games.'

In the multibillion-pound football industry, Accrington Stanley were investigated by the English Football League for allegedly recompensing their players illegally by buying them a McDonalds meal each if they won! All rewards, both financial and physical must be declared to the Governing body at the beginning of each season. Accrington Stanley omitted the McDonald's rewards.

Two old men, Abe and Sol, sit on a park bench feeding pigeons and talking about baseball. Abe turns to Sol and asks, "Do you think there's baseball in Heaven?" Sol thinks about it for a minute and replies, "I dunno. But let's make a deal — if I die first, I'll come back and tell you if there's baseball in Heaven, and if you die first, you do the same." They shake on it and sadly, a few months later, poor Abe passes on. Soon afterward, Sol sits in the park feeding the pigeons by himself and hears a voice whisper, "Sol... Sol... ." Sol responds, "Abe! Is that you?" "Yes, it is, Sol," whispers Abe's ghost. Sol, still amazed, asks,

"So, is there baseball in Heaven?" "Well," says Abe, "I've got good news and bad news." "Gimme the good news first," says Sol. Abe says, "Well, there is baseball in Heaven." Sol says, "That's great! What news could be bad enough to ruin that?" Abe sighs and whispers, "You're pitching on Friday."

In 2018 the Greek football league was temporarily suspended because the owner of PAOK Salonika invaded the pitch whilst being armed with a gun!

He just wanted to buy them a coffee.

Disgraced Olympic champion Asbel Kiprop from Kenya said he paid money to drug testers because he wanted to buy them a cup of tea, he certainly was not looking to bribe them.

A golfer was addressing his ball, getting ready to shoot. Just as he was about ready to hit, a voice came over the pa system – "Will the gentleman on the lady's tee please move back to the men's tee." He looked up, looked back down and then resumed addressing the ball again. The voice again – "Will the man on the red tees PLEASE MOVE BACK to the white tees?" He looked back at the starters shack and yelled, "Will the IDIOT on the pa shut up so that the man on the lady's tee can hit his second shot?"

David McNamara who was the referee officiating a women's football match between Manchester City and Reading forgot his coin for the toss and so used his initiative. He had the captains play rock, paper, scissors to determine kick off and ends. Some people would have thought this was a fair and sensible thing to do but not the referees association who hit him with a three-week suspension!

Serena Williams could not have possibly received coaching in the controversial US Open incident because she has a daughter! As she crashed to a 6-2 6-4 defeat at Flushing Meadows, Williams was warned for illegal coaching, penalised a point for breaking a racquet, before being docked a game for verbal abuse of chair umpire Carlos Ramos. Serena called the Portuguese official "a liar" and "a thief" as she broke down into tears on the court. In the defence to the allegation of cheating she somewhat bizarrely referenced her baby daughter as a reason why she would not have received the illegal coaching.

You cannot be serious!

Did you hear John McEnroe went for an audition for the latest Harry Potter film? They turned him down, saying "You cannot be Sirius!"

During the 1936 Berlin Games, Shuhei Nishida and Sueo Oe, two Japanese pole-vaulters who happened to be good friends tied for second place. Instead of competing again in a jump off they refused to compete anymore and upon their return to Japan, they cut the silver and bronze medals they received in half and fused the two different halves together so that each of them had a half-silver and half-bronze medal.

The Olympic torch is lit the old-fashioned way in an ancient ceremony at the temple of Hera, in Greece. The IOC recreate the whole Olympic tradition with actresses, wearing costumes of Greek priestesses. A parabolic mirror and the sun rays kindle (light) the torch.

The Stanley Cup existed before the NHL was formed! Canadian Governor General Lord Stanley of Preston was the benefactor and namesake on the Stanley Cup which was created in 1893. It was not until 1917 that the NHL was formed.

Super Bowl winning teams' players aren't the only ones to receive prestigious Super Bowl rings. All the NFL referees who officiate the final get rings.

The 2012 London games were the first Olympics in which all participating countries sent female athletes.

Up until 1914, ice hockey referees were really in the line of fire because rules stated that they had to place (with their hand!) the hockey puck on the ice between both centres' sticks. Being so close to the violent start of the game and with so many referees getting hand injuries the NHL changed the rule in 1914. Referees were able simply to drop the puck between the centres' sticks.

Ignorance or apathy?

Coach "Is your bad play due to ignorance or apathy?" Player "I don't know and I don't care!"

Unbelievable but true, a Swedish hockey player scored a goal by squatting in the net to dislodge the puck that was stuck in his hockey pants.

After setting the world record for most tennis hits in an hour where they managed 8156, the brothers Frank and Dennis Furhmann then went on to hit 50,970 strokes in a single rally!

In 1981, AAA baseball teams the Pawtucket Red Sox and the Rochester Red Wings took to the field. They ended up playing 33 innings. The game lasted a total of 8 hours and 25 minutes, making it the longest game of baseball ever played.

☺ "Did you hear the joke about the fast pitch?" "Forget it. You just missed it."

🏒 With a nickname, 'Le Magnifique' you know he has to be good. Mario Lemieux was very good, amongst many records he set, one was that he scored 5 goals in a unique way in a single game on December 31st, 1988. He scored an even-strength goal, followed by a short-handed goal, then a power-play goal, then a penalty shot goal, before finally putting one into the empty net with one second remaining.

☺ Harry walked over to the priest after services, "You know Father, I am really stuck in a quandary. I would like to attend church next week but I just can't miss the big game next Sunday, it's just out of the question." "Oh Harry," said the Priest putting his arm around Harry, "don't you know? With the technology we have nowadays you can record things and watch at a later date." Harry's face lit up. "You mean I could record your sermon?"

🏒 Ken Daneyko, New Jersey Devils longest serving player won three Stanley Cups, something not a lot of players can boast. But he holds another distinction. Daneyko scored a goal in February 1999 and didn't score again for more than 3 years until October 2002. That's a drought of 255 games, the most in NHL history.

🏎 Since Ayrton Senna death on May 1st, 1994 every single F1 car Williams has produced has had a memorial to Senna on it. They will have either Ayrton's face or logo on them in remembrance.

🎳 Some of us are lucky to get one strike in an entire game of bowling. Chad McLean of Florida got 12 tenpin strikes in just one minute in 2013.

Most FA cup replays.

⚽ Lincoln City and Coventry City were set to play an FA Cup soccer match against each other on January 5th 1963. However, the game was postponed due to heavy snowfall, and then postponed again, and again, and again! The two teams did not play each other until March 6th, after 63 days and an incredible 15 postponements.

🏀 The first game of basketball ever played took place on December 21st, 1891. It also holds another distinction. It was the lowest scoring game ever. The final score was 1-0. Dr. Luther Gulick, head of physical education at the School for Christian Workers (later renamed Springfield College), asked

Naismith to create an indoor game that would provide an "athletic distraction" for a rowdy class through the brutal New England winter.

Two hunters are walking through a forest looking for deer. When all of a sudden, a giant bear jumps out and scares them silly. They drop their guns and run like hell. One of the hunters stopped, opened up his backpack and laced up a pair of tennis shoes. His buddy looked at him and said, "What are you doing? Are you crazy? You can't outrun the bear!" To this the hunter said, "I know, all I have to do is outrun you!"

When the Detroit Pistons and the Denver Nuggets played each other on December 13th, 1983, they set quite a few NBA records. The triple overtime game had the highest score by a single team ever, highest score by a losing team and most points scored total, to name just a few. The final score was Detroit 186, Denver 184. Another interesting fact about this game is that Isiah Thomas for the Pistons and Richard Anderson for the Nuggets scored the game's only 2, 3-point shots!

Manute Bol not only was the joint tallest NBA player of all time but he also the tallest jockey of all time. He was licensed as a jockey by the Indiana Racing Commission as part of a fundraising event. As for real jockeys that actually raced horses, the tallest ever was probably Stuart Brown from Australia, who was 187cm, or about 6'3".

On April 29th, 2004, Christopher Bergland set the world record for distance running, on a treadmill. In 24 hours, he ran 153.76 miles, burning about 24,000 calories. But does it still count as long distance running if he didn't actually go anywhere?

Can you make it with a 5 iron?

Golfer: "Do you think I can get there with a 5-iron?" Caddy: "Eventually."

The average NBA basketball player is somewhere around 6'7". Muggsy Bogues, who played 14 seasons in the league, was 5'3", the shortest player ever. At different points in his career, he played with Manute Bol and Gheorghe Muersan, who both stood 7'7". Two feet and 4 inches is the biggest height difference ever between two players on an NBA court.

The record time for running a half marathon while pushing a stroller is 1 hour, 11 minutes and 27 seconds, set by Canadian Calum Neff in 2016. If you fancy a crack at this time you must be eligible, and this means the runner has to push the stroller the entire time and also there needs to be a baby in it. Neff pushed his 11-month-old daughter, Holland.

In 2012 Amadei Weiland from Germany ran 11 feet, 5.4 inches sideways and along a wall.

During a 2004 NBA basketball game between the Indiana Pacers and the Detroit Pistons, an all-out brawl broke out between the two teams. It would go down as the infamous "Malice at the Palace." The worst offender was Ron Artest who charged the stands and started throwing punches at a fan who threw a drink at him. That was enough to get Ron a full-season suspension, including the 73 remaining games and 13 playoff games; it was the longest suspension ever handed it out in the NBA.

Usain Bolt is the fastest person on two legs, but what about four? In 2014, Japan's Kenichi Ito 'ran' 100m in 15.71 seconds entirely down on all fours (he wore special gloves for grip).

Why do basketball players love cookies? Because they can dunk them!

The American, Ray Ewry proved to be the best standing jumper in the world. At his first Olympics, held in Paris (1900), he won gold medals in all three standing of the jumps which were;

- the standing long jump
- the standing triple jump
- and the standing high jump.

Incidentally, all three finals were held on the same day. Ewry was born in Beatrice, Nebraska and died in St. Louis, Missouri. Ewry currently holds the record for the most Olympic medals with a 100% record. 8 events entered, 8 individual golds won.

Oliver Kirk is the only boxer in Olympic history to ever win two gold medals in two separate weight divisions at the same games. In the 1904 St Louis games, Kirk first won gold in the featherweight and then shed almost 10 pounds in under two days to win gold in the bantamweight category. Kirk only had to win two fights to capture his two gold medals, in the bantamweight class only two boxers competed. In the featherweight class there were three boxers with Kirk earning the bye in the first round.

Ugly letter L.

The only Super Bowl game to not use Roman numerals was Super Bowl 50. The Roman numeral for 50 is L, and, because NFL ad designers felt that the 'Super Bowl L' title was too unattractive and unmarketable, they opted to use the number 50 instead.

What does a basketball player do once they lose their sight? They become a referee.

Stanislaw Kowalski was born in 1910. He began running at the spry age of 92, and in 2014 he set the record for being the oldest person in Europe to run a 100m race, finishing in 32.79 seconds at 104 years old. Over a century old and he is still running races.

In the UK, sports injuries account for about 2% of accident & emergency cases.

Why should you never date tennis players? To them, love means nothing.

According to research, football teams wearing red shirts have an advantage thanks to our deep-rooted biological response to the colour. Humans have a tendency to avoid the colour red or act submissively in its presence.

Doctor: "Do you do sports?" Patient: "Does sex count?" Doctor: "Yes." Patient: "Then no."

In 1906, the UK parliament banned women from participating in dangerous sports.

In the 1908 London Olympics, teams from United Kingdom police forces won all the medals in the tug-of-war event.

The earliest evidence of sport is depicted in cave paintings in Mongolia that date back to 7000BC. The paintings show crowds watching a wrestling match, but some argue that paintings in the Lascaux caves in France depict wrestling and sprinting as long as 15,000 years ago.

Before the All-England Club at Wimbledon introduced tennis in 1875, it was a croquet club

The word 'sport' was first seen in English in the 15th century. It was a contraction of the word 'disport', meaning a diversion from serious duties.

China didn't win until 1984.

The People's Republic of China (PRC) medal success in the Olympics hasn't always been so. In 1952 they only sent one athlete to the games. They were absent for the Summer games from 1956 until 1980. It was only after their return in 1984 that China won their first ever medal in the Olympics. Their first medal was a gold and it was won by Xu Haifeng in shooting. After this initial success, the floodgates somewhat opened. They won 32 medals that year including 15 golds.

In most American football games, around 10 balls are used in a match, however the home team are obliged to supply 24 in total.

Why do orphans like playing tennis? Because it's the only love they get.

The 1st ever Chinese Olympians were four tennis players, they attended the opening ceremony at the 1924 Olympic Games, but later withdrew from the competition. Nevertheless, this is the first appearance of Chinese people at an Olympic venue.

Boxing has its etymology from the Dutch/German word 'boke' for a blow, a strike or a hit. This dates back to the early medieval period of the 14th century. The English used the term for their organised punching/fighting art that developed around that time. It was originally visitors to England who applied the term 'boke', which the British adopted and subsequently modified to it to 'box'.

Anna Kopchovsky, was the first woman to cycle around the world way back in 1894. She had only learned how to ride a bicycle a few days before she set off. She covered the entire distance in 15 months and received a reward of 10,000 dollars.

During the 2002 soccer world cup, Ahn Jung-Hwan from South Korea scored a goal against Italy in injury time. Unfortunately, this was the goal that knocked the Italians out of the world cup. The next day, his contract with his Italian home club was terminated because the owner said he could not pay the person who had ruined Italian football.

The world record for the most consecutive push-ups was set in 1980 by Minoru Yoshida from Japan who managed to do 10,507 in a row.

Not too long ago, if you were to check the 30 fastest 100-metre sprints in the history of the sport, there are only nine that are not related or tainted by doping. All nine runs were completed by Usain Bolt.

James Fixx, the man credited with the word "jogging" died from a heart attack whilst jogging!

During the 2008 Olympic games in Beijing, it is said that Usain Bolt ate only chicken nuggets, as it was the only meal he recognised from home. Ultimately, he won three gold medals with this diet.

I don't give a toss.

'Fox tossing' was a popular sport in the 16th century in which two people held a 23-foot-long cloth on two opposite sides and then pulled it tight as soon as a fox ran over the cloth so that it flew into the air. The game continued until the animal broke its bones when it hit the ground and was then killed by a hunter.

Each year about 100 million bikes are produced worldwide.

Professional US swimmer Michael Phelps has won more gold medals than 80% of all countries in the history of the Olympic games.

Nissan only uses the number 23 on their race vehicles, since in Japanese number two is pronounced as "ni" and three as "san". Together this gives "ni-san".

Why doesn't the fastest land animal get to participate in any sports? Because he's a cheetah.

During the 1904 Summer Olympics in St. Louis, the American Frederick Lorz was the first to reach the finish line of the marathon race. It turned out, however, that he had covered about half the distance by car.

From 1912 to 1948 architecture was an Olympic discipline.

The game "Quidditch" from the Harry Potter novels is now a recognised sport, with its own leagues and even a world championship!

Octopus-wrestling was a popular trend in the sixties. A diver grapples with an octopus in shallow water and tries to bring it to the surface.

Dick Hoyt and his son Rick, who is fully paralyzed, have completed six Iron Man events together. Dick first swam 2.5 miles, pulling his son in a boat behind him, then rode a bicycle over the roads for 112 miles, before pushing him in a wheelchair for the final 26.2 miles.

Englishman Ben Smith ran 401 marathons in 401 days to raise money for the victims of bullying. With his "401 Challenge" he set a world record and covered a total of 10,506 miles.

In North Korea, basketball is played according to different rules. For example, the team loses points if it doesn't score on free throws and a dunk scores three points instead of the usual two.

I still don't believe it.

- American professional basketball player Shaquille O'Neal scored only one single three-point shot in his entire professional career!

- In 1949, a boxing match was held between boxer Gus Waldorf and a bear. The bear was given a muzzle and boxing gloves to create "fair" conditions for both fighters. In the end, however, it was the bear that won.

- Gladiators in ancient Rome were exclusively fighters who fought against other humans for life and death. People fighting exclusively against animals were called 'Bestiarii'. Also, the thumbs up, thumbs down expressions were from gladiatorial times. They were used slightly differently back then. To get a 'thumbs up' from the crowd was a bad thing because it meant the losing fighter would be spared and allowed to live. Thumbs down was death to the losing gladiator. Gladiators (apparently) wanted to die, if they lost in the arena.

- A blind man was describing his favorite sport-parachuting. When asked how this was accomplished, he said that things were all done for him. "I am placed in the door and told when to jump. My hand is placed on my release ring for me and out I go." "But how do you know when you are going to land?", he was asked. "Well, I have a very keen sense of smell and I can smell the trees and grass when I am 300 feet from the ground", he answered. "But how do you know when to lift your legs for your final arrival on the ground?", he was asked again. He quickly answered, "Oh that? That's the easiest bit. I just wait until the dog's leash goes slack!"

- In Amsterdam there is a gym where you can train naked.

- He's an ambidextrous fighter. He can get knocked out with either hand.

- The longest boxing match in the world took place on 6th April 1893 between Andy Bowen and Jack Burke. The fight went on for 110 rounds and lasted for more than seven hours. In the end, both fighters were too tired and exhausted to keep on fighting.

Originally no hand balls in football.

- Three years after the first football rules were agreed, the handball was introduced.

- In 1957, a lady had to be brought out of a baseball stadium after being hit in the face by a baseball. If the story is to be believed, when the paramedics were carrying her out, a second ball hit her.

In 2002, long-distance runner Tom Johnson competed against a horse in a 50-mile race. He ran the distance in five hours and 45 minutes, arriving ten seconds ahead of the horse.

The official length of a marathon was defined as 26.2 miles because it was exactly the length of the course at the Olympic games in London in 1908 and not because it corresponds to the historical distance between Athens and Marathon. That distance is only about 24.8 miles.

Miguel Indurain, five times Tour de France winner, had a resting heart rate of 28 beats per minute.

Dead rider wins race.

Frank Hayes was a unfortunate jockey who, on the 4th June, 1923, won a steeplechase despite suffering a fatal heart attack in the later part of the race at Belmont Park racetrack in New York, Somehow the dead rider stayed mounted and the horse continued on to win the race.

Archer Matt Stutzman holds the world record for the longest shot with a bow and arrow. He hit the bullseye from a distance of 930 feet. What makes this even more amazing is that Matt Stutzman has no arms and therefore uses the bow with his feet.

When Chinese basketball player Yao Ming first appeared for his new team in Houston, it was celebrated with 8,000 fortune cookies which were distributed to the fans. Ming was more than surprised, as he had never seen a fortune cookie in his life, as fortune cookies are not a Chinese, but an American invention.

Do you remember the Apple ™ advert with Yao Ming on the airplane? Where he easily reaches up, whilst seated, opens the overhead locker and removes his laptop from his bag.

What's harder to catch the faster you run? Your breath, of course.

There are no reported incidents of death by dehydration in the history of world running. But there are cases of people dying because of drinking too much water. A condition called Hyponatremia (abnormally low concentration of sodium in your blood) can be caused by several things including drinking excessive amounts of water. This excess can cause low sodium by overwhelming the kidneys' ability to excrete water. You lose sodium through sweat, and so drinking too much water during endurance activities, such as marathons, cycling and triathlons, can also dilute the sodium content of your blood. Sodium is super important and is an electrolyte, and it helps regulate the amount of water that's in and around your cells.

⚽ Since 1896, football pitches in Germany have had to be free of trees.

May the force be with you.

🤺 In France, the national fencing federation recognised light saber fencing as an official competitive sport in 2019. Instead of saber, foil or sword, the fighters use replicas of light sabers from the film Star Wars.

🏅 Kirani James was the first Olympian to win a gold medal for his home country Grenada. He achieved this in 400m at the London 2012 games. His homeland was so proud of it that there was a huge celebration for him and he was rewarded with over 220,000 euros. Even today he can be found on the country's stamps, a stadium bears his name and his hometown opened a museum about his achievements.

⚽ Before Alex Ferguson took over at Manchester United, Aston Villa were more successful than the Red Devils.

☺ Everyone should stop hating on Lance Armstrong. He won 7 Tour De France's on drugs! When I'm on drugs, I can't even find my bicycle.

⚽ In Gaelic, Pittodrie, the home of Aberdeen football club roughly translates as sh*t heap ('place of manure' or 'hill of dung' to be polite).

⚽ László Kubala is the only football player to play for three different (FIFA recognised) countries. Born to parents of Czech origin in Budapest, Kubala played for Czechoslovakia, Hungary and Spain. Former Real Madrid striker Alfredo Di Stefano played for Argentina, Spain and Colombia, however, his Colombia caps won in the early 1950's came at a time when the country's football association was not officially recognised by FIFA.

☺ Why did the football coach go to the bank? To get his quarter back.

⚽ Jimmy Rimmer is the only player to have won European Cup winners' medals with two different English clubs. He was on the Manchester United bench in 1968 and started for Aston Villa in 1982, however, he was forced off with injury and replaced by Nigel Spink against Bayern Munich.

☺ What does a cricketer and a magician have in common? They both do hat tricks.

Right person, wrong time.

Zlatan Ibrahimovic has played for six clubs that have won the Champions League, but he has never actually won the trophy himself. The striker has been at Ajax, Barcelona, Inter, Juventus, Milan and Man United.

The longest ever game of rugby league (which is normally 80 minutes) lasted 117 minutes. It was between Castleford and Featherstone Rovers in the Challenge Cup. In 1941, a golden point was used for the first-time. The match was 3-3 at full time and after the 20 minutes of extra time the scores were still tied at 5-5. It was decided to determine the winner by the next team to score wins. The game ended after 117 minutes when Castleford scored.

Giuseppe Bergomi played in four football world cups but did not appear in any qualifiers. The former Inter Milan defender played for Italy at the 1982, 1986, 1990 and 1998 world cups without exerting himself in any qualifiers.

How do you say "Floyd Mayweather Jr" in Chinese? Ka Ching.

Tommie C. Smith, is the man probably known best for his black power salute in the Olympic medal presentation of the 1968 games. In these games, Smith, aged 24, won the 200-metre sprint finals and gold medal in a time of 19.83 seconds, the first time the 20 second barrier had been broken. Tommie won gold, the other athlete giving the black power salute was bronze medallist John Carlos. The silver medallist was Australian Peter Norman who was actually wearing a OPHR (Olympic Project for Human Rights) badge in support of the 2 Americans. After these Olympic games Tommie would go onto play for the Cincinnati Bengals as a wide receiver.

The etymology of the word 'umpire' is from the old French nonper (from non, "not" and per, "equal"), meaning "one who is requested to act as arbiter of a dispute between two people", or that the arbiter is not paired with anyone in the dispute.

Before whistles were invented, referees used handkerchiefs to show a decision. Referee whistles were first introduced in 1884. The first whistle used by referees was called the Acme Thunder Whistle. Acme means 'the point at which something is at its best or most highly developed, the pinnacle.' Some people think it means American Companies Make Everything, but that is just true when it is used in cartoons!

What do you get when you cross a running back and the invisible man? Scoring like no one has ever seen.

A couple of years ago the English national team was about to start training in preparation for an important qualifying match when the manager at the time, Sven-Goran Eriksson, discovered a big turd in one of the penalty areas on the practice pitch. Ok boys, he said, who's shit on the ground? One of the strikers replied: "Me coach, but I'm good in the air!"

The horse racing classic known as the Oaks is named after The Oaks, an estate located to the east of Epsom which was leased to the 12th Earl of Derby in the 18th century.

What's the difference between LeBron James and time? Time actually passes.

The St Leger horse race was established in 1776, it's the oldest of Britain's five classics. The event was devised by Anthony St Leger, an army officer and politician who lived near Doncaster.

Physical education teachers were banned from the first modern Olympics in 1896 because they were classed as professional sportsmen.

The 1988 Seoul Olympic games has the rather illogically titled sport of solo synchronised swimming.

Rugby players wore bow ties.

Rugby school's first rugby kit involved them wearing a bow tie.

The odds of hitting 2 holes in one in the same round are one in 67 million.

In 1903, the three largest stadiums in the world were all in the same city. Glasgow, Scotland is the home to Celtic Park, Ibrox and Hampden Park

Great Britain - World baseball champions.

Great Britain beat the USA in the first ever amateur world baseball final. Just before you get too carried away. The 1938 tournament only had 2 teams in it. Great Britain won 4 out the 5 games in the series.

Why is suntanning not an Olympic sport? Because the best you can ever get is bronze.

The Empire stadium (which went on to be renamed as Wembley, now the old Wembley) was built in exactly 300 days at the cost of £750,000. It was ready only 4 days before the FA cup final in 1923. The FA had not considered admission by ticket, grossly underestimating the number of fans on match day. Such was the eagerness of fans and casual observers to attend the final at the new national stadium that vast numbers of people crammed into the stadium, significantly exceeding its official capacity of 127,000. The crowds overflowed onto the pitch as there was no room on the terraces. Estimates of the number of fans in attendance range from 240,000 to well over 300,000. It is estimated that another 60,000 were locked outside the gates. The final has the highest ever unofficial 'non-racing' sports attendance in the world. Bolton Wanderers won the final 2-0 against West Ham.

In London, England, a ton is slang for 100 pounds sterling. Some sports have adopted it into their language. In darts, a ton (or ton up) is a score of 100 or more points with three darts. In cricket, a ton is a score of 100 runs.

In the first modern Olympics of 1896, the gold medals were made of silver!

In the longest ever tennis match between Isner and Mahut in 2010 which Isner won 70-68 in the fifth, the scoreboard on courtside only went up to 47 games until IBM quickly rectified the situation. Online scoring only went to 50 games and at 50 all, the games were reset to 0 and spectators were asked to add 50.

When the distance between the cricket wickets was decided, a length of chain (used in factories at the time) was one of the few reliable forms of measurement because it was unlikely to stretch like rope. A chain was 22 yards in the Imperial measure and cricket rules were written by the British. So, the length of the cricket pitch is 22 yards. The outfield has curved boundaries. There are no fixed dimensions for the field, but its diameter doesn't usually exceed 150m. Cricket, golf, aussie rules and baseball are unusual among major sports in that there is no official rule for the fixed shape of their grounds.

Putt is a Scottish word that originally meant "to shove" or "to push," and came to include the golf meaning in 1743. To putt is to hit a golf ball softly with a club, usually when you're close to the hole.

Road greys.

In baseball, the away team or the road team will generally wear a grey or dark colour uniform referred to as the 'road greys'. The term 'home whites' originated in the early days of Major League Baseball. Typically, the visiting team had no access to laundry or cleaning facilities and thus the players were unable to clean their uniforms on the road. By wearing grey or another dark colour the visiting team was better able to conceal the dirt and grass stains that had accumulated on their uniforms over the course of the series on the road. The home team, having access to laundry facilities, was able to wear clean white uniforms each day, hence the term 'home whites'.

Abebe Bikila after winning the Tokyo Olympic gold for the marathon returned to Ethiopia to a hero's welcome. Amongst other rewards he was given a top of the range white Volkswagen Beetle by the Emperor.

Originally there were no official referees in sumo wrestling, if there were any close matches the emperor would determine the winner. It was not until the early 16th century, that gyōji (sumo referees) started to make an appearance. Gyōji usually enter the sumo world as teenagers and remain employees of the Sumo Association until they retire aged 65.

The rink, as in ice rink comes from the Scottish dialect which they took from the from old French 'renc', which meant row, or line. It was used as the name of a place where curling was played. The name has been retained and used as a description of ice areas for other sports.

Looking down the stairs at an American football game, a fan spots an open seat on the 50-yard line. He asks the man sitting next to it if the seat is taken. "No," he replies. "I used to take my wife to all the games, but ever since she passed away, I've gone alone." "Why don't you invite a friend?" "I can't. They're all at the funeral."

World's worst golfer.

Maurice Gerald Flitcroft is known as the world's worst golfer, after hitting a score of 121 in the qualifying competition for the 1976 Open Championship. This is the highest score ever recorded in the Open Championship. Following this, the rules were changed to prevent Flitcroft from attempting to enter again. The rule changes however didn't prevent him from trying and he regularly attempted to enter the Open, either under his own name or under pseudonyms such as Gene Paceky (as in paycheque), Gerald Hoppy, and James Beau Jolley.

Brace (as in a brace of goals), is an old English word meaning a pair (2) of something (bird or animal) killed in hunting.

Barbados needed to beat Grenada by two clear goals in the 1994 Shell Caribbean Cup qualifications in order to reach the finals. Barbados were 2-0 and progressing as planned to the finals. Unfortunately, though Grenada scored making it 2-1. There would not be enough time for Barbados to score twice in the regulation 90 minutes and so they deliberately scored an own goal, taking the game into overtime with the golden goal rule. The whole tournament had a regulation that there would be no tied matches and a result would be determined with extra time. The golden goal was worth 2 goals in the old rules of the tournament. Barbados scored first and qualified for the finals. There wasn't the fairy tale ending with Trinidad and Tobago eventually winning the competition.

Regatta (as in boating) dates back to the early 17th century, from Italian (Venetian dialect). It literally means 'a fight or contest'. In the 1650's there were boat races between gondoliers held on the Grand Canal in Venice.

First team to average 100 points a game.

The Boston Celtics became the first NBA team to average more than 100 points per game.

What do you call 11 millionaires gathered around the TV to watch the Champions League Final? Manchester City's first team.

When ChemGrass™ was first installed in the Houston Astrodome, the groundskeepers would dress up as astronauts between innings and use vacuum cleaners to keep the turf clean during the game. ChemGrass™ would go onto be called Astroturf.

An average USPGA green in the summer takes 2000 litres of water a day, imagine that times 19 holes! I do not mean the bar! Remember there is a practice green on each course.

Fiji play in the Europe Open of women's netball.

When Italian giants Juventus marked the opening of their new stadium in 2011, they chose to play against English side Notts County. This is because Notts County are the very reason that Juventus wear black and white, rather than pink that they originally wore. In 1903, the Englishman John Savage, who played for Juventus, arranged for replacement shirts to be sent to the Turin club because their pink number were fading in the wash. As a result, the club known as the 'Old Lady' adopted the black and white stripes of Notts County.

What's the difference between England and a teabag? The teabag stays in the cup longer.

The Lance Todd Trophy is given to the man of the match in the rugby league Challenge Cup final. Lance Todd was a Kiwi player and coach who was killed in a car crash in 1942.

You can't even cook.

☺ A lady was sprawled on the living-room couch watching her favorite show on the Food Network when her husband walked in. "Why do you watch those food shows?" he asked. "You don't even cook." Glaring back at him, I asked, "Then why do you watch soccer?"

⊘ The famous words, "he's a poor lad." were said by rugby league commentator Eddie Waring after the 1968 Challenge Cup final between Leeds and Wakefield. In the game often referred to as the 'watersplash' final, a match that certainly would be postponed today because of the waterlogged Wembley pitch. Wakefield's goal kicker, Don Cox found himself in the last minute of the match with a conversation directly in front of the posts to tie it up. Up until this point Cox had been man of the match and prior to the kick his man of the match award had been announced to the 87,000 spectators. That kick would have been the icing on the cake for the Lance Todd Trophy winner. However, that is exactly where the fairy tale finishes, and the nightmare started. He slipped on the approach and missed the easiest kick of his career handing Leeds the victory.

⊘ In 1920, the University of Texas football players ate their mascot (Bevo the pig) at their annual sports banquet. At the time the university was short on cash and the cost of tending to Bevo wasn't a top priority. Since he was not tame enough to roam wild, they ate him.

☺ How many teeth does an ice hockey player have? Don't you mean tooth?

⊘ The Yankees became the first team to present rings to players after their championship win in 1922, four years before it was adopted as a league-wide practice. Before that, players were awarded pocket watches or medallions.

His first pass was to himself.

⊘ Brett Favre's first regular season pass completion when he was playing for the Falcons in 1991 was to himself! Believe it or not, Favre's first attempt was deflected by a defender and Favre himself caught it for a seven-yard loss.

🎾 Goran Ivanisevic smashed three rackets in one match during in the 2000 Samsung Open in Brighton. He had to forfeit the match because he had no more rackets to play with!

⊘ New Orleans Saints kicker Tom Dempsey set the record for the longest NFL field goal with a 63-yard kick in 1970. It was only beaten in 2013. The placekicker, who was born without toes on his right foot and fingers on his right hand, played for five teams in an 11-season NFL career.

Australia opener Alyssa Healy had some explaining to do when she failed to turn up for jury service in early March 2020. She received a letter from the local sheriff inquiring about her absence. Her excuse was he was playing in the women's T20 world cup final against India. She was required to send a picture of her participation to convince them to accept it as an acceptable reason for absenteeism. Lucky, she did play because she hit 75 from 39 balls in front of 86,174 at the MCG to win the player of the match award.

The Liverpool FC manager flies to Kabul to watch a young Afghani play football and is suitably impressed and arranges for him to come over. Two weeks later Liverpool are 4–0 down to Chelsea with only 20 minutes left, the manager gives the young Afghani striker the nod and on he goes. The lad is a sensation, scores five goals in 20 minutes and wins the game for Liverpool. The fans are delighted, the players and coaches are delighted and the media love the new star. When the player comes off the pitch, he phones his mum to tell her about his first day in English football. "Hello mum guess what?" he says, "I played for 20 minutes today, we were 4–0 down but I scored five and we won. Everybody loves me, the fans, the media, they all love me." "Wonderful," says his mum. "Let me tell you about my day. Your father got shot in the street and robbed, your sister and I were ambushed and beaten and your brother has joined a gang of looters, and all whilst you were having such great time." The young lad is very upset. "What can I say mum, but I'm really sorry." "Sorry? Sorry?" says his mum, "It's your bloody fault we came to Liverpool in the first place!"

At the first modern Olympic games in 1896, Australian Edwin Flack, who had originally come to spectate the games, ended up deciding to compete in the athletics events. He ended up winning both the 800m and 1500m events.

An effect of the light.

The 'stripes' you see on an athletic field or football pitch are caused by light reflecting off the blades of grass.

The victorious allied countries held an athletic competition in 1919 for those who had served in their militaries during WWI. Among the events at the first and only Inter-Allied Games was a hand-grenade throwing competition, won by a U.S. chaplain.

In 1950 India qualified for the world cup in Brazil, but ultimately was forced to withdraw for two reasons. The first was they couldn't afford to travel to

Brazil and the second was FIFA's requirement that players wore footwear during the matches. Indian footballers in 1950 were not accustomed to playing in shoes and preferred playing in barefoot!

What sport is played by angry French people? Lacrosse.

There is currently no conclusive evidence that human growth hormone (HGH) enhances athletic performance. It does make you bigger and as the saying goes, a good big one will beat a good little one.

Cricket fielders (except of course the wicket keeper) are not allowed to wear gloves to catch. If they do, the offending team concedes 5 runs and the catch doesn't count.

All of Ethiopia's Olympic medals (more than 50) have been won in athletics.

Georgetown University's athletic team is named 'the Hoyas'. Hoya translates directly to Ancient Greek as 'what'. Therefore, were you to ask 'What is a Hoya?' You would actually be correct.

The arses.

FC Barcelona supporters are nicknamed 'the arses'. This less than glamorous nickname is said to hold its origins in the early days of the club, back when they used to play in their first stadium in the neighbourhood of Les Corts. Supporters of FC Barcelona are called 'culés', coming from the word for bum or backside in Catalan. According to legend, from outside the old Les Corts stadium, all that could be seen of the spectators in the stands was their backsides!

What is it called when a dinosaur gets a goal? A dino-score.

Up until 1964, no substitutions were permitted in rugby league. When they were first introduced, they were only allowed for injuries and only until halftime. From 1969 onwards substitutions as we know them now were allowed.

The Dickinson High School (North Dakota) athletic teams are known as 'The Midgets'. Quite rightly so, in this new world of political correctness the school considered changing the name, but the 'Little People of America' stated that they were not offended by it, influencing the school to keep their traditional mascot.

In athletics, if you move as the gun sounds, you have considered having false started as the human brain cannot hear and process the noise of the starting gun in under 0.10 seconds.

The USA has nearly 3 million female high school athletes, of these only 3% are cheerleaders. Yet cheerleading accounts for about 65% of injuries in girls' high school athletics.

About 40% of the top honours in men's long-distance international athletics since 1980 have gone to the Kalenjin which is a tribe from Kenya.

The All-Blacks rugby union team have a winning record against everyone!

At the age of 100, Fauja Singh broke 8 world records for centenarians in athletics in a single day. Singh broke the records for the 100, 200, 400, 800, 1500, 3000, 5000 meters and the mile. That totals more than 12500m of racing in a day!

Life can't get any better.

I just bought a €2 million house and a €500,000 sports car with my beautiful new wife and signed a new 5 contract to play for Bayern Munich. Yes, my life has certainly gotten better since I took up lying.

Why are umpires always overweight? It's their job to clean their plates.

The athletic brand ASICS is an acronym for 'anima sana in corpore sano' which translates as 'a sound mind in a sound body'.

Elite athletes have an area of the brain that performs 82% faster than the average person under intense pressure.

St. Francis Xavier University Athletics teams from Nova Scotia, Canada are officially known as the X-Men and X-Women.

Why does a pitcher raise one leg when he throws the ball? Because if he raised them both, he'd fall down.

Michigan requires 1,460 days of education and training to become an athletic trainer, but just 26 to be an emergency medical technician.

My favourite sport of rugby says a lot about my life. It has frequent breakdowns, and so do I.

Paid to grow moustaches.

- In the early seventies, the Oakland Athletics paid their players to grow moustaches.

- The Indian government (and some private companies) give free jobs to athletes to compete on their agency/department teams, similar to how universities give out athletic scholarships.

- In rugby union if a ball falls off the kicking tee, part of Rule 9 states that a player can't return and put it back on but must first ask permission from the referee. It is known as the 'polite rule.'

- I'm thinking of taking a job as a crowd estimator of sporting events. I wonder how many people are in that field?

- Although tennis has been around for centuries, the first lawn tennis court was in Birmingham, England. In 1859 Harry Gem and his friend JBA Perera first experimented with a game recognizably the forerunner of the modern game of lawn tennis, in the garden of Perera's house.

You can't lose a homing pigeon

- If you think about, you can't lose a homing pigeon. If during a race your homing pigeon doesn't come home, then all that you have lost is a pigeon!

- There are principally four different tennis surfaces played on.

  - Grass – Wimbledon
  - Clay – Roland Garros
  - Hard – Australian and US
  - Carpet – Indoor competitions

- Under Franquismo (which was general Franco's dictatorial rule over Spain), the Catalan language and its symbols were banned. In 1939, FC Barcelona was forced to change its name to Club de Football Barcelona. The Catalan flag was removed from the shield of the club. The stadium however, remained one of the rare places where Catalan could be spoken and Catalan flag could be shown freely. A previous president of FC Barcelona, Joan Laporta, who was a self-proclaimed nationalist, required all foreign players to learn Catalan. It was only in 1974 the club changed its name back to the Catalan, Futbol Club Barcelona.

England is the only northern hemisphere team to win the rugby union world cup.

If having low confidence and low self-esteem was an Olympic sport. I would probably get bronze.

Quite an ordeal.

The boating store was having a big sale on canoes. There were lots of people there, It was quite the oar deal.

After the 1996 Atlanta games the sport or yachting ceased to exist and the new Olympic sport of sailing started.

Swimmers go faster underwater than on the surface! In the 1956 Olympics in Melbourne. Japan's Masaru Furukawa won Olympic gold by swimming the 200m breaststroke underwater, only coming up to breathe in the turns. David Berkoff entered the 100m backstroke in the American qualifiers for the Seoul Olympics. He won his races, setting two new world records, with a best time of 54.91 seconds. Berkoff spent most of his races underwater, surfacing 40m into his first length, and 20m into the second. He actually only swam on the surface for 40 metres. There are several factors that allow swimmers to go faster underwater. Very simply they are

- Friction - This is the friction between the water on the swimmer's body. This friction is produced by surface movements that bring the swimmer's body into contact with a greater surface area of water.

- Form drag - This could also be called hydrodynamics. Water is much denser than air and its resistance is 1,000 times higher than that of air. When a swimmer is underwater, their position favours penetration into the masses of water, thereby producing more efficient gliding than on the surface.

- Wave drag - Swimmers at depths greater than half a metre avoid wave drag. Believe it or not there are waves in the swimming pool, you can't surf on them, but they are there. The energy dissipated by surface waves slows down forward movement. By passing beneath this wave turbulence, underwater swimming is more efficient.

For several reasons including safety and the sport of swimming as a spectacle, FINA (World Governing Body of Swimming) came up with an appropriate restriction. Today, swimmers cannot remain submerged for more than 15 metres after a start or a turn. The 15-metre limit (shown by a line hanging above the pool) is measured to the swimmer's feet, not the head.

In the pursuit of signing Diego Maradona in 1982, not only did Barca pay a then world record fee of 5,000,000 pounds sterling but hey also changed the training timetable so he could sleep in, in the mornings!

Liam Botham followed in his father's footsteps by playing county cricket for Hampshire but, he became a rugby union wing for Cardiff, then Newcastle, and briefly made the England squad. When Leeds Rhinos came calling, Liam completed an unlikely sporting hat-trick by switching codes to rugby league.

What are we to do with all the cancelled sporting events due to Covid? Well, we are going to televise the world origami championships live, it will be on 'paper view'!!!

In 1969, Rodney George Laver of Australia became the first man to win a pure 'open' grand slam, by taking all four major titles in the same year. He also won 'the grand slam' as an amateur in 1962. Laver was also the first player to develop a top spin back hand as opposed to the slice.

Iconic Italian cyclist Gino Bartali the three-time Giro d'Italia and two-time Tour de France champion, saved the lives of more than 800 people during WW II. Bartali risked his life to deliver false documents on training rides and defy the fascist party ruling Italy at the time.

Feisty chickens.

Most of the weight categories in boxing are obvious. Like heavyweight, middleweight and lightweight. This one is a little different, bantamweight apparently takes its name from the bantam, named for a particularly feisty kind of chicken, originally from Bantam in Java.

Athletic trainers are called 'sneakers' because when they were invented people to remark how quiet it was wearing them. You couldn't hear your own footsteps. The word 'sneak' comes from the old English word 'snican.' At first, the word meant 'to desire, reach for' and evolved into 'to creep or crawl.' By the 1500's, 'sneaking' came to mean 'to move or walk in a stealthy or slinking manner, as if ashamed to be seen.'

Fred Perry was an English tennis and table tennis player. He was world No. 1 in both sports at different points of his careers. In Tennis he won 10 Majors including eight Grand Slams and was world table tennis champion at 19.

Jim Brown is often regarded as the greatest American football player of all time (he's the only running back to average more than 100 yards a game). His sporting skills didn't end there, and he was also one of the greatest lacrosse players.

If football had never existed, Messi would've been just a normal guy. Maybe I'm the best player of a sport that doesn't exist and that's why I'm a normal guy.

The US military made their WWII hand grenades the same size as baseballs to assist soldiers throwing them.

The national sport of Afghanistan is buzkashi. Buzkashi is a sport in which horse-mounted players attempt to place a goat or calf carcass in a goal. The sport is played across several other central Asian countries.

Russia were 12 days late to 1908 Olympics because they were still using the Julian Calendar (introduced by Julius Caesar in 45 BC). In the 1500's most Roman Catholic countries adopted the Gregorian Calendar (established by Pope Gregory XIII to compensate for the errors in time that had built up over centuries). Russia, for one did not convert to the Gregorian calendar until after the Russian Revolution in 1917.

Inventor of basketball with a losing record!

James Naismith was a physical education teacher, physician, Christian chaplain and innovator having invented the game of basketball and written the original 13 rules of this sport. He went onto to be head coach for 9 seasons at the University of Kansas. In the 9 season they played 115 games and only won 55. To this day he is the only head coach in the universities history to have a losing record!

What is cardboard's favorite sport? Boxing.

The longest ever game of basketball was on January 6th, 1951 and was between the Indianapolis Olympians and the Rochester Royals. It lasted 78 minutes and involved six overtimes.

Deion Sanders played 16 years in the NFL (from 1989 to 2005) for the San Francisco 49ers, the Dallas Cowboys, the Washington Redskins, the Baltimore Ravens and the Atlanta Falcons, winning the Super Bowl with both the 49ers and the Cowboys. In baseball, he made his debut in 1989 for the New York Yankees, before his retirement in 2001 he would also go onto to play for the Atlanta Braves, the San Francisco Giants and the Cincinnati Reds.

Why did the soccer ball quit the team? He was tired of being kicked around.

It was partly Henry Kissinger, who convinced Pelé to play in the USA.

Althea Gibson not only won 5 tennis grand slams but she also became the first black player to compete on the women's professional golf tour.

What was Sean Connery's favourite sport and when did he play it? Tennish.

A 'podium' is a platform used to raise something to a short distance above its surroundings. It derives from the Greek 'podi' meaning foot.

Boxers may pummel each other, but they do not pommel each other. The pommel refers to one of the handgrips fitted onto the pommel horse, which gymnasts grab in this Olympic and gymnastic event. The grips resemble pommels on the saddles for actual horses, which jut out, knob-like, from the front. These get their name from the French word 'pommel' meaning 'little apple.' The root is from Latin word 'pomum', meaning fruit.'

Pentathlon is derived from Greek: combining the words pente (five) and áthlon, meaning 'contest' or 'prize'.

Biathlon / bicycle, the prefix 'bi' has its derivation from Latin, and its Greek variant di, both mean 'two.' The Latin prefix is far more prevalent in common words, such as biathlon, biceps, and bicycle, the more technical Greek di- appears in such words as dioxide and dilemma.

If you listen to the pronunciation 'deuce' you could forgive yourself for thinking that this word means to be in a 'tight squeeze' at 40 points each. But alas the origins of this tennis word 'deuce' are from the French language where the term 'a deux de jeux' means to be two points away from the game or 'to both is the game'.

To shake up and down.

Jog doesn't really mean what the popular pastime we enjoy today is, it really means 'to shake up and down,' a bit like jogging your memory. It was perhaps altered from middle English 'shoggen' which means 'to shake, jolt or move with a jerk'.

The serve and serving has its roots in tennis and royalty. Some affluent players didn't want to bend down and pick balls up and so would have their servants throw the ball to start the rally.

The word 'boycott', entered the English language during the Irish 'Land War' and derives from Captain Charles Boycott, the land agent of an absentee landlord, Lord Erne, who lived in County Mayo, Ireland. He was the subject to social ostracism organized by the Irish Land League in 1880.

What US state loves a sport so much they named themselves after it? It's tennis, see.

After Achilles was born, his mother wanted to protect him from harm. She held him by the heel and dipped him into the river Styx. In Greek mythology, the river Styx was located in the Underworld and had special powers. Achilles became invulnerable everywhere but at his heel where his mother held him. All sports participants have their 'Achilles heel' or weakness.

I was told once I had the body of a god. The only problem it was Buddha!

Danny went golfing with his buddy, Tom. He stood over his tee shot for what seemed an eternity, looking up, looking down, measuring the distance, figuring the wind direction. Finally, his exasperated partner says, "What the hell is taking so long, just hit the damned ball!" Tom answers, "My wife is up there watching me from the clubhouse. I want to make this a perfect shot." "Give me a break!" Danny retorted. "You don't stand a chance in hell of hitting her from here!"

Highest foul count in basketball.

On April 9th, 1990 the Utah Jazz committed 52 fouls in a 119-115 loss to the Phoenix Suns. The most fouls ever committed by an NBA team. Here are the offenders and their violation count.

John Stockton	six
Thurl Bailey	six
Bobby Hansen	six
Eric Johnson	six
Karl Malone	five
Blue Edwards	five
Mark Eaton	four
Darrell Griffith	four
Mike Brown	four
Delaney Rudd	four
Eric Leckner	two

- Luc Alphand, is one of skiing's greatest, winning five World Cup globes, including the downhill, super-G and overall world cup titles in 1997. Once retired from skiing in 1997 at the age of 32, he turned to motor racing, competing in the Le Mans Series, the FIA GT Championship and in 2006 he won the Paris-Dakar rally.

- I'm sporting a quarantine beard. I didn't like it at first, but now it's growing on me.

- Between March 24th, 1993 and November 9th, 1993 Michael Williams playing for the Minnesota Timberwolves made 97 free throws in a row. On the day he failed (against the San Antonio Spurs), he still made 9 of his 10 attempts.

- Why doesn't Cinderella play sports? Because she has a pumpkin for a coach and runs away from the ball.

- Cornelius McGillicuddy (December 22, 1862 – February 8, 1956), better known as Connie Mack, was an American professional baseball catcher, manager, and team owner. He was the longest-serving manager in Major League Baseball history. He managed the Philadelphia Athletics for the club's first 50 seasons of play, starting in 1901, before retiring at age 87 following the 1950 season.

- How many Manchester United soccer fans does it take to change a lightbulb? None – they're quite happy living in the shadows.

- The Sri Chinmoy Self-Transcendence 3,100 Mile Race is the world's longest running race. The race is around the same single block in New York. Runners head out on the sidewalk down 84th Avenue, past a playground, along the busy Grand Central Parkway, around Thomas Edison High School, down 168 Street and back on to 84th. The competitors complete this loop 5,649 times. The race is so long that runners need a haircut during it and some get through 20 pairs of shoes. They run more than two marathons a day, for almost two months!

What is a calorie?

- The calorie is a unit of energy that is defined as the amount of heat needed to raise a quantity of water by one degree of temperature. There are two versions of the unit in use. Historically, it is defined as the amount of heat energy needed to raise the temperature of one gram of water by one degree Celsius. This is spelled with a small 'c' and known as a small calorie. This is the calorie mostly used in nutrition description. The large calorie, is spelled capital "C' this is defined as the amount of heat needed to raise the temperature of one kilogram of water by one degree Celsius. Sometimes written as kc, a kilocalorie. 1C = 1kc =1000c

A boxer had written on his tombstone: "You can stop counting. I'm not getting up."

A bit of a technicality here, a substitute in football is not allowed to take a throw in until they have entered the field of play. They can step onto the pitch and then step off to take the throw. Also, the substitute isn't permitted onto the pitch until the player being substituted has left the pitch. Otherwise, the team will be deemed as having 1 player more than is permitted. If the team plays with an extra person, the referee will remove the offending player and a free kick is given against offending team in the position the player either entered the field of play or interfered with play. If a goal was scored whilst a team had an extra player on the field of play, if that goal was scored by the offending team the goal would be chalked off, however if the goal was scored by the non-offending team then the goal would stand.

27 a side and parking the bus.

In 'calcio fiorentino' which is an ancestor of the football we know today each team has 27 players, of which 5 are goalkeepers.

In 1987 Craig Stadler was playing the Shearson Lehman Brothers / Andy Williams Open at Torrey Pines Golf Club, he was doing rather well and finished tied second winning $37,333.33. But he was disqualified after the final round because of a rules violation he had committed a day earlier. The rule he was deemed to have broken was action of building of a stance to play a shot. Stadler placed a towel under his knees while hitting a shot from a kneeling position. The ground was very damp, and he wanted to keep his trousers dry. He did not get any advantage from kneeling on the towel and official didn't see it as an offence. However, tournament officials were alerted to the infraction by a television viewer who called in to report it. The violation carried a two-stroke penalty. Unfortunately, Stadler had failed to declare the penalty after the round (maybe he didn't even know it was an offence), and therefore signed an incorrect scorecard. For this he was disqualified.

A player can still play after fouling out in an NBA game. If the team does not have five able-bodied players due to either injury or ejection, then any player who fouls out can stay in a game. However, the downside is that each subsequent personal foul made by that player also being called as a technical foul. This isn't the case in college basketball, where players cannot play with more than five fouls, and teams would be reduced to four players on the court in this instance.

When fat is lost, the majority (about 85%) is exhaled as carbon dioxide. The remaining 15% is excreted as water. During the conversion of energy, carbon dioxide and water are by products or waste. They are excreted via urine, perspiration, and exhalation. The average person loses about 200g of carbon every day and about a third of that occurs when we sleep. Simply replacing one hour of inactivity with moderate intensity exercise, such as jogging, cycling or swimming removes an additional 40g of carbon from the body, raising the total by about a ⅕ to 240g.

Disaster drafts.

There have been instances over the ages of entire teams being wiped out due to disasters. Manchester United football club lost 8 players in the 1958 Munich air disaster. North American sports addressed the unthinkable and created 'Disaster Draft' scenarios.

- In the National Basketball Association, if a disaster occurs in which five or more players die or are dismembered, that team would be able to rebuild by taking players from other NBA teams. Those teams unaffected by the disaster would be allowed to protect five of their players. The league would then hold a 'Disaster Draft' to enable all teams to fill their rosters.

- National Football League has a 'near disaster,' in which if fewer than 15 players are killed or lost for the season, teams would be required to play out the season but would receive priority on all waiver claims. In a full 'disaster,' in which 15 or more players are killed or lost for the season, the commissioner decides whether the team will continue for the remainder of the season. If this is the case a 'near disaster' plan would be implemented. If not, the affected team would get the No. 1 pick in a restocking draft that would take place in the offseason.

- National Hockey League has the following. If the disaster occurs resulting in the death or disability of five or more active players. The affected club would be allowed to restock its roster by buying players from other teams (who can protect 11 players) using money from an indemnity insurance policy. Once the affected club returns to a playing strength of 15 players, including 1 goalkeeper (NHL teams often have 20 active players), an emergency rehabilitation draft can be enacted to finish the re-stocking process for all teams.

- Major League Baseball does have a plan, but it is not publicly available.

Unlike muscles, tendons and ligaments have a very poor blood supply meaning that they do not have any blood vessels that travel through them. This makes them very strong and resistant to stretch. However, this is also why they do not heal quickly, because they lack that direct blood supply. RICE (Rest Ice Compression Elevation) is the standard treatment for muscle injuries, but heat is the way forward for tendons and ligaments. Heat through patches, a warm shower or massage stimulates blood flow to the affected area and promotes healing. Sometimes however they need operations if they become unattached.

Football club for sale (spares or repairs).

Even though it wasn't his, a disgruntled Stoke City fan (jokingly) put the football team up for sale on eBay. His description read, 'Stoke City FC First Team Squad. Condition is for parts or not working. Dispatched with Royal Mail 2nd Class.' The reason for sale was 'Not suitable for task for which bought, unreliable and unpredictable, job lot of below average footballers, attitudes questionable, work ethic poor, not advisable to use as dog walkers as cannot hold onto a lead.' There were at least 35 bids made and the auction reached £590 before the listing was removed.

In American football, the rules prohibit a team from using consecutive timeouts within the same dead ball period. It doesn't result in a penalty if a team tries to go back-to-back, but referees are instructed to not allow the second timeout. That's all.

If a basketball player accidentally tips the ball into their own basket, the closest player on the other team gets credit for the points!

Squash is a descendant of the sport of rackets, having probably originated around the middle of the 19th century at Harrow School in England. Students who were unable to get playing time on the limited number of courts took their exercise by hitting an India-rubber ball, which squashed when hit against a wall. The players found they preferred the bounce of the rubber ball to the hard one used in rackets.

Playing with an extra (illegal) player on the pitch in American football will result in a 5-yard penalty. The Australians in Aussie rules have gone a lot further to prevent the issue arising in their game. If a team fields too many players at any time, their entire score up to that point is wiped away to zero.

The NBA and NCAA permits the use of 0 and 00 as team numbers and there have been some great players wearing them. Russell Westbrook wore 0, and Robert Parish wore 00. The governing bodies do not permit the team to use both of these numbers though. The reason being that when a foul is called it would lead to uncertainty who the infringing player was as the official's signal would be the same.

Beijing had to remove more than 1 million tons of algae from the Olympic sailing venue. This was after a giant bloom left large areas of the course green!

The 1908 London games had a 100m swimming pool in the centre of the running track. This enormous pool was unique because it was the first time any Olympics had used a purpose-built facility for swimming. Normally they would have used lakes or rivers. The White City stadium had a capacity of nearly 70,000 spectators. Although the swimming events didn't fill the stadium, it is still officially recognised as the largest ever swimming venue.

Why are ice hockey players so good at making friends? They're quick to break the ice.

Debut for the wrong country.

The Indian, Sachin Tendulkar made his international debut against Pakistan in 1989 as a 16-year-old. However, the first time he stepped on an international arena as a player, he actually turned out for Pakistan! On January 20th, 1987 in an exhibition match in Mumbai, between India and Pakistan to mark the golden jubilee of Cricket Club of India. Tendulkar was only 13 at the time when he got the opportunity to field. Some of the Pakistan players were going to the team hotel to rest. Imran Khan asked the Indian captain if he could get three-four players to field. Two youngsters were the close by, they were Khushru Vasania and Sachin Tendulkar. Onto the field they went as substitutes for Pakistan. It was towards the end of the match and Sachin fielded for about 25 minutes.

Horsepower refers to the power an engine produces. It's calculated as the power needed to move 550 pounds, one foot in one second or by the power needed to move 33,000 pounds, one foot in one minute. The power is gauged by the rate it takes to do the work. The term 'horsepower' was coined by Scottish inventor James Watt, who is often wrongly credited with inventing the steam engine. In simple terms, he needed to be able to demonstrate the power and efficiency of his industrial machines and so compared their power to the power of horses.

Something was very unusual in the 3000-metre steeplechase final at the 1932 Olympics. It was actually a 3460-metre steeplechase, as the officials made an error, and all the runners ran an extra lap! The official whose job it was to ring the bell to tell the athletes they were starting their last lap was watching the decathletes taking part in their long-jump event. Eventually the mistake was realised, and the Finnish man, Volmari Iso-Hollo came home to claim the gold medal.

- Pelé's farewell match organised for him on October 1st, 1977, was between New York Cosmos and Santos. He played one half for each team and the match resulted in a 2-1 victory for the Cosmos.

- 'Bigorexia' is a medical condition that sees people strive to get bigger and is the opposite of 'anorexia.'

- Swimmers can flex their toes to the ground. Flexibility is extremely import for range of movement and swimming efficiency. Foot and ankle flexion are extremely important for swim performance, swimmers work hard on increasing the toe-point. Swimmers can sit or lay down with their legs stretched out in front of them and point their toes all the way down to the ground. Whilst keeping their heels on the ground.

- Goalkeeper Rogério Ceni scored an amazing 131 goals in his 25-year career as a professional footballer. He played for Sao Paulo and was a dead ball specialist taking direct free kicks and penalties.

- Kenyan Reuben Kipyego won the prestigious 2019 Abu Dhabi Marathon and $100,000 in prize money. Rueben hadn't really read the script as he was employed as a pacer. He didn't even have a race number on the front of his shirt, just 'Pace M2'. He ended up beating the entire elite field and winning in a time of 2:04:40. This is not the only time the pace maker has upset the field, it also happened in Los Angeles and Berlin. Paul Pilkington won $65000 as an American winner of the 1994 Los Angeles marathon. He also won a brand-new Mercedes Benz and just to top it off he was still paid his $10,000 fee for pace making duties. Other top athletes in the race complained about the fact they let him build up a sizable lead thinking he would drop out and that he continued onto to win, but there is nothing in the rules that says pacemakers can't win. Similarly, on the 10th September 2000, Simon Biwott won 50,000 Deutsche Mark for his race win in the Berlin marathon and another 30,000DM in time bonuses plus several more thousand for his work as a pacemaker.

It's not a cup!

- The FIFA world cup is wrongly named, it should be called the FIFA World Lump! Ever since the Jules Rimet Trophy (which was a cup) was permanently awarded to Brazil, its successor the World Cup Trophy is best described as a lump. There is absolutely no cup to be seen and it would be impossible to drink Champagne out of. In the near future, they should bear this in mind because there is only enough space for a few more winning teams' names to be engraved on the base of the trophy. A new trophy and this time hopefully a cup will be needed in 2030 (which will be the tournaments centenary year.)

George Louis Eyser was an American gymnast with a wooden leg who won six medals, including three gold, in a single day at the 1904 Olympics. He was the only Olympian to have competed with a prosthetic limb for more than 100 years, until 2008. Oscar Pistorius was his successor, Pistorius qualified for the Beijing games in the 400m event.

Because of a sandwich, French rugby player Gaston Vareilles missed his international debut against Scotland in 1910. The team train stopped at Lyon and Vareilles jumped of quickly to buy himself a sandwich. Unfortunately, by the time he returned to the platform, the train had left without him! He was never picked for his country again.

Lionel Messi was a child prodigy and being that good, Barcelona were desperate to sign him. So desperate indeed, that they used a napkin for the basic contract be written on. This was back in 2000 when he was playing for Newell's Old Boys in Argentina. Also, when he tried to activate his release clause in 2020, he sent in his request by fax. Lionel was also named after Lionel Ritchie!

Since the mid 1800's, boys would customarily play sport in short pants in the summer and knickerbockers (also known as knickers or knee pants) in the winter. Plus fours were introduced in the 1920's and became popular sports attire, particularly amongst golfers and game shooters. They allowed for more freedom of movement than the knickerbockers. Plus fours are breeches or trousers that extend 4 inches (10 cm) below the knee. They were four inches longer than the traditional knickerbockers. There are other less used variations on the theme such as Plus 2's.

In football we have already mentioned a brace being two and a hat trick being three goals in a single game, but did you know

- 4 goals is a haul or poker
- 5 goals is a glut or re-poker
- 6 goals is a double hat trick
- And 7 a haul trick?

You have reached the end of the book. I'd like to think reading it has seemed like a sprint and not a marathon. We obviously associate sport with success but for every winner there must be at least one loser. Some sports however (often) end in failure and they are the high jump and pole vault. I hope you enjoyed 'Interested in Sport.'